Maria
Woodworth-Etter

FOR SUCH
A TIME
AS THIS

A SPIRIT-FILLED CLASSIC

Maria
Woodworth-Etter

FOR SUCH
A TIME
AS THIS

by
Wayne Warner

Bridge-Logos
Gainesville, Florida 32614

Bridge-Logos
Gainesville, FL 32614 USA

Copyright ©2004 by Wayne Warner

04   1

Library of Congress Catalog Card Number: pending
International Standard Book Number 0-88270-935-6

Dedication

With Love and Appreciation to

My Brothers and Sisters

Lawrence, Ellis, Josephine, Leonard, Ernest,

Helen, Lester, and George

Who Helped Me Grow Up

At Wendling, Oregon

and to

Two Favorite Mohawk High School Teachers

Rosella Pavelich and Lois Sparkman

Who Taught Me to Write and Type

Contents

APPENDICES

Preface

In the late 1960s—a few years before Alex Haley's book *Roots* and its powerful television drama took America by storm, and a couple of decades before the History and Discovery Channels eased their way into our living rooms—history books were on the wane, and history teachers were looking for other fields of employment. The study of history had definitely seen better days, giving way to physics, computer science, and the like. Trend watchers were beginning to believe the oft-quoted trash statement attributed to Henry Ford: "History is bunk!"

During this changing period, while working as a book editor for a religious press, I received a letter from a man in Seattle who had an unusual request—at least, unusual for a diminishing interest in history. He suggested our company reprint a 1922 book that had long been out of print, *Marvels and Miracles*, by the late Evangelist Maria B. Woodworth-Etter.[1] I couldn't remember ever hearing of the book or the author.

After a brief search I found a copy of the 568-page book, which I discovered was a homespun journal of the author's 45 years of ministry on the sawdust trail. Then someone suggested I should talk with a Pentecostal veteran, J. Roswell Flower. He and his wife had known Maria B. Woodworth-Etter as early as 1912.

I told Flower of the suggestion from our correspondent in Seattle, and he began to tell me about the relationship he and his wife had enjoyed with the woman they affectionately called Sister Etter. She was definitely used of God, he said, and was honored throughout the Pentecostal movement in its early years. However, he doubted whether a reprint of the book would find a market simply because the evangelist was not well known in the late 1960s, having died more than 40 years earlier.

Flower's comments, no doubt, were wise counsel because the book probably would not have sold in the late 1960s.[2] Since that time, however, a great number of people in numerous denominations and para-church ministries have discovered Maria B. Woodworth-Etter and are recognizing her important contribution not only to the Pentecostal movement but also to the Christian Church worldwide.

Authors and speakers frequently use her name and tell of the phenomenal results she had in praying for the sick and spreading the Pentecostal message. Several of her many books have come out in "classic" reprints. Authors have written magazine articles about her exploits. True, many of the stories become apocryphal as they are retold. No doubt Woodworth-Etter wouldn't even recognize some of the accounts attributed to her because they have swelled in numbers—like the numbers healed, converted, fallen in the Spirit (trances), and baptized in the Spirit.

As time went on, I could not get this woman's life and ministry out of my mind. I hoped someone would separate the fact from fiction and publish a definitive biography. My initial effort to give her the prominence she seemed to deserve came in 1977 when I compiled a collection of stories told by early Pentecostals and which was published as *Touched by the Fire*.[3] I used two incidents from Woodworth-Etter's *Marvels and Miracles* in my compilation. But my interest did not stop there. I began to think more and more about doing a new work on the legendary evangelist.

Over the next several years—before the seemingly miraculous internet system was developed—my research took me into several states, with primary concern centered on old newspaper files and interviewing the last remaining people who knew her. I discovered that newspapers everywhere, beginning in the 1880s, thoroughly covered the Woodworth-Etter meetings: geographically, papers from the Salem, Oregon, *Statesman* to the Boston *Herald*; and in size and reputation from the Muscatine, Iowa, *Journal* to the *New York Times*. With the help of both Tom Slevin, one of Woodworth-Etter's descendants, and the indispensable interlibrary loan system, I compiled scores of photocopied news stories and editorials covering Woodworth and the high-energy meetings. Her circus-like meetings to rural areas, small towns, and cities were the biggest stories of the time. Many editors viewed her as a fraud—a "travesty on religion," wrote one—but to them she was news. If news was slow, they could wish and pray for a Woodworth campaign to hit their city with its explosive impact. It certainly topped news of family reunions, weddings, obituaries, bar room brawls, small-town gossip, or nothing at all.

In addition to the newspaper stories, I read scores of authors in an effort to determine just how they perceived Woodworth's place in American holiness and Pentecostal history. I uncovered an abundance of primary source material for a biography; my major problem was to condense it to a coherent narrative form.

I became aware what some people who had never met Woodworth thought about her—both critical and uncritical. But I wanted to get the opinions of her contemporaries—those who watched her ministry and life from about 1880 to her death in 1924. The list was long, including historians, preachers, doctors, reporters, editors, professional people, factory workers, farmers, the poor and the rich, and public servants. It was not difficult to find pro and con views in each of these groups in books, magazines, and newspapers.

I discovered that to some people this small town Ohio farm woman was a mystic because she believed in visions and experienced other spiritual phenomena that defied the imagination. To some, Woodworth was a hypnotist because hundreds and thousands of people in her meetings—both believers and unbelievers—were struck down by a trance similar to what the apostle Paul experienced on the road to Damascus and what many others experienced in the 19th-century Kentucky camp meetings and in the meetings Evangelist Charles G. Finney conducted. To others, Woodworth was a psychic healer, simply because they could not explain why multitudes could claim wellness after she prayed for them.

Despite Woodworth's many critics, American church historian Grant Wacker called her the most prominient healing evangelist of the era and that "no one commanded greater awe in Pentecostal circles."[4]

And not only awe, Open Bible Churches historian, R. Bryant Mitchell, calls her 19th and early 20th century ministry in Iowa "refreshing wellsprings" that helped prepare the soil for later Pentecostal revivals.[5]

She "anticipated" the Pentecostal movement, believes historian Edith Blumhofer, pioneering the salvation-healing meetings that later Pentecostals imitated. Harvey Cox, in his *Fire from Heaven*, calls Woodworth "a woman of fabled eloquence"; and historian Carl Brumback referred to Woodworth as an evangelist whose meetings sparked church planting, describing her as "looking just like your grandmother, but who exercised tremendous spiritual authority over sin, disease, and demons."[6]

To her friends and supporters, she was a woman sent from God to preach the same message that the apostles of the first century took to the known world. She was the woman who broke the male domination on the Christian pulpit—

becoming a forerunner for Aimee Semple McPherson, Kathryn Kuhlman, Marilyn Hickey, and Joyce Meyer. Like Esther of the Old Testament, Maria B. Woodworth-Etter seemingly was "born for such a time as this."

Most readers who are somewhat familiar with the Woodworth legend, focus on the big crowds, conversions, healings, and trances—all attributed to an anointed vessel and a powerful wave of the Holy Spirit. I invite the reader to keep the Woodworth mystique in mind, but keep an eye on how she perceived her calling, and the characteristics and practices that helped solidify her place in the hearts of people of her day and now:

- Her cooperation with other groups in the Kingdom;

- Her outspoken championing of women's rights in the ministry in a day long before the 19th Amendment gave women the right to vote in national elections;

- Her love for Clara Barton and William Booth's poor and disinherited;

- Getting along with a husband when most males believed a woman's place was in the home and pew rather than in the pulpit;

- Her gracious reaction to heavy criticism and persecution;

- And her maturing views and practices in racial relations.

I view her as a crusader with a megaphone crying in the wilderness, "Out with gender discrimination; out with racial discrimination; Jesus is the only answer to those awful sins and debilitating sicknesses; you don't need any of this trash from the pit of hell!"

She held her ground in courageous fashion that could inspire a Super Bowl team defending its goal line in the last 10 seconds of the game.

Happily, Scarecrow Press agreed that my book would fit in their Studies in Evangelicalism series. They published it for a limited market in 1986 as *The Woman Evangelist, The Life and Times of Charismatic Evangelist Maria B. Woodworth-Etter*. With sales geared only for libraries and scholars, they allowed it to go out of print a few years ago.

After off and on research for the next 20 years and a revision of the above book, this more definitive work will answer some of the questions posed in my earlier edition. Naturally the views of the author must enter the writing of a biography; concurrently, certain objectives must be maintained throughout the research and writing. My attempt is not to canonize Maria B. Woodworth-Etter. Neither do I try to hide the "warts" in this legendary character. In some cases the information gathered from original sources and presented in this biography will dim slightly the halo that time and well-meaning people have created for her. Overall, the biography will probably reduce her to a mere mortal. But realizing that she was human is necessary to understand and appreciate the unique personality, ministry, and challenges of this Esther-like woman "born for such a time as this."

ENDNOTES

1. Woodworth's name should be pronounced Mah-rí-ah, instead of the more common *Mah-ree-ah*. Her maiden name was Underwood. She married P. H. Woodworth, whom she divorced in 1890; he died in 1891. Her second husband was Samuel Etter, who died in 1914.

2. In 1980 Harrison House publishers in Tulsa, Oklahoma, reprinted Woodworth's *Signs and Wonders*, which was originally published in 1916. According to a company spokesman, the book has had steady sales. Other authors and compilers have discovered and published books on this legendary character since, following Harrison House's success.

3. Published by Logos, International, Plainfield, N.J., 1978. Reprinted as *Revival* by Harrison House, Tulsa, Okla., 1983.

4. Grant Wacker, *Heaven Below: Early Pentecostals and American Culture* (Cambridge, MA and London, England: Harvard University Press, 2001), pp. 84, 114.

5. Robert Bryant Mitchell, *Heritage & Horizons* (Des Moines: Open Bible Publishers, 1982), p. 120.

6. Edith Blumhofer, *Restoring the Faith* (Urbana and Chicago: University of Illinois Press, 1993), pp. 20, 24; Harvey Cox, *Fire From Heaven* (Reading, MA: Addison-Wesley Publishing Co., 1995), p. 124; Carl Brumback, *Suddenly ... From Heaven* (Springfield, MO: Gospel Publishing House, 1961), p. 271.

Acknowledgements

I owe a debt of gratitude to many people who responded to my questionnaires and correspondence for this and the earlier edition; others, such as archivists, librarians, editors, historians, and individuals lent important primary sources and offered advice. Several of these deserve special mention because they offered a tremendous amount of help and encouragement: Edith Blumhofer, Glen Ellard, Gary McGee, William W. Menzies, R. Bryant Mitchell, Cecil M. Robeck, Jr., Tom Slevin, and Grant Wacker. Descendants of Thomas Paino, Sr. (who was converted in Woodworth-Etter's meetings and who later became the pastor of the church she founded) also offered their able assistance.

Joyce Lee, archivist for the Flower Pentecostal Heritage Center, read this edition of the book and made helpful corrections and suggestions. And others of my staff at the center shared tidbits of information and showed interest in my research and writing. These include Glenn Gohr, Brett Pavia, Sharon Rasnake, David Ringer, Janice Stefaniw, Eloise Thomas, and Faye Williams.

Without the support of my family, this book project would still be gathering dust in the libraries and archives from the Atlantic to the Pacific.

CHAPTER 1

Early Life and Call to Ministry

"Soon after I was converted I heard the voice of Jesus
calling me to go out in the highways and hedges
and gather in the lost sheep."
Marvels and Miracles[1]

The sun had long set on the city of Indianapolis on that
September night in 1904, and the service inside the big
Gospel tent was winding down to probably its last hour.
Evangelist Maria B. Woodworth-Etter strolled back and forth
across the rough platform, waving her arms for emphasis as
she directed her remarks toward saints and sinners who sat
on folding chairs, fanning themselves in the muggy tent.

As the sermon came in staccato rhythm, sinners heard
an urgent plea to get right with God; believers heard the
hopeful news that a more powerful and holy life was within
their grasp; and the sick heard a clarion voice that divine
healing was available for their bodies wracked with pain
and weakness.

It was a typical Woodworth-Etter theme, one that she
had preached for twenty-five years.

Suddenly Woodworth stopped in the middle of her
exhortation, stepped from the platform, and walked down
an aisle to warmly grasp the hand of a gray-haired man who
had come in late and was making his way through the straw
toward the front of the tent.

The congregation and the ministers on the platform watched intently and whispered to their neighbors as the evangelist led the man to the front where she introduced him to her husband, Samuel P. Etter. The crowd watched and waited for an explanation. Who would be important enough to interrupt Evangelist Maria B. Woodworth-Etter, one of the best-known evangelists of that period? Was it the mayor? the governor? a dear friend? a famous preacher? Who could it be?

The crowd didn't have to wait long for an answer.

"This is the man who first led me to Christ," Woodworth told the audience. "He is Mr. Charles Stratton, now a manufacturer at Muncie."[2]

The evening's sermon was forgotten as the delighted evangelist told an emotionally charged story of her conversion 25 years earlier. It happened when she was visiting in Damascus, Ohio, during a religious revival. Despite the excitement in town and the many conversions, Woodworth didn't want to get involved. Now standing on the platform in Indianapolis in 1904, she told of a wonderful change. "Finally this man here, who was taking an active part in the meetings, earnestly solicited me to attend just one meeting. I might see things in a different light, he told me." [3]

Woodworth did attend that 1879 revival at the urging of Charles Stratton, and according to her testimony, she was converted within an hour. And then she told the Indianapolis crowd, "I owe much to this man."[4]

After leaving Damascus, Woodworth—without theological training, began preaching in her own area a few miles away and finally launched her evangelistic meetings that had taken her from coast to coast in the intervening twenty-five years. She had not seen Stratton since the revival in Damascus.

Woodworth began to write an important new chapter with the experience in Damascus, but to get a more complete picture of her life we must go back to her place of birth, Lisbon, another small eastern Ohio community.

Lisbon, Ohio

Traffic on U.S. Highway 30 slows down long enough to cross Little Beaver Creek, passes through the business section of Lisbon, and then crosses Little Beaver again and moves on toward Canton to the west or Pittsburgh to the southeast.

Unlike so many of the industrial towns and cities of Ohio, Lisbon is a pleasant residential community. Things are pretty slow and peaceful in Lisbon. But this is what makes it attractive to the residents.

The population is not great as county seats go—just a shade under 3,000—but historians here proudly tell you that their hometown is rich in history, and at one time was even bigger than the giant Cleveland, which has gobbled up so much of the shoreline of Lake Erie. But that was a long time ago, in 1820, when Lisbon boasted 746 people while Cleveland could count but 606.

Today the city tour-bus guide will tell you that Lisbon was founded and first called New Lisbon by Lewis Kinney in 1803—which gives the city Bicentennial status.[5] The guide will also point out Kinney's stone house, now serving as headquarters and museum for the Lisbon Historical Society and which is the oldest stone building in the state. Another historical building still standing along West Lincoln Way, Hamilton's Drug Store, holds the distinction as the first brick building constructed in Ohio.[6] Continuing the ride, tourists will see the house in which the parents of President McKinley were married at 431 West Lincoln Way.

One of the fascinating stories from the past is Lisbon's part in the "Underground Railroad," the system of mercy that was responsible for secretly moving slaves from the South into Canada. Sympathetic residents of Lisbon provided a stopover for the slaves, which included room and board and directions to the next point of safety in their flight to freedom.[7]

Throughout her ministry Woodworth championed the rights of blacks and other minorities. No doubt the operation of the Underground Railroad in Lisbon and the opinions of the abolitionists in the area helped shape her attitudes on the matter as she was growing up during those pre-Civil War years.

The year 1844 marked the election of James K. Polk as president. It was also the year that a mob in Carthage, Illinois, stormed the jail and killed Mormon leader Joseph Smith. But the most important event of 1844 in the Samuel and Matilda Underwood farm home near Lisbon occurred July 22, when their fourth daughter, Maria Beulah, was born.

The neighbors around Lisbon would never have thought this couple—ordinary, hard-working farmers—would rear a daughter who would later become a famous evangelist. Neither Samuel nor Matilda Underwood had much time for religious matters, even though they did join a Disciples Church in 1854 when Maria was ten.[8]

Years later Woodworth looked back on her early life with regret that she had received little religious training in the home and church. As it was, the family's joining the Christian Church came only a year before her father's premature death in July 1856, a result of sunstroke. Woodworth, her seven brothers and sisters, and her mother would never forget that traumatic experience during a raging storm, which Woodworth described as the first great sorrow of her life.

Samuel Underwood had left for the fields that morning, apparently in good health. But something happened no one would have planned or dreamed. "It was a terrible blow to our young hearts to see our father carried into the house, cold and stiff in death," Woodworth wrote. Her mother fainted as fast as friends and family could revive her. "We children were screaming and the storm was raging in all its fury."[9]

In a later book Woodworth revealed her hatred for alcohol, which had trapped her father who was "a fine looking man, very intelligent, and full of energy, but addicted to the accursed cup."[10] He spent much of their income on alcohol and little remained to support a family of eight children. Woodworth, however, was left with at least one pleasant memory in the tragedy as her father lived a few hours after he suffered the sunstroke and died praying for his family.[11] Following Samuel Underwood's shocking death, Woodworth and her older sisters had to leave the home to find work. Woodworth longed for schooling, but knew that their circumstances prevented further formal education. Her career, which included successfully ministering to hundreds of thousands of people over a span of more than 45 years, was nothing short of remarkable when one considers her educationally deprived childhood and young adult years.

She gave credit for her conversion to Charles Stratton, as related at the beginning of this chapter. This experience in 1879 when Woodworth was 35 years old, however, could have been classified as a "reclaiming" because her books give an account of her conversion at the age of 13 at the Christian Church.

With no father to care for the family, with little hope for an education, and prospects of a rather unhappy future, young Woodworth looked for a stabilizing force in her life. She found it when she trusted Christ as her Savior during the revival meeting a Dr. Belding (probably physician-evangelist Warren Asa Belding) conducted at the Disciples Church in 1857. This year, incidentally, was also the beginning in New York City of what was known as the Prayer Meeting Revival, which led to a major awakening the following year.

Young Maria was seated in the back of the nearly filled sanctuary and was the first to respond to Dr. Belding's invitation. "It seemed so far to the front seat," she wrote, "that it looked as though I could never make it."[12]

She did make it to the front where Belding took an interest in her, encouraged her, and prayed that her life "might be a shining light."[13] Little did Belding realize that the 13-year-old fatherless girl at his mourner's bench would someday preach to as many as 25,000 people in a single service. Neither could he know that young Maria Underwood would be used as a modern John the Baptist to herald the coming of the 20th Century Pentecostal Movement and that she would stay around long enough to help it get off to a good start. And she would become far better known than Belding.

Looking back on that 1857 revival meeting, and as much as she appreciated Dr. Belding's preaching and his spiritual counsel, Woodworth said she remained unsatisfied when she walked away from the altar that night. She could not believe she was converted, because she did not think the Disciples Church taught that a person could have a changed heart and nature. She believed her conversion actually took place the next day during the baptismal service at a nearby creek.

"Praise the Lord, He did not leave me in the dark," she wrote about an experience she would treasure the rest of her life. "The next day, as they took me down to the creek to baptize me, there was a great crowd around.... I asked the Lord to save me, fully trusting myself in His hands; and while going into the water, a light came over me, and I was converted. The people saw the change, and said I had fainted."[14]

The dramatic conversion—whether it took place at the creek or the night before—was what this young teenager wanted. Woodworth immediately began to experience a new life of peace and joy. She felt that she should separate herself from places of amusement and give her time to worship and service at the Christian Church. This dedication brought her to the church building for four meetings on Sunday and that many more during the week.

Now she was more anxious than ever to obtain an education so she could be "useful in the vineyard of Christ."[15] But the formal education would never come; what preparation she made for Christian service came at home, at her church, or in conversations with ministers who had been privileged to receive an education during the nineteenth century. Consequently, her formal education or training was not nearly as complete as the average preacher of the day. She was never considered brilliant, yet neither was she ignorant nor unrefined.

Even though she was only a young teenager, Woodworth knew she would someday minister in some capacity. She viewed it as a divine call. "I heard the voice of Jesus calling me to go out in the highways and hedges and gather in the lost sheep. Like Mary, I pondered these things in my heart, for I had no one to counsel with."[16]

Woodworth became fearful that the church members would ridicule her if she dared mention anything about her call. Having never heard of women ministering in public except as missionaries, she could see no opening without marriage, providing an earnest Christian would ask her to marry him. Then they could minister as a team. But the man who asked for her hand in marriage was not the man in her teenager dreams at Lisbon.[17]

A Whirlwind Courtship Brings a Life of Sorrow

During the Civil War, Maria B. Underwood met Philo Harrison Woodworth, a returned veteran who had been discharged after suffering a head injury in a battle. The couple was married after a brief courtship and settled near Lisbon, Philo Woodworth as a farmer and Maria as a housewife. They worked hard during the next few years, trying to make a living; but they were anything but successful. As she confessed: "Everything we undertook seemed to be a failure."[18]

Philo had no inclinations toward spiritual matters, and it appeared that Maria's dream to work in "Christ's vineyard" was just that, a dream. And their growing family took her further and further away from her childhood call to the ministry. But yet the call remained, even though it seemed ludicrous that anyone in her situation would dare dream that she would find a place to serve.

She was a woman, which was the first strike against her. Also, she had little formal education and no theological training. She had a family to rear. She was married to a man who had no interest in the ministry. To make matters worse, Woodworth herself was sickly. Then came the deaths at young ages of five of her six children.

She said the sorrow affected her husband permanently, describing his condition as derangement. She said he would go around their farm looking for their deceased son Willie, saying someone had taken him away. "He has never been well since," she added.[19]

The only remaining child of the six was the firstborn, Lizzie. Even though Lizzie survived the illnesses, which took her brothers and sisters, she would not outlive her mother. Just a month before Maria Woodworth died in 1924, Lizzie was injured in a bus accident in Indianapolis and died a few days later.

The Persistent Call

Throughout the long ordeal of losing five of six children, Woodworth was not well, but the call to the ministry that she had received as a teenager never left her. And the repeated calls she relates in her books are woven with the miraculous that are not unlike the calling of people in the Bible for certain ministries. However, Woodworth, like Moses in his calling at the Burning Bush, continued to offer excuses.

The Disciples Church was not the only tradition in the 19th century to sentence a woman to the home and never allow her behind the pulpit. With a few exceptions, the other Christian churches agreed with Woodworth's Disciples Church. But the more she read the Bible, the more she encountered women as Miriam, Deborah, Hannah, the Marys, and those in the ministry of Paul. "The more I investigated," she wrote later, "the more I found to condemn me.... I had one talent, which was hidden away."[20] As she pondered the words of the prophet Joel, she became more convinced than ever that there was a place for women in the ministry.

Years later she would become very defensive whenever men tried to take the pulpit from her and other women who felt similarly called. At one point she had taken about as much criticism as she could bear. Knocking the males who preached that women should keep silent in the churches and learn from their husbands at home, she thundered, "If some women had to depend on their husbands for knowledge, they would die in ignorance."[21]

Then she offered advice to her disenfranchised friends: "My dear sister in Christ, as you hear these words may the Spirit of God come upon you, and make you willing to do the work the Lord has assigned you. It is high time for women to let their lights shine; to bring out their talents that have been hidden away rusting, and use them for the glory of God, and do with their might what their hands find to do, trusting God for strength, who has said, 'I will never leave you.'"[22]

Ironically, though, women are seldom mentioned as contributing much to Christian Church history. George R. Stotts, in a paper devoted to Mrs. Woodworth-Etter, detects a male bias in the history books. He cites *Modern Revivalism* as rightly claiming history had not treated American revivals fairly, but he adds that the author overlooked the contributions of women in American church history. "In one sentence devoted to each, he makes short shrift of Aimee Semple McPherson and Kathryn Kuhlman."[23]

Stotts has a point, and a good example of this bias can be found in Canton, Ohio, just 40 miles west of Woodworth's birthplace. Canton Baptist Temple built the Christian Hall of Fame and had inducted 79 persons by 1971.[24] Incredible as it may seem, not one woman can be found among the 79. Certainly one can understand why a Baptist church would not recognize the pulpit ministry of a woman, but it is difficult to understand how the selection committee could overlook the contribution of such outstanding women of the Christian faith as Madam Guyon, Amanda Berry Smith, Mary Slessor, Frances Havergal, Phoebe Palmer, Fannie Crosby, Evangeline Booth, Ida Scudder, Lillian Trasher, and so many others. Is it any wonder that women (and fair-minded men) have objected to the limitations that men and other women have placed on their efforts to minister the Gospel?

Being a woman was not Woodworth's only fear in going into the ministry. Her thoughts always returned to her limited formal education and lack of theological training. When she prayed that there would be some way that she could study the Bible and overcome the handicap, she said the Lord showed her a vision of a large open Bible and verses standing out in raised type. Then she said Jesus repeated the call: "'Go, and I will be with you.' I cried, 'Lord, I will go. Where shall I go?' And Jesus said, 'Go here, go there, wherever souls are perishing.'"[25]

Woodworth could only praise the Lord for His goodness in revealing the Bible and His will for her life "to such a poor worm of the dust." And she believed that years of Bible study would not have given her as much as she had seen in the vision. "Praise His Holy Name," she exclaimed. "I saw that I must not depend on anything that I could do, but to look to Him for strength and wisdom: 'Not by might, nor by power, but by my Spirit,' saith the Lord. I was to be the vessel of clay God was going to use to his own glory. I was to be his mouth-piece. I must trust God to speak through me to the people the words of eternal life."[26]

Seemingly the more Woodworth resisted the call of God on her life, the more intensely the calls came. She wrote that God gave her many visions of people in need and others in hell. Yet she continued to resist the call for months and even years.

Finally after the death of her fifth child in 1880, when Woodworth was about 35 years old, she settled the call upon her life—which she described as similar to the Apostle Paul's on the Damascus road (her call was in Damascus, Ohio). In another vision she saw angels come into her room. They took her to the West, over prairies, lakes, forests, and rivers. She saw a long, wide field of waving golden grain. Then she began to preach in the vision and saw the grain begin to fall in sheaves, similar to Ezekiel's vision. She told it often that Christ spoke to her as the grain began to fall, explaining that just as the grain was falling in the vision, so would people fall as she preached. Later, when people fell prostrate in her meetings, she said the Lord spoke to her with the meaning of this earlier vision: "Sister, don't you remember the vision about the grain?"[27]

Through the series of visions and calls, Woodworth knew she could not be happy nor please the Lord unless she yielded. Without formal training, though, she knew she needed divine help. She asked God for the power He gave the Galilean fishermen, to anoint her for service.

"I came like a child asking for bread. I looked for it. God did not disappoint me," she testified. Always quick with symbolic language, Woodworth described her experience as the power of the Holy Ghost appearing in a bright cloud. "It was brighter than the sun. I was covered and wrapped up in it. My body was light as the air. It seemed that heaven came down. I was baptized with the Holy Ghost, and fire, and power which has never left me. Oh, Praise the Lord! There was liquid fire, and the angels were all around in the fire and glory."

She added, "It is through the Lord Jesus Christ, and by this power that I have stood before hundreds of thousands of men and women, proclaiming the unsearchable riches of Christ."[28] Woodworth had resisted the call to preach long enough. Now she was ready to go.

ENDNOTES

1. Woodworth-Etter, *Marvels and Miracles*, pp. 3-4.

2. "Gray-Haired Man Hears His Convert. Woman Evangelist Finds in Audience the One Who Led Her to Accept Christianity," *Indianapolis Star*, Sept. 18, 1904.

3. Ibid.

4. Ibid.

5. "A Proud Heritage: A History of Lisbon, Ohio." The name of New Lisbon was changed to Lisbon in 1894. The city observed its Bicentennial Celebration during 2003.

6. Lisbon Historical Society publications.

7. "A Proud Heritage."

8. *The Life, Work, and Experience of Maria Beulah Woodworth,* Rev. edition, 1894, p. 17. The church they joined was probably the Christian Church on East Washington. The building was constructed in 1841 and is still in use.

9. Ibid., pp. 17-18.

10. *Marvels and Miracles,* p. 2. No doubt the sad memory of her father's drunkenness was one reason Woodworth fought liquor so vigorously in her lifetime. Shoving out of her memory the suffering her mother and the children experienced as a result of the alcohol was difficult. And it gave her deep compassion for alcoholics and their families. In her books she reports with obvious satisfaction of people who were delivered from alcohol, and newspaper reports tell of people in her meetings who signed an abstainer's pledge.

11. Ibid. Underwood was struck by lightning according to Woodworth's report in *Holy Ghost Sermons,* p. 3; but later books say death was a result of a sun stroke.

12. Ibid. p. 3. Belding (1816?-1901) was reared in Portage County, Ohio.

13. Ibid.

14. Ibid.

15. Ibid.

16. Ibid., pp. 3-4.

17. Ibid.

18. *Life, Work and Experience,* p. 20.

19. *Life and Experiences of Maria B. Woodworth,* 1885, p.33.

20. *Marvels and Miracles,* pp. 13-14.

21. *Signs and Wonders,* p. 211.

22. Ibid. , p. 215.

23. George R. Stotts, "Maria Woodworth-Etter: A Forgotten Feminine Figure in the Late 19th and Early 20th Century Charismatic Revival," p. 1. A paper presented at the National Convention, Church History Section, The American Academy of Religion, Washington, D.C., October 26, 1974. Stotts adds that church historian J. Edwin Orr "unwittingly has neglected feminine figures" in his several volumes of church history.

24. Elmer L. Towns. *The Christian Hall of Fame* (Grand Rapids, Mich.: Baker Book House, 1971). See also Canton Baptist Temple web site.

25. *Marvels and Miracles*, pp. 12-13. It is easy to accuse Woodworth of being anti-education and accepting the popular theory that if one "opens his mouth, God will fill it." Other early Pentecostals were afraid that education—religious or secular— would take the fire out of their preaching, create doubt concerning what they believed to be the essential doctrines and practices, and take time from their ministry. Now with almost every Pentecostal organization operating their own Bible college and/or seminary, comparatively few Pentecostals hold this view.

26. Ibid. It is interesting to note that Woodworth quotes Zechariah 4:6, which later became the theme verse for the Assemblies of God, the largest of the Pentecostal denominations. Woodworth was never a member of the Assemblies of God but worked closely with its early leaders. Perhaps one of the reasons she did not join was that during the early years a woman could serve as a missionary and evangelist and could participate in church business at a General Council, but she could not vote. Neither could a woman pastor a church in the early years of the denomination—which would have hampered Woodworth when she founded her own church in Indianapolis in 1918.

27. *St. Louis Post-Dispatch*, Aug. 31, 1890.

28. *Marvels and Miracles*, p. 11. This book was published in 1922, about 21 years after the modern Pentecostal Movement began. The testimony is almost identical to the one given in Woodworth's 1894 book, *Life, Work and Experience*, except for

one sentence. In 1894 she wrote, "It has been fourteen years now since I received that anointing power, which John said, "abideth" page 33). In 1922 she revised the sentence to read, "I was baptized with the Holy Ghost and fire, and power which has never left me." Obviously she equated the "anointing power" with the Pentecostal baptism. The symbolic descriptions of Woodworth's experience might defy the imagination, but her evangelistic results were unparalleled for women until Aimee Semple McPherson burst on the scene when Woodworth was in her 70s. Equipped with the powerful evangelistic organizations that D. L. Moody, R. A. Torrey, and Billy Sunday enjoyed, no doubt historians would have given Woodworth a more prominent place in American church history.

CHAPTER 2

A Daring Pulpit Feminist

"I opened the meeting and repeated the text. As I did so the power came, and it seemed that all I had to do was to open my mouth. The people all through the house [church] began to weep. I talked one hour and a quarter. The power came as it did when I received the anointing."—*1894 report*[1]

Sister Woodworth, the novice evangelist, could not have asked for a tougher place to launch her ministry than in the little community where she and her husband had formerly lived. There she looked out across her curious audience and recognized her husband's relatives who wondered what P. H. Woodworth's poor wife was doing in the pulpit. What a challenge!

As was her custom throughout her preaching ministry, Woodworth went into this pulpit with very little preparation besides prayer. She really needed all the prayer power she could muster, especially with those skeptical relatives occupying the pews in front of her. Apprehensively she glanced around the audience and saw that every eye was riveted on her as she waited for the introduction. As she rose to speak, a text came to her mind: "Set thy house in order, for thou shalt die, and not live." With that, the "man-fearing spirit" left her, and she said that the Holy Spirit gave her the words faster than she could deliver them. "My sister-in-law broke down and left the house," she reported. "We continued the meeting a few days and 20 claimed to be

17

converted. People were converted all through the neighborhood.[2]

Another night the church was crowded with several hundred people, and Woodworth could not find a text from which to preach. Naturally, she became frightened that she would make a fool of herself. She went to prayer, reminding the Lord that He had called her to preach, that a starving multitude was waiting, and she had nothing to feed them. Again her prayer of desperation was answered. The words of Pilate came to her, and she turned the question to her audience: "What are you going to do with Jesus, that is called Christ?" (Matthew 27:22). Jesus seemed to whisper in her ear, "I am with you; be not afraid" as she began her hour and a quarter sermon. And the power came. "It seemed that all I had to do was to open my mouth. The people all through the house began to weep."

During the message something dramatic happened to Woodworth. "I received the baptism of the Holy Ghost. It seemed as if the house was full of the glory of God. I felt as if I was drawn up over the people. Glory to God for helping a worm of the dust."[3]

The Woodworth ministry was launched, and this prophetess received honor in her own country—or at least in her husband's own country!

Woodworth became an immediate success at reviving other churches in her home area around Columbiana County, Ohio, and planting new ones—something she now knew would be her life's work. Before she left home for extended revival tours—"going West," as she called it—in a period of about a year and a half she held nine revivals, organized two churches (one of these started with 70 members), organized a Sunday school of about 100 members, preached in 22 meeting houses and four school houses, and delivered 200 sermons. And all of this was on an ecumenical basis for eight separate denominations. According to Woodworth, "God blessed my labors in this short time with more glorious results than I had expected to see in years, or perhaps in a lifetime of labor.[4]

Several church groups recognized her preaching and organizing ability and approached her with attractive offers. The Friends Church wanted her to travel for a year with a minister and his wife to conduct revival meetings.[5] The United Brethren wanted her to take charge of the Women's Missionary Society or take a circuit of churches. A group called Bible Christians wanted her to join their forces and take charge of three large churches. The Methodists offered her a church.

With the exception of the Friends' offer, which was an itinerant ministry, these preaching opportunities were within ten miles of her home, and each of the groups offered Woodworth a good salary.[6] The itinerant ministry that the Friends offered appealed most to Woodworth because she felt that God had called her to be an evangelist, and her eyes were set on other sections of Ohio and points west.

All around eastern Ohio sinners and saints alike excitedly accepted Woodworth's new ministry, but in her own household her husband and daughter thought she had lost her mind. P.H. Woodworth had been converted in a Methodist church after they were married, and Mrs. Woodworth described his conversion as "very bright" and he "seemed to speak with other tongues." They had a happy home for a while, Woodworth wrote in one of her first books, but when trials came, her husband became discouraged.[7]

P.H. reluctantly consented that his wife could minister in their local area, but a traveling ministry was out of the question. If she wanted to preach, there were enough sinners around Columbiana County she could reach without going off on a foolish venture into the West.

In the meantime, she joined the United Brethren Church and preached in neighboring communities. One of these places was the notorious Devil's Den, a rural area that was widely known for its religious infidelity and skepticism.

An old church building in which conversions were unheard of was made available for Woodworth's meetings. She knew other ministers had tried to start revival fires at Devil's Den and had gone away discouraged, but Woodworth was either too naive or was filled with too much faith to be turned away from this challenge.

A large curious crowd met her on her arrival at Devil's Den, and they expected another short-lived, unproductive revival meeting. This woman evangelist would flee in disgrace, they laughed. But they were in for the shock of their lives!

Woodworth could hardly believe people anywhere were as hard and uninterested as the ones she met at Devil's Den. Whoever had named this place wasn't fooling. For three days Woodworth did everything she knew to break the hardened hearts. She prayed, she sang, she preached, and she called for day meetings of prayer—all in an effort to combat the evil influence of the area and start a revival fire. Finally on the fourth day some of the residents were converted, and the news quickly spread that Devil's Den was being stirred for God. Soon the neighborhood rang with joyous singing and praises, and the old church building could not hold the crowds who gathered to see the excitement. Hundreds milled around outside, eagerly waiting for someone inside to leave so they could get in.

Woodworth recognized the 2-week meeting as a spiritual breakthrough. Seventy-five of Devil's Den people, most of whom were over 20, were converted. An elderly couple of 75 and nine of their children were in the number. "Some of the hardest sinners in the whole country were converted,"

Woodworth reported. "They had to confess that God was there in wonderful power."

As a result, Woodworth organized a Sunday school of 150 and placed a converted drunkard in charge. She organized two weekly prayer meetings and meetings each Sunday. The critics had good reason to doubt whether such a church would last very long, given the foundation of new believers. When Woodworth left, they said, the work would fold in Devil's Den. In her 1885 book, Woodworth boasted, "Bless God, I have heard of only one who went back to the world!"[8] Any church planter with the best of foundations would be pleased at that drop-out rate.

Even at this early point in her ministry Woodworth knew the value of conserving the results of evangelistic efforts—something she probably learned from the Friends and United Brethren. This method of organizing a church and placing someone in charge was a pattern she used throughout the 1880s and 1890s. In this regard she was not simply an evangelist in the modern sense, but she was the biblical evangelist who not only planted the seed but also made certain the seed was nourished and watered so God's purpose could be carried out in the new disciples. Woodworth felt a keen responsibility for these new believers, and she did her best to channel them into existing churches if available. If there were no churches, she planted her own, as happened in Devil's Den.

But still her eyes looked toward the West and her prayers continued night and day that P. H. Woodworth would give up the plow and give her a chance to reach people beyond Columbiana County's borders. Doubts came. What if she would have to spend the rest of her life ministering only in Columbiana County's 500 square miles? It can't be, she would reason, because *God had called her to a ministry far away from Lisbon*. She knew it, but yet P. H. appeared as stubborn now as he was when she first told him God wanted her to preach. *Why didn't God speak to him?*

P. H. Woodworth Surrenders

Finally, in what Woodworth reasoned was an answer to her desire and her intercessory prayer, Philo Harrison Woodworth agreed to accompany his wife on her evangelism mission to the West, which was endorsed by the United Brethren Church. Woodworth wrote that P. H. became willing and even anxious to go with her to fulfill the burden on her heart.[9]

Why did P. H. finally agree to give up farming and enter the unpredictable evangelistic ministry with no promise of salary, a place to stay, or food to eat? He knew the career offered few comforts of life and little financial remuneration.

From past experiences he knew Woodworth's determination. Maybe he knew that she would eventually go without him unless he agreed to go. Maybe he saw the business potential in an evangelistic organization that could attract hundreds and even thousands to a single service. We do know he developed a commercial enterprise in connection with the meetings that included food, books, and Woodworth's photograph for sale. (Newspaper reporters and editors often criticized his business, likening it to the moneychangers that Christ drove out of the Temple.) Maybe he thought one trip west would get the itinerant ministry foolishness out of Woodworth's system, and then she would settle down again on the farm.

Another possibility is that P. H. Woodworth felt called to the ministry after he saw firsthand how his wife had developed overnight from a little-known farmwife to an evangelist of no little reputation in eastern Ohio. Even though Woodworth's contribution to his wife's ministry was not at the pulpit, the Churches of God (Winebrenner) later granted him exhorter's credentials.

P. H. Woodworth's motives regarding the ministry remain unanswered, but few people would question the sincerity that took his wife from the farm to the pulpit. When the opportunity came to pull up stakes at Lisbon and head west to Willshire on the opposite side of the state, she joyfully took it without asking questions. She knew it was nothing less than the call God placed on Abraham, David, the Apostles, and others through the centuries. It was the will of God!

Despite the fact that few women were preaching the Gospel in the latter part of the nineteenth century, Woodworth was determined she would answer the call on her heart and continue her evangelistic preaching on a wider scale to reach more people in need of a Savior.

The call would take her to Willshire, but that was only the beginning. For the next 45 years she would crisscross the country, and only a recording angel—if they do such things—would know how many sermons she would preach, how many sinners would respond to her passionate appeals, and how many people would claim physical healings. Even Woodworth would not be able to keep count of the churches she would establish and how many young men and women she would influence for the ministry. Her 500-page autobiographies could only record the high points of her evangelistic ministry that in duration surpassed two of her more famous male contemporaries, Dwight L. Moody and Billy Sunday—each of whom preached for 39 years.

Religious Enthusiasm, 19th-Century Style

During the legendary 19th century revivals and camp meetings, various vocal and physical manifestations were as common as the emotional appeals for sinners to get right with God. But it did not begin there. Going back to the mid-18th century revivals with the noted pastor and theologian

Jonathan Edwards, emotional responses were acceptable behavior. Edwards' 1741 sermon, "Sinners in the Hands of an Angry God," elicited emotional responses that not even Edwards could have predicted.

Because of Edwards' preaching, English evangelist George Whitefield, and others, revivals burst out in the colonies—a movement later called the Great Awakening. Beginning at the end of the century and rolling into the 19th century, after the United States came into existence, other revivals of conversion with spreading influence were called the Second Great Awakening.

While the Great Awakening centered on New England and the middle colonies, the second movement knew hardly any boundaries—with the American Frontier and Kentucky's Cane Ridge receiving most of the publicity and attracting the huge crowds.

Despite the great good that revival, evangelistic, and camp meetings produced, they were often scenes of utter confusion. Those in charge often allowed the congregation to "do their own thing" or "go with the flow"—to use modern vernacular terms—whenever the "Spirit" moved them. People in the audience took advantage of the freedom and would frequently cry out, pray aloud, run, dance, bark like dogs, and give vent to their emotions through other various physical manifestations—much of which happened while the preacher tried to make himself heard.

That is not to say that people were not converted and churches established. But to deny that the emotional displays were excessive is to try to defend everything that went on at Corinth in the first century.[10] In defense of the emotional responses of later revivals, proponents take the critic back to 18th and 19th century meetings for proof that what happened in their Holiness, Pentecostal, or Charismatic gatherings was solid because it had precedent. The critic rejoins that the Bible is the guide rather than experiences of another generation on the Kentucky frontier or at the Azusa Street Mission.

Because of the licensed disorder, critics wrote them off as only emotional displays with no solid teaching or preaching. History supports the claims of the Christian church, however, that these periods produced genuine spiritual awakenings. Sadly, the awakenings in both North and South could not prevent the greatest tragedy in the nation, the Civil War.

When Dwight L. Moody thundered onto the scene with his big evangelistic campaigns, he frowned on audience participation except for three things: singing, giving, and responding to his altar calls. He taught his co-workers to break into a hymn if the services ever "got out of hand." Other 19th century evangelists and pastors followed Moody's lead. Later during the Billy Sunday meetings, a worshiper took the chance of being thrown out of the meeting if he or she interjected an "Amen" or "Hallelujah" while the former baseball player dramatized his sermon at the pulpit.[11]

Woodworth operated with a different style manual. Forbidding the audience from participating in the service was not her way of worshiping God and converting sinners. Her association with certain Holiness groups that were products of the earlier revival efforts, led her to believe that the shouting, dancing, and falling were norms for the church service. She believed that a service should have singing and preaching, but she would not try to discourage emotional displays if she felt they were in order. Admittedly a subjective role. She believed that a lack of physical manifestations was only a sign of apostasy and used the Methodist church as an example.

She remembered from childhood that the Methodist Church was the most powerful and most spiritual. "The people fell under the power of God, shouted, danced, got healed from diseases and did lots of other things," she wrote. "They had an amen corner in every church and when the preacher would come in he would not stop for anything but go to the pulpit, open the Bible and begin. There were no secondlys nor thirdlys nor anything of that kind, they did not have time, and the amens came from all over the house. They obeyed God, and they were happy people, they had great power."

In contrast, Woodworth described the same church during her preaching ministry: "They are saying 'We don't know God. He left us. We don't see Him.' So today there is not an amen nor a shout from anybody. They do not like any fuss or see any need for it. And if one sister gets blessed and the power of God comes on her and she shouts, three or four good sisters get around and she never shouts again."[12]

It isn't any wonder, then, that Woodworth's meetings took on the characteristics that marked the early Methodist meetings of her childhood and the Frontier camp meetings. She was not a lecturer or entertainer. Without audience participation her meetings would have had far less impact on her times. Maybe they would have folded and Woodworth would have been back in Lisbon.

Evangelizing in the West

Citizens of western Ohio soon learned that Woodworth was in their area. Although she reported nothing outstanding concerning the one service she conducted in the Methodist church at Willshire, Ohio, what happened during the next 16 days in Fairview was to establish some sort of pattern for at least one feature of her meetings for the rest of her preaching career. This feature was the unusual experience commonly called trances or falling in the Spirit. Because of this phenomenon and others associated with the Fairview meetings, Woodworth said that she had never seen the power of God "so wonderfully manifested as at these meetings."[13]

Trouble had been brewing in the Fairview church for years; some of the members had left, and in Woodworth's manner of judging the spiritual climate, the church had lost its power. But she felt impressed that God would restore love and harmony in the church and that she had been brought there as His instrument of peace. She visited estranged families, and within three days the trouble was settled. What Woodworth described as happening in the Fairview service one night more than a century ago could be an apt description of innumerable Pentecostal and Charismatic services since:

"All who were present came to the altar and made a full consecration and prayed for a baptism of the Holy Ghost and of fire, and that night it came. Fifteen came to the altar screaming for mercy. Men and women fell and lay like dead. I had never seen anything like this. I felt it was the work of God, but did not know how to explain it, or what to say. I was a little frightened, as I did not know what the people would think or what they might do to me, as I was the leader of the meeting."[14]

While Woodworth stood watching the phenomenon, a vision she had seen before she started preaching flashed through her mind. In the vision she saw a field of wheat, representing the multitudes that would hear her preaching; in the field were sheaves falling, or those who would be "slain" by the Spirit. Now it was happening in Fairview, Ohio. As she stood and watched the scene, Woodworth said the Spirit of the Lord assured her that He would fight for her and that this particular manifestation was needed to bring sinners to Him.

No doubt Woodworth was relieved when people began to come out of the trances after some two hours. They "sprang to their feet as quick as a flash, with shining faces and shouted all over the house." She had never seen such "bright" conversions or such excitement and shouting. "The ministers and old saints wept and praised the Lord with a loud voice. They said it was the Pentecost power."[15]

During a meeting Woodworth conducted at Bethel Chapel, St. Mary's Circuit, Ohio, about 135 came to the altar for salvation. But two young unnamed men became an illustration of those who reject the call to repentance. They were under the conviction of the Holy Spirit but refused to yield—even though Woodworth, who could make sinners smell the smoke and feel the heat of hell, repeatedly pled with them. Finally she told the two that she was convinced they had one last chance to get right with God. "They turned pale, but did not yield," Woodworth recalled. After the meeting closed the two young men became sick about the same time and died within a matter of days. Woodworth was certain they went out of this life "without a ray of hope."[16]

This would be only one of many "deathbed" experiences Woodworth would relate in her books. Some responded to the Gospel while others would—like the two men—resist and reject the invitation. Woodworth believed these experiences were real, that hell was real, and that people without Christ were eternally lost. More than anything else, these convictions motivated her to witness and preach wherever she had opportunity.

Western Ohio and eastern Indiana soon became aware of the Woodworth zeal as she labored among not only the United Brethren, but also Methodists, Baptists, and others during 1883. The leaders of the churches recognized her unusual abilities of stirring up their dead charges, bringing in the unconverted, and persuading people to seek a deeper walk with the Lord.

The pattern was similar; only the towns differed in those early years. In Ohio she started revival fires at Willshire,

Fairview, St. Mary's Circuit, Lima, Dayton, and Zion; and in Indiana at Pleasant Mills, Ft. Wayne, and Monroeville, to list only a few.

The Monroeville, Indiana, revival is perhaps a model of the meetings Woodworth conducted while she was with the United Brethren. In November 1883 the Monroeville Methodist church had no mourner's bench, or altar. In fact, it had been about eight years since the church had any use for the bench. For Woodworth to preach the Gospel without an altar was like asking a fisherman to throw a line into the lake without a hook. So Woodworth found the church sexton and asked him to dust off the old mourner's bench and bring it back into the sanctuary so it could be used in the revival. He laughed at the strange request, but agreed to bring it back:

"When the people saw the mourners' bench they said it would be a good joke on me; that we would have no use for it," she recalled. While preaching that night she shouted victory as did the Children of Israel as they marched around Jericho. "[I] told them to clear the altar—for the house was crowded—and called for seekers."

What had been a dead Methodist church suddenly took on new life, like the dead bones of Ezekiel's day. The crowd sitting in the pews became penitents and began crowding around the altar. And this continued day and night for three weeks. It was a new day in Monroeville.[17]

How could one uneducated farm woman impact hardened sinners and dead church members alike? How did she strike others who listened to her preach? Newspaper reporters probably described Woodworth better than anyone else of the period, but often their descriptions were colored by obvious bias against women in the pulpit and the particular style that characterized Woodworth's preaching.

"She is of medium size, forty years of age—though she does not appear thirty-five," a writer for the *Indianapolis Times* wrote in 1885. In a further description, he wrote, "[She] has brown hair worn in a high knot above her head, gray eyes, fairly good-looking ... has in the corners of her mouth a firmness suggestive of the picture of Andrew Jackson."

Woodworth was not particularly intellectual and did not look like a fanatic, he judged. But her machine gun delivery caught his attention: "As a talker [she] is coherent and evidently sincere. Once started on the subject of religion she can get in as many words to the hour, and as many hours to the day, as the most accomplished lightning-rod agent that ever plied his calling."[18]

A Stormy Relationship with the Churches of God

After Woodworth severed her association with the United Brethren Church in 1884, the 39th Indiana Eldership [District] of the Churches of God granted her a license to preach and appointed her as Eldership evangelist. Her relationship with the local churches in the denomination was generally favorable, but certain church officials criticized her whenever the opportunity arose. Finally in 1904, church officials asked Woodworth to return her Churches of God credentials, thus ending a rather stormy 20-year relationship.[19]

During that 20-year period Woodworth was heralded as the greatest woman evangelist in the history of the Christian Church. She conducted meetings that attracted as many as 25,000 people to a single service. She planted churches that thrived for years. She attracted unbelievers to the church and remarkable "hard case" conversions were recorded. She revived dead churches and inspired ministers to "preach the whole Bible." She prayed for the sick and recorded some astounding results. She introduced believers to a subsequent spiritual experience following their conversions. And newspaper reporters wrote hundreds of stories about her and her meetings.

Paradoxically, Woodworth was also the most criticized woman evangelist during that same 20-year period. And much of the criticism came from her own denomination, the Churches of God.

The Church Advocate, which is still the official periodical for the Churches of God, regularly carried reports of Woodworth's meetings beginning in 1885. The early stories carried reports of another phase of Woodworth's ministry: divine healing. She began to pray for the sick even though she was at first worried that it would take too much of her time away from evangelism. This aspect of her ministry, along with the other Charismatic phenomena, would create a controversy within the denomination that threatened to split it wide open. *The Advocate* became a sounding board for the healing controversy during an eight-month period between July 1887 and February 1888. Nothing was settled, as is usually the case, but the Churches of God constituency certainly read enough on the issue to form some definite opinions.

In evaluating Woodworth's ministry with the Churches of God, the long-time editor of *Advocate*, C. H. Forney, could see both positive and negative elements. Forney criticized Woodworth and P. H. for breaking church rules. The first infraction came when a minister in Chambersburg, Pennsylvania, Joseph H. Martin, invited the Woodworths to his church for a series of meetings in the fall of 1885. Churches of God rules stated that a minister in one eldership could not accept ministry within another eldership without first joining the second.

Apparently the Woodworths were unaware of the rule. One can understand this oversight because prior to associating with the Churches of God, they had operated independently, working as harmoniously in one denomination as in another. No denomination could have put Woodworth in a prescribed box—not even a box as big as the 39th Indiana Eldership.

Ironically, and probably not what Forney wanted to publish, Martin wrote a glowing report for the *Advocate* concerning the ministry the Woodworths conducted in his church. With praise like Martin used, it is no wonder that Forney and other church officials stepped up their efforts to censure Woodworth.

Martin wrote that cold professors of religion were revived and sinners were converted; the Chambersburg church was destined to prosper as a result of the Woodworth revival. He wrote that Woodworth was filled with the Holy Ghost and power. "Her words are sharp as a sword and pierce the heart." Pastor Martin wrote favorably of a "peculiar feature" of the meetings when large numbers of people went into trances. He called it a beautiful picture with "the joy of the Holy Ghost beaming in their eyes." He added that Woodworth made plain the subject of heart purity.[20]

Given his position on the Woodworth ministry, it is commendable that Forney published both sides of the physical healing and trance controversies. But later he came out strongly against Woodworth in his history of the denomination. "Proof abounded," he wrote, "that she built with wood, hay, and other inflammable materials."[21]

After the Churches of God called for Woodworth to surrender her credentials in 1904, Forney evidently lost touch with her. His book, which was published ten years later, states, "Mrs. Woodworth was a revivalist of remarkable power; but after a brief period of constant activity she relapsed into obscurity."[22]

Forney should have looked into Woodworth's "obscurity," because it appears that even though she was 70 years of age when he published that statement, Woodworth was just getting her second wind. True, she had no meetings that attracted 25,000 as some of her meetings in the 1880s did, but no other Pentecostal evangelist could attract the crowds as Woodworth did in such places as Dallas, Chicago, Atlanta, and Los Angeles between 1912 and 1918. Her name was almost magic when it appeared on revival posters during the early years of the Pentecostal Movement.

In all fairness to C. H. Forney, and a tribute to Woodworth, Forney did write some positive statements concerning her ministry. "An encouraging effect of Mrs. Woodworth's wonderful revivals was the inspiration to energetic endeavors felt by ministers and churches in the work of evangelism and Church extension." He added that despite all the defects, her work "was of a very serious character, and it suggested the propriety of 'days of fasting and solemn prayer for revivals' in many localities. Gratifying results followed."[23]

In more recent times, the Churches of God constituency appears more in sympathy with Woodworth and her contribution to their history than some of the ministers of the 19th century. Most of today's members had never heard of Woodworth until a Churches of God pastor, Jon R. Neely, wrote an article in 1975 concerning Woodworth's life and ministry while she was with the denomination. Ironically, the article, which is sympathetic and conciliatory in tone, was published in the same *Advocate* that C. H. Forney edited for so many years.[24]

Neely is convinced that the Churches of God were privileged to have Woodworth ministering in their churches. She was "a powerful and persuasive evangelist," but the church failed to capitalize on Mrs. Woodworth's efforts— which was tragic, but not surprising in Neely's view because of the incompatibility. "The Churches of God were rural and small town, and middle class," he wrote. "Maria Woodworth's ministry was primarily to big cities and to the lower classes."[25]

Neely cites examples of church leaders who were too slow in providing leadership for the churches and missions Woodworth and her husband had planted. P. H. Woodworth had even called the Church "cold hearted" because of their reluctance to establish intercity missions to reach the poor.[26] He adds that in the 1880s the Churches of God were more concerned with converting doctors and lawyers than blue-collar workers. "In her selection of audiences," he writes, "Mrs. Woodworth's taste was as bad as John Wesley's or George Whitefield's."[27]

The Churches of God in 1975 had a similar dilemma as it faced in 1884 with Woodworth, in Neely's view. The Charismatic movement was challenging his denomination and others worldwide. "The church can respond by resisting, turning inward, and alienating the bearers (however awkwardly) of new life; or, she can learn from, add guidance to, and harness the new power being offered."[28]

Few women were in the pulpit during the last quarter of the nineteenth century—at least 20 years before men could trust women to even cast a vote in a national election. The most influential and best known was this humble wife of a farmer from Columbiana County, Ohio. She had her critics— one minister dubbed her "Saint Maria"—yet she touched a group of people, thousands of them, many of whom were not attracted to conventional church services.

Her mission, as she saw it, was to make the Gospel alive and available to everyone. She was accessible to people, and her personal attention won friends among the wealthy as well as the poor, among the professional as well as the factory workers and farmers.

As a woman in the pulpit, she endured wagonloads of criticism and abuse—in and outside the Christian church. A weaker person would have dropped out after a hoodlum threw the first rotten egg or the editor published the first critical editorial. Her enemies, however, could never match her stamina, determination, and patience. She believed she was called to preach the Gospel and—with God's help—she determined that she would fight for righteousness as long as she had breath.

The sawdust trail has never seen anybody quite like Maria B. Woodworth-Etter. And it probably never will.

ENDNOTES

1. Maria Beulah Woodworth, *Life, Work and Experience* of Maria Beulah Woodworth (St. Louis: Commercial Printing Co., revised 1894), p. 43. In her later writings, Woodworth uses the term "baptism in the Holy Ghost" for the "anointing."

2. *Spirit filled Sermons*, p. 18. Her future son-in-law, John F. Ormsby, who married Elizabeth Woodworth, was converted in this meeting. He died in 1943 at the age of 89 and is buried beside his wife and Mrs. Woodworth-Etter in Memorial Park Cemetery, Indianapolis.

3. Ibid., p. 19.

4. *Marvels and Miracles*, pp. 19-20. It should be noted here in the 1880s that Woodworth possessed a powerful preaching style even without the Charismatic phenomena that characterized her later ministry.

5. *Life, Work and Experience*, p. 34.

6. *Marvels and Miracles*, p. 19.

7. *Life and Experiences*, 1885, p. 28.

8. *Life, Work and Experience*, pp. 44-45. The more famous

Devil's Den is a bloody part of the Gettysburgh Battlefield.

9.   The Church of the United Brethren in Christ amalgamated with the Evangelical Church to become the Evangelical United Brethren Church (E.U.B.), which in 1968 became a part of the Methodist Church and is now called The United Methodist Church.

10. To read certain secondary sources regarding the ministry of Charles Finney, one could get the idea that Finney supported all the emotional displays that seemed synonymous with his great revivals. However, Finney said in *Reflections on Revival*, p. 38, that to encourage an unhealthy degree of excitement in revivals was an error. There would be a certain amount of excitement in revival meetings, he agreed, but "it should always be understood that excitement, especially where it exists in a high degree, exposes the sinner to great delusions....When the feelings are greatly excited, the will yields to them almost of necessity."

11. *Vision of the Disinherited*, Robert Mapes Anderson, p. 38. Anderson quotes *Modern Revivalism: Charles G. Finney to Billy Graham*, by William G. McLoughlin, Jr. (New York: Ronald Press, 1959), pp. 193-94; and *They Gathered at the River*, by Bernard A. Weisberger (New York: Fleming H. Revell, 1930), pp. 159, 224.

12. *Spirit filled Sermons*, p. 136. Woodworth attended a D. L. Moody meeting in New York in the 1880s, reporting simply that she "assisted in the work." On this same trip she attended one of A. B. Simpson's meetings but "was surprised to see it so cold. Not one saved or healed, and no signs of the Holy Ghost baptism," *Acts of the Holy Ghost*, p.118.

13. *Life, Work and Experience*, p. 52.

14. Ibid., p. 53. It should be noted that this quotation is from a book Woodworth wrote at least as early as 1894—six years before the modern Pentecostal Movement came into existence under the leadership of Charles F. Parham at Topeka, Kansas.

15. Ibid., pp. 53-54.

16. Ibid., p. 57.

17. Ibid., pp. 87-88. See Appendix B, "Woodworth's Wand," for a report of perhaps a typical meeting before the turn of the century as seen in the eyes of a newspaper reporter.

18. *Indianapolis Times*, May 12, 1885. The *Times* seldom had a kind word for Woodworth. P. H. Woodworth also sat in on this interview. Because of certain critical newspaper accounts the *Times* had published about Woodworth's recent meetings, the reporter described P. H. as "full of hostility to newspaper reporters." He sat nearby and "exercised a lawyer-like surveillance over the interview."

19. A common belief is that Woodworth was associated with the Church of God, with headquarters at Anderson, Indiana, an organization that Daniel S. Warner, a holiness preacher, helped found. Woodworth actually belonged to the Churches of God, General Conference, which was started in 1825 by a German Reformed minister, John Winebrenner. Daniel S. Warner also was associated with the Winebrenner group before helping to start the Church of God. In a letter to the author, John W. V. Smith, a historian for the Church of God (Anderson), said Warner's credentials were revoked in 1878 because "like Maria Woodworth he encountered some difficulty because of his enthusiasm for holiness preaching." It is understandable how Woodworth's connection with the Churches of God could be confused with the Anderson group. The church names are similar and she ministered throughout Indiana and established a church at Anderson even before Warner's group set up their headquarters there. The Winebrenner group has their headquarters and two schools in Findlay, Ohio. Their early church history is recorded in a massive volume, *The History of the Churches of God in the United States of America*, by C. H. Forney (1914).

20. *The Church Advocate*, Nov. 11, 1885.

21. *History of Churches of God*, p. 210.

22. Ibid.

23. Ibid. Forney added that Woodworth, in a four-year period between 1885-89, was responsible for starting about a dozen churches, adding 1,000 members, erecting six churches, starting several Sunday schools. In addition, 12 preachers were licensed as a result of her ministry.

24. "Maria B. Woodworth-Etter and The Churches of God," by Jon R. Neely. *The Church of God Advocate*, Aug. 1975, pp. 2-7.

25. Ibid., p. 6. In the Feb.17, 1887, issue of the paper, P. H. Woodworth called on the church to provide pastors for the new congregations they were forming. Many of the new congregations simply failed to get beyond the infancy stage, as Forney, Neely, and others agree. It is interesting to view P. H. Woodworth's assessment after he and Woodworth separated in 1889. The Cincinnati *Enquirer*, in their Jan. 8, 1891, issue, quoted P.H. as saying of the 75 churches they had established "all have gone to the devil but three—those at Kokomo, Anderson, and Muncie." P.H. at this time (1891) accused his wife and helpers of deceiving the people, which caused the churches to fold. He said nothing about his earlier contention that the Churches of God failed to provide leadership.

26. Ibid., p. 7. P. H. Woodworth's article appeared in the Jan.5, 1887 issue of *The Church Advocate* as "Indianapolis, Indiana."

27. Ibid.

28. Ibid. Neely received but one negative letter as a result of the article.

CHAPTER 3

The *New York Times* Takes Notice

"The reports from the Hartford City religious craze, carried on under Mrs. Woodworth, are beyond belief. Mrs. Woodworth is well-known in the State and enjoys a good reputation. A letter from there gives some instances of the so-called conversions which rival and outdo the celebrated 'Yerks' in Kentucky a half century ago."— *1885 New York Times.*[1]

When Woodworth hit the Midwest with her forceful evangelistic blitz in the 1880s, oldtimers wagged their heads and agreed that nothing in their memories could compare with the impact she made from town to town and state to state. Woodworth's thrust into the heartland affected not only the cities and towns in which she ministered, but also turned surrounding communities, counties, and even states upside down. And she was crowned both as a mighty conqueror and as an emissary from the netherworld—it all depended on who made the calls.

But in spite of the frequent opposition along the way, Woodworth won more battles than she lost during her 19th century blitz. Unnumbered people were attracted to her meetings, hundreds and thousands professed conversion, others claimed physical healings, while still others claimed to have experienced a subsequent spiritual happening that for all practical purposes wasn't unlike the Pentecostal experience of the Book of Acts and which was repeated in Topeka, Los Angeles, and many other places around the world at the turn of the century.[2] In addition, Woodworth's efforts established many new churches and revived numerous dead ones, and many young men and women were challenged to enter full-time Christian service.

The Woodworth blitz was unprecedented for women evangelists, and it is doubtful whether even Moody and Finney had any more impact than Woodworth did in any given area. It is difficult to understand now, 125 years after Woodworth burst on the scene, why many historians overlook the impact Woodworth made on both the Christian church and unchurched people. Unless one reads a Pentecostal church history, it isn't likely Woodworth's name will be found. Some church historians have never heard of her. Others perhaps have read about her, but discount the reports simply because she was a woman and/or she was a Charismatic.

She may be ignored now by historians, but people in every walk of life during the latter part of the 19th century had little doubt about the impact of her ministry. And that impact deserves a careful examination.

Woodworth was 40 years old and had been preaching about five years when she began to receive national attention in 1885. Earlier meetings had been sensational, but received limited coverage in regional newspapers; however, beginning with her opening crusade in Hartford City, Indiana, in January 1885 the meetings seemed to grow in attendance, results, and news coverage. She had no need for a publicity agent. Thousands of people heard about the meetings through word of mouth or through newspapers, and then they packed churches, courthouses, skating rinks, tents, and camp grounds, trying to get close to the celebrated evangelist who orchestrated the mass meetings usually from her improvised pulpits on rough platforms.

When success and popularity came, Woodworth was a little slow in being able to pace herself. She was "hot" and she believed her evangelistic message should be preached—week after week—with hardly a day set aside for rest. Often she would preach three times a day, each service running into the next. And it was not uncommon for the services to continue into the early hours of the morning.

After conducting a dozen meetings in Indiana during the first nine months of 1885, Woodworth's voice developed a hoarseness and she was simply worn out. Limp as a dishrag. In spite of the physically drained condition, one reporter described Woodworth "as full of religious zeal, and as capable of making impassioned appeals to the throngs who assemble at her services as when she began her labors."[3]

While Woodworth conducted a meeting at Xenia, Indiana, in August 1885, the same reporter from neighboring Wabash tried to analyze the factors that gave Woodworth her amazing appeal. First of all, he viewed her negative qualities—at least considered negative in terms of the usual qualities that attract the masses:

"Mrs. Woodworth, according to the *Courier's* connoisseur in female loveliness, is not a handsome woman, indeed, she is not passably good looking. Of medium height, a trifle inclined to embonpoint, she possesses a mobile countenance, by the expression of which her auditor almost imagines he can discern the shades of emotion as they come and go. At times her countenance is illumed with a smile so cold, so palpably artificial, that it begets a feeling of absolute repugnance."[4]

It is understandable, with the grueling schedule Woodworth was following during 1885, that it was not her best appearance she presented by the end of the summer when the *Courier* published this report. The amazing thing is that she was still alive after the night-and-day evangelistic effort.

But the reporter suddenly switched gears in his story and turned to another side of Woodworth—her platform behavior, which she, of course, attributed to the anointing of the Holy Spirit. "Once, however, she ascends the rude platform to inspire the multitude with religious fervor," he began, "criticism of her personal appearance is cast to the winds, and her hearer, though he may scoff at her methods, cannot fail to admire this most remarkable woman."[5]

The amazing Woodworth revivals between 1885-89 would easily fill a book, and it isn't my aim to focus on this brief period. However, some of the high points during this period must be included in this chapter and Chapter 4, for this is the period when Woodworth gained her greatest success prior to the advent of the Pentecostal Movement in 1901.

Woodworth Has Hartford City in Her Sights

It would be hard to imagine any city anywhere being jolted more with Woodworth's "heavenly batteries" than this county seat of Blackford County, Indiana, experienced during a five-week revival during January and February 1885. People were not attracted just to see the trances—although this aspect of the Woodworth meetings was always a drawing card—but multitudes were convinced they needed to get right with God. That conviction rested mightily on some of the town's worst sinners, professional people, most respected church members, and at least one pastor.

More than a score of reporters—one from as far away as Boston—were summoned by the excitement at Hartford City. Their papers published the stories widely and then other papers reprinted them, which resulted in a tremendous amount of publicity not only for Woodworth as the evangelist, but also for the many testimonies of conversions and subsequent spiritual experiences.[6] Woodworth had conducted a revival in Hartford City in 1884, but the impact was minor compared to this second meeting at the beginning of 1885. She had received several invitations to return to Hartford City and finally felt it was in the will of God to open the meetings in the Methodist Church. Later, because of the crowds, the meetings were moved to the courthouse and then to the spacious opera house. Even the opera house was too small to hold the crowds that swarmed to this Hoosier revival center like bees to a clover patch.

Spiritually the Methodist church was as cold as the January weather; it had drifted into formalism and some of the members were admitted skeptics. Woodworth knew that the Holy Spirit would have to move in an unusual manner or the meeting would accomplish very little. Her battle plan was simple: she asked five people to join her in prayer. They prayed that God would display his power, that the sinners in the town and surrounding area would know God's reality, and that a strong conviction of coming judgment would grip the people. One way this would happen—the most dramatic and effective in Woodworth's opinion—would be the trance experience. And so they prayed that believers and sinners alike "might fall as dead men; that the slain of the Lord might be many."[7]

Woodworth began her Hartford City crusade with little advance publicity—it wasn't even known when she would begin her meetings. The night she arrived in this pre-radio day, the news circulated by the ringing of the church bell. Methodists and others responded to the bell and soon the building was filled to overflowing that first night.

A child's experience and testimony actually ignited the revival fire in Hartford City. It happened when a son of a church leader fell under the power of God. Then Woodworth said their prayers were answered. "He rose up, stepped on the pulpit, and began to talk with the wisdom and power of God," she wrote. His father could not contain himself and began to shout and praise the Lord." Woodworth added, "As the little fellow exhorted and asked the people to come to Christ they began to weep all over the house. Some shouted; others fell prostrated. Divers operations of the spirit was seen."[8]

From then on nobody would stop this awakening.

Newspaper headlines from Indiana to New York called attention to the strange happenings in the small Midwestern city some 50 miles northeast of Indianapolis. Most of the 20 reporters who came to Hartford City wrote sensational and critical stories, but this only served to increase interest for miles around. Although the reporters in most cases were not given to this type of religious excitement, some of them tried to give an objective view—which frequently corroborated the accounts Woodworth gave in her books.[9]

Among the many remarkable happenings were the conversions—especially the conversions of well-known and respected citizens in the community. One of these was 62-year-old John Cantwell, a leading lawyer in the state and widely known for his disdain for spiritual matters. Ministers in the city had given up hope of ever seeing his conversion.

But something happened that changed Cantwell's mind and his life.

Cantwell was fascinated when he saw Woodworth in a trance, by this time a frequent happening for the evangelist. He watched as Woodworth stood at times with her face and hands raised toward heaven, and then at other times as tears streamed down her face—all the while going through the motions of preaching and pleading with sinners to come to Christ. Then Cantwell saw Woodworth lying for hours in trances. He had never seen anything like this and wanted to know more about it.

The lawyer invited Woodworth to his home, assuring her that he wanted light on spiritual matters. There, in Cantwell's home, the amazing Woodworth simply told him of her own experiences. This proud lawyer had never listened any closer to an opponent's argument before the bench than he listened to this unlettered woman preacher. Woodworth told the story in her book, saying that the power of God fell in the room, and she was almost blind with the glory of God.

John Cantwell would never be the same. He began to weep and then knelt, not caring what others would say or do. Woodworth added with a note of victory, "This was the first time this strong man, this tall cedar, had ever bowed before the living God."[10]

One might as well have tried to quiet a steam engine rolling through Blackburn County as to keep Cantwell's remarkable conversion a secret. The news soon spread around the city, and that night Cantwell came boldly to the crowded opera house and knelt at the altar. His dramatic conversion touched the heart of another attorney, Elisha Pearce, and he soon joined Cantwell at the once despised mourner's bench. Cantwell testified that he had served Satan for 62 years, but now was converted and had "come to the great fountain of everlasting life, drank at its sacred shrine" and was redeemed.[11]

Another well-known citizen to respond to the "anxious seat" was John M. Ruckman, postmaster and former editor of the *Hartford City News*. Ruckman told the audience how he had been translated from the darkness of sin to light and then, when he gave an earnest appeal for others to follow his lead, the audience responded with "an enthusiasm seldom witnessed."[12]

A *Fort Wayne Gazette* writer treated Ruckman's conversion in jest and doubted that Woodworth could work the same kind of wonders with Fort Wayne editors. "[She] will have poor luck we fear when she strikes Ft. Wayne and attempts to bring the ungodly editors of our contemporaries from their evil ways. The toughest job will be to get Shober [apparently an editor] on his knees."[13]

But the excitement of Hartford City's revival was only beginning. A local man, whose drinking habits were generally known, was determined to break up one of the services. He marched within ten feet of the pulpit and let out a torrent of profanity. Neither he nor anyone else was ready for what happened next. Suddenly a power seemed to grip his vocal chords. His tongue refused to obey him. And what made it all the more mysterious is that Woodworth seemed oblivious to his standing there just a short distance away. Later when the bewildered man was asked about his strange experience, he replied, "Go up yourself and find out."[14]

Newspapers of the day and Woodworth's writings tell of people who joked about the trances and then went into trances themselves. In one of her earlier books, she told about a party where several young women thought they would have fun mimicking and acting out a trance. They were struck down by the same power that had stopped the drunk's abusive language, and their mocking quickly turned to loud praying, pleading to God for mercy.

While the Hartford City revival was at high tide, an editor at Kokomo, 40 miles away, took note of the phenomenon, agreeing Hartford City needed not only a religious revival, but also a strong disinfectant. He had never seen in one town such a bunch of gamblers and liquor dealers, or a dirtier set of loafers. "It is pardonable exaggeration," he wrote, "to say that the carrion-crows fly a mile from the courthouse to get fresh air."[15]

Then the editor vividly described Woodworth's camp meeting style:

"She goes at it like a foot pad tackles his prey. By some supernatural power she just knocks 'em silly when they are not looking for it, and while they are down she applies the hydraulic pressure and pumps the grace of God into them by the bucketful. While in this semi-comatose condition, her subjects go 'galivanting' over the gold-paved streets of the New Jerusalem, conversing with departed friends, and having a good time in general."[16]

The writer expressed reservations about the methods used and the trance as a viable Christian experience. He certainly wouldn't want to be riding in a train knowing that the engineer was given to trances: "I will thank him to stop and let me off at his earliest convenience. And I know no reason why I should trust his judgment more in a spiritual journey than a temporal one."[17]

Others agreed with the Kokomo editor and heaped scorn on Woodworth and her converts at Hartford City. But in spite of the criticism, Woodworth pulled out all of the stops in her usual style. She believed what was happening was a ministry of the Holy Spirit and an answer to the prayers of that small group she pulled together when she first came to Hartford City.

And who can deny that much good was accomplished through this 1885 meeting in Hartford City? The Methodist Church was not complaining. They received 40 new members. The city knew something had happened. An estimated 500 people were converted, unnumbered people reported that they received a deeper spiritual experience, and others received calls into the ministry. Hartford City and surrounding communities were indeed revolutionized. Woodworth said it was the fear of God falling on the city that had produced the results. Even the police remarked that they had never seen such a change in the city. With no fighting and swearing on the streets, the police had little to do. Woodworth noticed the change, even though it might be for a season: "There seemed to be a spirit of love and kindness among all classes, as if they felt they were in the presence of God."[18] Other newspaper reports stated that the saloons were empty, and the saloonkeepers locked their doors and went to the meetings themselves.

Hartford City, Indiana, during the winter of 1885 would not be Woodworth's biggest revival by any means, but it was the place she gained national attention and a place where conversions and trances gained a certain degree of respectability.

And not only Hartford City, but also neighboring New Corner, Indiana, received a spillover from the revival fountain. New Corner believers invited Woodworth to visit their town, and despite invitations to Cincinnati, Fort Wayne, and other cities, she felt the Lord calling her to this small town just 15 miles away. Here she remained a week where a reported 500 persons were converted. Regarding the New Corner experience, Woodworth quoted a story from the *Indianapolis Journal* (no date given) in her 1894 book: "Many superstitious persons stay away for fear of Mrs. W.'s power to overcome them," the report claimed. "Others refuse to shake her hand."[19]

The reporter probably summed up best these Indiana meetings early in 1885 that helped set the tone for Woodworth's ministry during the next 40 years: "Whatever may be said of the trances, there is no denying the fact that her meetings are productive of great good, and that when the sheaves are finally bound for eternity, many will bless the name of the great evangelist."[20]

Selected Regional and National Headlines
During Hartford City, Indiana, Meetings
January and February 1885

Cincinnati *Enquirer* (Jan. 25, 27, Feb.17)

CATALEPTIC REVIVAL
An Evangelist's Wonderful Power

Her Subjects Fall Rigid in and Away from the Church

THE LADY EVANGELIST
Her Great Work Still Progressing

The Excitement Unabated and the Attendance on the Increase

THE GREAT REVIVAL
Wonderful Work of the Evangelist

Old and Young Entranced by the Inspiration of Her Teachings

The Most Hardened Sinners Crowding Around the Anxious Seat Seeking a Better Life

Indianapolis Journal (Jan. 25):

A REMARKABLE REVIVAL
Extraordinary Character of the Meetings Now in Progress at Hartford City

New York Times (Jan. 24, 26, and 30):

SAID TO BE RELIGION
Strange Scenes at "Revival Meetings" Held in Indiana

AN EVANGELIST AT WORK
A Revival in Indiana Conducted by Mrs. Woodworth

RELIGIOUS CRAZE IN INDIANA
One of the Female Converts Explains the Sensation of a Trance

Fort Wayne Gazette (Jan. 23):

SISTER WOODWORTH
She Knocks 'Em Cold at Hartford City

The Unregenerate Fall in Spasms of Religious Emotion

Fort Wayne Sentinel (Jan. 31):

RIGID RELIGION
Mrs. Woodworth, the Evangelist, at Hartford City, Revolutionizing the Town

Citizens Neglecting Their Business to Witness the Wonderful Manifestations

Trances Becoming Fashionable—Saloon Business Demoralized—Glimpses of New Jerusalem

ENDNOTES

1. *New York Times*, Jan. 30, 1885.

2. The modern Pentecostal revival is usually associated with two American cities that experienced Holy Spirit baptism accompanied with speaking in tongues: Topeka, Kansas, in 1901, under the ministry of Charles F. Parham; and Los Angeles,

in 1906, under the ministry of William J. Seymour.

3. Wabash (Indiana) *Weekly Courier*, Aug. 21, 1885.

4. Ibid.

5. Ibid.

6. In her *Life, Work and Experience of Maria Beulah Woodworth*, p. 189, Woodworth said she received the gift of healing while ministering at Columbia City, Ind., in March and April 1885.

7. Ibid., pp.174-75.

8. Ibid., pp. 174.

9. Woodworth appreciated the Cincinnati *Enquirer*, which usually treated her fairly. *Enquirer* paperboys in Hartford City made a good living while the revival was going on as people were anxious to read the reports from a big city newspaper.

10. *Life, Work and Experience*, p. 178.

11. Cincinnati *Enquirer*, Feb. 17, 1885.

12. Cincinnati *Enquirer*, as quoted in *Trials and Triumphs of Maria B. Woodworth*, p. 192.

13. *Fort Wayne Gazette*, Feb. 12, 1885.

14. *Indianapolis Journal*, Jan. 30, 1885. This unnamed drunk gained probably more publicity in that moment than he gained in a lifetime, for this same story was published in the *New York Times*.

15. *Kokomo Dispatch*, Feb. 5, 1885.

16. Ibid.

17. Ibid. About three years later in Decatur, Illinois, it was reported in the *Daily Republic* (Sept. 19, 1887) that a Wabash engineer who was scheduled to go out on a run at midnight went into a trance earlier in the evening in one of Woodworth's meetings. He never made the run that night and was still

entranced the following afternoon.

18. *Life, Work, and Experiences*, p. 175.

19. Ibid, p. 183.

20. Ibid.

CHAPTER 4

Gaining a Powerful Momentum

*"It was a wonderful sight to see so many old people, many with
white hair, who had come into the fold of Christ at the eleventh
hour, plucked as brands from the burning, coming up out of the
water with their faces and hands raised to heaven, praising
God ... I organized a church in the grove. Two hundred and
ninety-five names were enrolled."*
— 1886 meeting in Anderson, Indiana[1]

After Woodworth wrapped up the highly successful
campaign at Hartford City in February 1885, she
conducted back-to-back revival meetings throughout central
and northern Indiana—gaining phenomenal publicity and
results with every campaign. Her stops included the towns
of New Corner, Summitville, Fairmount, Columbia City,
Elwood, Tipton, and Pendleton.

Riding high as a result of outstanding success in these
smaller towns, Woodworth drew a bead on Kokomo, a larger
city named for a Miami Indian chief, with a reputation of
being one of the most wicked cities in the state. Here she
battled long and hard for three weeks against fierce
opposition from most of the churches and the city's *Dispatch*
newspaper.[2]

But by this time Woodworth had added a new weapon
to her spiritual arsenal: divine healing. At Columbia City
during March and April, Woodworth said the Lord called her

to pray for the sick, which she was reluctant to do because she thought it would distract from her evangelistic efforts. Nine years later she wrote that thousands had been won to Christ after seeing others healed.

One of the names on her Pendleton healing list that spring was a well-known unbeliever, a Dr. Troy, who was healed of diabetes. After his conversion, Troy began to preach, and a year later could report that more than a hundred people had responded to his invitations. "I am 58 years old," he told a camp meeting audience in 1886, "and the last year has been the happiest of my life."[3] In 1890, while Woodworth came under strong criticism and legal action initiated by two St. Louis doctors, the same Dr. Troy came to her aid and was quoted in the St. Louis papers.

In addition to Dr. Troy, other medical doctors joined the Woodworth steamroller in 1885. These included A. B. Pitzer, Tipton; William Cooper, Kokomo; T. V. Gifford, Kokomo; and a woman physician, a Dr. Guy. The medical profession in general, however, usually avoided becoming involved in Woodworth's type of salvation and healing.

Another exception came after the turn of the century when Woodworth was laboring in the Quad City area of Iowa and Illinois. A medical doctor, O.W. Looker, saw so many of his patients healed, he investigated the revival meeting in Moline, Illinois. Woodworth wrote that he was one of the finest men in the city, but the churches could not reach him. "He was converted and became an earnest worker."[4]

Three cities, in addition to Kokomo, that felt big time impacts from Woodworth's Midwestern blitz and that are selected for a closer look as being representative of the period are Alexandria and Anderson, Indiana, and Springfield, Illinois.

Kokomo, 1885

Woodworth was no stranger to Kokomo, having conducted a meeting here in 1884, and because of the news she had generated in nearby cities. Some of the residents had gone to the other meetings held in Indiana during the winter and spring and they could hardly wait for Woodworth to turn her weapons on wicked Kokomo.

Woodworth opened the Kokomo crusade in the Friends church, Saturday, May 24, and fired off the first shot in her battle with a sermon based on Elijah's question on Mount Carmel: "How long halt ye between two opinions?" She promised her hearers that Kokomo would experience an outpouring of the Holy Spirit, and that first day 4,000 people tried to get in to see what would happen. It was obvious that if the city was to have an outpouring of the Holy Spirit, it would not happen in the Friends church alone, simply because the building wouldn't hold the crowds.

The next day Howard County officials permitted Woodworth to move her meeting to the courthouse. But even the spacious courthouse proved far too small for this meeting. So Woodworth moved again, this time to the skating rink, which held 2,500. Finally, in a building that would hold most of the enthusiastic crowd, Woodworth began to reach what one editor called the Sodom and Gomorrah of Indiana. "When Kokomo, the combined Sodom and Gomorrah of modern times, begins to succumb to the entreaties of the evangelist," he wrote, "then indeed is her work successful. The average Kokomoke has heretofore been considered beyond redemption."[5]

One of these considered beyond redemption was Charles Snowden, who was described as a brilliant intellect from a good family and a graduate of Earlham College. Snowden's first visit to the revival meeting proved quite embarrassing. He had been making the rounds of Kokomo's saloons that day and then wandered into the Woodworth meeting. When Woodworth opened the floor for converts to give testimonies, Snowden arose and in a very eloquent manner gave an account of his checkered life. The more Snowden talked, the more he revealed just how drunk he was. Someone called police officers who escorted Snowden to the city jail.

But Woodworth determined the devil would not keep Snowden bound in alcohol. She called the saints to prayer for this "misguided wreck of once noble manhood."[6] The next morning Woodworth sent to the jail for Snowden, who was brought sober and very repentant to the rink by an officer by the name of Imbler. Soon both officer and prisoner knelt at the altar, where they remained for an hour; then they arose to testify of their conversions.

The *Kokomo Gazette Tribune*, which repeatedly promoted the meetings, commented on Snowden's conversion, calling him a remarkable man who came from a good family and was brilliant. But alcohol had bound him. The writer hoped his conversion would save him and make a productive citizen out of him. "Now, if, after a long career of dissipation and sin he can break loose from the chains that bind him, there will be thousands of amens all over Indiana and Ohio."[7]

Woodworth's meeting in Kokomo will have accomplished a great work, the editorial writer added, if Charley Snowden could be restored to his wife and children. Although Woodworth did not choose to reprint this editorial in her books, she must have been one of those who shouted "amen" for just one more victory in her blitz against the devil and his crowd.

The other major newspaper in Kokomo, the *Dispatch*, gave Woodworth and her methods bad marks and sought out ministers to get their reactions. They came up with mixed reviews. Some were extremely critical, while others preferred to give Woodworth the benefit of the doubt, reasoning if some good came of the meetings they should be supported.[8]

Ministers Divided in 1885 Kokomo Meeting

Dr. Lewis Kern: "I believe it is genuine, old-fashioned Methodist religion, just such as we had in the times of Finley [possibly Evangelist Charles Finney], Mrs. Fletcher, and Peter Cartwright, all wool and a yard wide. No one who believes in the Methodist doctrine can say aught against Mrs. Woodworth's plan and teachings."

I. H. Ellis: "I like it the best of anything I ever saw in the way of a religious meeting. Hope it will go on till every sinner in Kokomo is stretched out stiff on the mourner's bench."

Elder E. L. Frazier: "I do not at all endorse it nor accept her claims. The whole work and results may be accounted for without God.... No one who has respect for Holy things or reverence can give bold utterances to such as 'a cyclone of the Holy Ghost'... I have not witnessed the like since I attended the meetings of the poor black slaves in Kentucky, thirty years ago."

Father Lordemann: "I believe Mrs. Woodworth's meetings are a reproach and a disgrace to the religion of God."

J. B. Carter: "I think Mrs. Woodworth is reaching a class of people that the churches can not—or do not—reach , and I say amen to her work."

Elder Joseph Reese: "I don't believe the Woodworth theory of conversion. Don't believe God has anything to do with the so-called Woodworth trance. The plan is not rational neither is it desirable."

W. B. Elson: "It's nawthun but flap-doodle and wind.

—*Kokomo Dispatch*, May 28, 1885

The same *Dispatch* reporter who surveyed the area ministers told his readers in a story that took up most of the front page that Woodworth couldn't preach as he understood the meaning of the word. He then labeled her as an exhorter, "and the burden of her discourses is 'Come to Jesus.'"[9]

How Woodworth would have loved for a Kokomo jury to find her guilty of urging people to come to Jesus! She could smile with satisfaction when she read this intended criticism. Indeed, reaching people with the Gospel of Christ was her trademark, her driving passion.

As in most of the meetings of this period, the greatest criticism of the Woodworth meetings was on the trance experience. Although Woodworth appeared to have mellowed in her teaching on the trances in later years, she always held that the trance was a viable religious experience and was equivalent to an anointing of the Holy Spirit, receiving the power, or being baptized in the Spirit, and was usually accompanied by a vision. Here in Kokomo, however, reporters understood her teachings to mean that the trance was the way of conversion. For this unorthodox interpretation, ministers and others opposed her campaigns.

A lengthy and well-written editorial in the June 4 *Dispatch* dealt primarily with the Holy Ghost baptismal experience—which Woodworth defended as being the same as Cornelius received in Acts 10.

Outspoken against the trance as a means of conversion, the writer called the experience "ecstasy." He quoted several doctors and authorities of the day who had given their opinions in earlier meetings. Sinners could be saved without the Woodworth trance, the editor believed. And if the trance was the only way to be saved, he reasoned, one out of 100 people would obtain righteousness.

On the other side of the issues stood the *Dispatch's* competition, the *Gazette Tribune*, which took a more sympathetic view of the meetings—including, surprisingly, the trances—and saw much good in Woodworth's unconventional circus-like campaign, especially conversions such as Charles Snowden experienced. In a story published two weeks after Woodworth opened the Kokomo campaign, a *Gazette* writer called a Sunday meeting "a phenomenal day in the religious history of Kokomo."[10]

Summarizing the events of the revival to that point, the writer noted the success Woodworth was enjoying despite the critics who predicted she would fall on her face in Kokomo. Even the critics had to admit the now sanctified skating rink was seldom empty and that thousands from out of town were being drawn into the city. At every service scores of people—many of them prominent citizens—lined the once-despised altar to receive pardon and to be "led into a better experience."

In an obvious answer to the rival *Dispatch's* ministerial survey, the *Gazette* writer reasoned that surely not all the new converts were "dealing in flap doodle, poppy cock and humbuggery." And for the good that was being accomplished at the revival meeting—despite the unusual methods employed—the paper went on record to encourage the meetings, an effort that leads people "from sin and degradation up towards the Divine Father."[11]

With support from one of the leading Kokomo newspapers like this, Woodworth had no need of paid advertisements for the Charismatic phenomena taking place in Indiana. Even the critical *Dispatch* gave generous coverage of the closing meeting in Kokomo and couldn't help but compliment Woodworth and the positive results of the meetings—despite the trances.

She would be far more efficient if she would no longer use trances, the *Dispatch* argued. "That would certainly lessen her drawing power, but it would enlarge her possibilities for doing good. She is a woman of remarkable natural power, honest, and deeply spiritual but self-deceived as to the divinity of the trance."[12]

The *Dispatch* compared the trances to Methodist meetings of 20 years earlier. The only difference the writer could see was that although in the Methodist meetings the trances were a side issue and not encouraged, Mrs. Woodworth's trances were considered essential "and are spoken of at almost every meeting, and are encouraged to the utmost degree."[13]

Woodworth closed the Kokomo revival with a spectacular baptismal service in Wildcat Creek, the "religious Ganges and Howard County's Jordan"—a festival-like scene attracting upwards of 12,000 people. Eighty-two men and women and boys and girls walked into the Wildcat to be baptized by one of Woodworth's associates, William Hile, whom the *Gazette Tribune* called "a brilliant young Wesleyan Methodist preacher."[14] Woodworth did not go into the water, but helped prepare the candidates and with a practice Methodists approved, sprinkled two of the converts.

What was accomplished in Kokomo during the three weeks and 66 meetings in which Woodworth pounded the pulpit, went into trances, prayed for the sick, and pleaded with sinners to get right with God?

Converts numbered in the hundreds; 82 people were baptized on the last day of the meetings, and a few weeks later Woodworth returned to the Kokomo battlefield and baptized 62 more; a Daniel's Band was started with 320 members, which later developed into a local church.[15]

Kokomo, the wicked "Sodom and Gomorrah," would never be the same after this Woodworth blitz. The next year ecumenist Woodworth returned and reported she met several young men who had gone into the ministry as a result of the 1885 meeting. Always inspired by military symbolism, she described pitching tents, sounding the battle cry, and calling for soldiers of the cross. "We had a grand reunion; several hundred converts of the meeting of one year before were there; also many others, with their bright testimonies, that God had kept them through all the persecutions; many had been healed of all manner of diseases."

Woodworth learned that many had gone into the evangelistic field and pastorates. She said, "One day there were present twenty young ministers, who had been licensed by the different churches; all converts of my first meeting at Kokomo."[16] Woodworth added that the congregation under the leadership of Pastor Hile had built a "fine church edifice at Kokomo, and have the most powerful church in the city; also the largest congregation."

Alexandria, 1885

In her 1894 autobiography, Woodworth describes the Alexandria, Indiana, camp meeting held in September 1885 as the "most wonderful meeting I ever held."[17]

If gauged by numbers alone, few people would argue with Woodworth's assessment of this meeting she orchestrated in Madison County between Alexandria and Muncie. Here, an estimated 20,000-25,000 people gathered to hear and see the signs and wonders that had become the hallmarks of Woodworth's meetings. It proved to be the biggest single gathering of any meeting Woodworth conducted in her more than 45 years on the sawdust trail.

As was customary, Woodworth took time for hundreds of converts to give their ringing testimonies—which only set the stage for others to be converted. One morning after the testimony service, Woodworth preached about the power of the Holy Ghost. Before she finished, she said the power of God moved from her preaching to grip the congregation. "Many fell to the ground," she wrote. "Others stood with their faces and hands raised to heaven. The Holy Ghost sat upon them. Others shouted, some talked, others wept aloud. Sinners were converted and began to testify and praise God."[18]

No tent at the time could possibly hold the crowds that surrounded the campsite, so a high platform was built in a grove of trees for Woodworth's pulpit. Then she faced the largest crowd she had ever seen. God gave her a deep subject, she said, which resulted in a two-hour sermon, several healings, and hundreds converted.

It is hard to imagine up to 25,000 people standing in one place to hear a speaker without the benefit of a microphone and public address system. It is difficult to imagine, too, how the crowd managed to find enough to eat, places to stay, and restroom facilities during the several days the meetings were held at the grove—which was five miles from the nearest town.

A *Muncie Daily News* reporter who was there to perform his duty, not to get religion, described Woodworth's appeal to the sinners. "She tells her hearers that the Holy Ghost is about knocking at the heart of each one and may never come again, and if they do not heed its call he may be angered and they will be damned irrevocably and unredeemably."[19] Mrs. Woodworth understood human nature, the reporter averred, and "seems to move her people more by the fear of hell than by the love of God."

Although Woodworth and other believers could hardly appreciate everything this reporter wrote—including the extreme alliterations used in the headlines—the story is colorful and descriptive and representative of both the secular reporting of the day and possibly a model of scores of other meetings in other cities and towns. (See Appendix B for the complete story as published in the September 21, 1885, issue of the *Muncie Daily News*.)

Anderson, 1886-87

Anderson, Indiana, the county seat of Madison County, is known in evangelical circles as the home of one of the 200 American church groups and separate congregations that use the name "The Church of God." This Indiana group, founded by Daniel S. Warner and others in 1881, is usually identified with "Anderson" in parentheses.

Before Warner moved his headquarters to Anderson, Woodworth had already been here. She conducted a revival meeting here, which resulted in a local church being established for the Churches of God (Winebrenner), the very group Warner had left a few years earlier because of his support of the entire sanctification experience.

For two years prior to her first meeting in 1886, a few believers in Anderson had been asking Woodworth to conduct a meeting in their city. They had attended nearby revival efforts and were certain their city could use Woodworth's brand of religious fervor. Finally in the summer of that year, Woodworth threw down the gauntlet against Satan and evil in Anderson by opening a tent crusade on the county fair grounds.

The previous year, the Anderson *Weekly Review* had set the stage of opposition by referring to Woodworth as "the great paralyzer" during a meeting she orchestrated at Elwood, Indiana. They disapproved of her methods, which they described as "perfectly awful and shameful."[20]

Having read her press clippings, Woodworth had a pretty good idea what she faced in Anderson.

The very first service found the tent packed to capacity, but it was a strange crowd that waited impatiently for Woodworth to start her meeting. Most of the people were unbelievers. Many of them had come out of curiosity. Some of these unbelievers, surprisingly enough, were there to support Woodworth because most of the church members of the city—along with the ministers—were outspoken about Woodworth stepping foot inside Anderson's city limits and simply boycotted the meetings.

Woodworth loaded her cannons, mounted the Anderson platform, straightened out her skirts, and preached one of her patented fiery sermons that left no doubt the people would split hell wide open unless they repented. Ministers and newspaper editors headed the list. Church membership alone would not take care of their sins that were an abomination unto God. When she concluded her no-holds-barred sermon and threw the altar open for the penitents, scores of people rushed to the front where they fell on their faces in prayer. Before the three-week meeting came to an end, Woodworth's first effort in Anderson had touched the entire city—despite the ministerial boycott and negative newspaper reports.

But Woodworth saw her work in Anderson as an unfinished symphony. Ten days after the first Anderson crusade closed, she returned to the city, following a series of meetings in a nearby town, and opened a second three-week campaign in a grove of trees. If the first campaign was a breakthrough, this one was an explosion. If the first was basic training, this was the battlefield.

The first service saw 28 people respond to the altar call, and conversions totaled 20-50 a day during the remainder of the revival. Many of these converts had been attracted to the meetings from different parts of the country. How the out-of-state people heard about the meetings isn't known, but they came, were converted, and then took the message back to their homes.

Critics often claimed that Woodworth's converts could be corralled in a building set aside for the mentally challenged, with a few religious zealots thrown in for good measure. Not so, supporters would counter. At Anderson, Judge William R. West, and an influential farmer, Casper Hartman, unashamedly added their names to the growing convert list.[21] After a Mrs. Simpson was converted and healed of heart disease, her physician, a Dr. Riggs, attended one of Woodworth's meetings, and both he and his wife were converted.

Many others—doctors, lawyers, drunkards, agnostics, and church members—"from the tallest cedar down to the weakest" were shown their need of the Savior and bowed unashamedly at the camp meeting altar.[22] One lawyer who was converted in the meeting gave a ringing testimony of the conversion of his brother who had written concerning the far-reaching effects of the revival. Woodworth reported the event in her book, noting that the brother who had written had never seen her, nor attended any of her meetings. "What he had seen and heard of them from a distance and by reading my book, he was converted and was going into the ministry," Woodworth wrote. And furthermore, he had "several hundred dollars worth of infidel books, and he had made a fire and burned them."[23]

When Woodworth set a day for the baptismal service in the White River, the city of Anderson was unprepared for what happened. Hundreds of people streamed into the city in wagons, buggies, and other vehicles to watch the 194 persons follow the Lord in baptism. At the appointed time, an impressive parade of new converts—marching four abreast and with arms locked not unlike the Civil Rights parades during the turbulent 1960s—moved toward the river as thousands lined the banks to watch.

One of the leaders broke into the first verse of "The Star of Bethlehem," and the crowd picked it up as the procession moved across a steel bridge and down the bank on the other side.

Supporters of the revival meeting built a pier of planks extending 30 feet into the river under the bridge. As the converts and workers sang on the shore, Woodworth walked each convert onto the pier, where a minister in the water performed the ordinance.

Being able to reach older adults with the Gospel became another trademark with Woodworth, now 42 years old, as she seemed to place a high priority on the ones closest to the grave, and obviously they responded to her interest in them. Anderson was no exception. Many were past middle age, some as old as 85.

"It was a wonderful sight to see so many old people, many with white hair," she wrote in a report, "who had come into the fold of Christ at the eleventh hour, plucked as brands from the burning, coming up out of the water with their faces and hands raised to heaven, praising God"[24]

She added that nearly all who were baptized came out of the water shouting. And in what could have been a pretty risky baptismal service, some "fell under the power of God, and had to be carried out."

Before the second Anderson meeting closed, Woodworth organized a Church of God with a charter membership of 295. The group later built a new brick building on South Brown Street, which Woodworth helped dedicate the next year.[25] By the time the building was dedicated, the membership had grown to 400.

For Woodworth, it was an emotional dedication service as her eyes roamed from one smiling convert to the next.

She guessed some 500 people in attendance were converts from her meetings during the previous two years—many of whom had gone into some phase of Christian ministry—just another indication of her ability to reproduce herself with no gender or denominational distinction.

In January 1891, about four and a half years after Woodworth held her first campaign in Anderson, she returned to conduct a revival meeting in the new church building. Several healings were reported, including the healing of a blind woman. Although Woodworth overlooked the blind woman's story for her book, the *St. Louis Post-Dispatch* published an article titled, "Remarkable Cures. The Deaf Hear and the Blind See at Mrs. Woodworth's Command." The paper cited one of the most remarkable cases was that of a Mollie Bowers, "a prepossessing young woman from near Alexandria and a woman of more than ordinary intelligence."

The story related that Mollie had been attacked with measles 12 years earlier, leaving her totally blind in one eye and the other very damaged. "The young lady, kneeling upon the rostrum, pleaded with burning fervor that her eyesight be restored." Unlike some of the other newspaper reports, the St. Louis reporter gave his readers the benefit of any doubts:

"The prayer was a remarkable one, in which the fair petitioner recited her trials and temptations and the grievous annoyance that the loss of her eyesight had been to her. Mrs. Woodworth laid her hands across the young lady's eyes and, quoting a passage of scripture appropriate to the occasion, commanded her to arise. She did so and saw. For a few moments she stood bewildered, and finally realizing that her eyesight had been fully restored she turned to her father and fell upon his neck, sobbing bitterly."[26]

One could get the impression that the meetings in Anderson were without controversy, and everybody marched to the beat of Woodworth's drum. A closer look reveals otherwise.

Some of the newspapers were extremely critical of the meetings, giving Woodworth a "sound roasting." And Woodworth was involved in a libel suit while in Anderson, which created some hard feelings toward her.[27] Despite the many conversions and the rapid formation of a thriving church in the late 1880s, the congregation fell on hard times before the turn of the century. The membership had dwindled and the church was in debt in 1898; as a result, the mortgage was foreclosed and the property was sold.[28]

What happened to the believers who came shouting out of the White River baptismal service and later united with the thriving Church of God established in Anderson? Woodworth is silent on the later troubles, and we can rely only on the report given by C. H. Forney, the historian for the Churches of God. Forney blames Woodworth for the church's demise because of her later "meddling" in the affairs of the congregation.

Regardless of the cause of trouble at Anderson, the genuinely converted seemed to have found a place in other congregations to worship and serve. Some probably united with Daniel S. Warner's group that had set up its headquarters there a few years before the Woodworth church dissolved.

Some critics would take the Anderson episode and claim the "Woodworth revival wave" was more of a mirage than a wave, more of a puffy white cloud than a cloud burst.

But in all fairness to Woodworth, her gifts were in evangelism and church planting—not supervising and organizing weekly pastoral duties. And as one of the leading Churches of God ministers of that day reasoned, it wasn't easy to form a church with the types of people she gathered in her revivals. R. H. Bolton wrote in *The Church Advocate* that it would take a minister with patience and special tact, and then it would have been a "herculean task" to bring harmony to the converts who had come from every walk of life. "Where men took hold of this work with these qualifications they have succeeded admirably," he argued. Likewise, "Where men failed to possess qualifications to harmonize contrary elements they most signally failed."[29]

Anderson was stirred for God during those early campaigns in 1886-87. And many appeared genuinely converted and became dedicated workers for the Master. Woodworth and her workers saw that fruit, and could say that the meetings were worth every prayer, tear, sacrifice— and yes, every stinging criticism.

Springfield, Illinois, 1888-89

During 1887-88 Maria Woodworth conducted meetings in Illinois—Boiling Springs, Decatur, Urbana, and a few other small towns—before moving into Springfield in June 1888 for what proved to be her most successful salvation-healing campaign in the Prairie State. Although Woodworth didn't know a soul among the 24,000 inhabitants before the Springfield meeting began, she believed the time had come to hit the center of state government. Springfield was ripe to launch a Gospel offensive.

As in previous campaigns, Woodworth's Springfield meetings attracted thousands of people, and before the dust settled—or the mud dried up in this campaign—she founded a Church of God. Remarkably, within a year a new church building housed Springfield's newest and largest congregation.[30]

But the harvest in the opening days of the crusade was not as ripe as Woodworth had thought. Only a Lutheran church responded to her invitation to participate in the meetings in which she purposed to "build up the Temple of our God" and to battle the "mighty." Certainly she was disappointed at the lack of response, but that had never kept her out of the battle for righteousness, she must have told herself as she rolled into Oak Ridge Park.

Standing like a sentry here is the 117-foot Lincoln Tomb, reminding visitors of the awful price the nation suffered as angry forces ripped it apart in the Civil War. Beginning the Springfield meetings in June 1888, Woodworth pitched her tent and attracted a grand total of 18 persons to the first service.[31]

Despite the ministerial boycott, which no doubt had something to do with the small crowd on the opening night, Woodworth shouted victory in the tent, which was being drenched by unseasonably heavy rains. Before the meetings closed that summer, the congregation of 18 curious persons had exploded to thousands, and even those who opposed the meetings had to admit Woodworth and her team accomplished what their own local churches had not been able to do in the Illinois capital city.

One of the few outside factors in Woodworth's favor was the positive newspaper reporting in the *Springfield Journal*. Reporter C. E. Kalb gave Woodworth probably the most favorable reporting she had received up to that time. He was impressed with Woodworth's preaching, the crowds, the healings, and the deeper spiritual experiences Woodworth encouraged. There were embarrassing moments brought on by overzealous converts, but Kalb—who later went into the Presbyterian ministry—blamed the individuals involved, not Woodworth and her practices.[32]

A *Journal* story, which appeared about two weeks after the meetings began, commended Woodworth to its readers. Then Kalb not only invited readers to the meetings, but he also challenged ministers and doctors to attend, reasoning that they would reflect no discredit on themselves if they would attend and investigate Woodworth's ministry.

The ministers did take up a challenge, but it wasn't what the reporter had in mind, and certainly not in a manner Woodworth welcomed. Avoiding the meetings, as they had in the begining, was easier for Woodworth to take compared with the new tactic. Now they viewed the tent meeting as something like a plague, and the best place for Woodworth and her crowd was in Peoria or Decatur or anywhere except in Springfield. Taking the lead, Dr. John B. Briney, pastor of the Christian Church and later editor of the Disciples' *Christian Standard*, told his congregation he was going to prove Woodworth to be a fraud and drive her out of the city.

When Woodworth returned to the city during the winter of 1888-89, she faced more criticism from Briney and the other ministers. Battle lines soon separated Woodworth's troops from the traditional churches that Briney represented. He fired the first salvo at Woodworth in a paper he wrote, challenging her interpretations and practices.

Woodworth wrote that the other minister selected Briney—whom she called the "great theologian and champion debater"—to debate her.

She had taken on the devil and his demons, but Woodworth recognized her limitation in this kind of theological warfare. While Briney had degrees hanging on his study wall, she had not completed grammar school. She knew she would have little success in a debate and had no plans to go up against Briney. Finally, however, she gave in to the pressures of her newfound friends and agreed to accept Briney's challenge. Woodworth admitted it was an enormous challenge just to stand on the same platform with Briney. "He boasted of his college course, of his education, of his wisdom, of his popularity, and made it appear that I was a poor ignorant, blinded crank."[33]

They had brought together "history, doctor books and the devil's works to prove that the power of God had been taken from the church," Woodworth added, and she was ready to defend what she had preached from the Bible.

But how would she answer Briney's charges and compete with his education and intellect? Years earlier she learned that God would go before her, and she seemed unafraid and anxious for the debate to get started. Holding the paper Briney had written, which claimed she was a fraud, Woodworth referred to each argument and believed that she proved to the people, who packed out the hall to hear the debate, that her accuser did not have Scripture to back up his arguments. Then she used a tactic which no doubt caught Briney by surprise.

Among her own followers were people who could send a message to Briney and his side. "I said the best proof of our being called of God to preach was the fact that souls were saved," she said. "I asked all who had been converted in these meetings to stand up, and over two hundred arose."

If that wasn't enough, Woodworth asked all who had received healing by the power of God to stand. About 50 people stood. Her followers assured Woodworth that—despite the fact that the arena was not her turf, Briney was a highly respected scholar, and it looked like David and Goliath's confrontation—she had won the debate. And it wasn't even close. "The people said that before I had taken the Bible in my hand, I had cut his head off with his own sword," she wrote.[34]

Woodworth claimed she put Briney on the run by answering his arguments with only the Bible. She wrote, "I proved him to be wrong on every point. Glory to God for victory! With all his boasted wisdom, God chose a weak woman to confound and condemn, and show to the world that it was useless to fight against him or the Holy Ghost power."[35]

During the exciting days Woodworth conducted meetings in Springfield, all classes of people were attracted and testified of beneficial results. Woodworth wrote that infidels, skeptics, gamblers, harlots, drunkards, and dead church members had been reached. Two members of the legislature responded to her altar call, and after their conversion, gave their testimonies of what God had done for them and what He was doing for others through them.

An 82-year-old infidel, O. G. Wood, was converted during the first meeting at Oak Ridge Park in the summer of 1888. Wood also claimed to have been healed of rheumatism, which had crippled him for 15 years. Both Woodworth's books and the *Journal* tell of Wood's past life—which included close friendship with Robert Ingersoll, the noted infidel—and Wood's newfound faith. He told the audience that he would write to his old friend Ingersoll and "tell him what a fearful mistake he was making and try to persuade him to turn."[36]

A few months later while Woodworth preached in Louisville, Wood—the former infidel—gave support in the meetings and gave his testimony. After he returned to Springfield, he suffered a stroke, and on his deathbed, he sent a message to Woodworth: "Oh, sinners, hear the dying testimony of the converted infidel. Tell Sister Woodworth she was the instrument in God's hands of saving my soul. I have never had a doubt of my experience with God since my conversion. All is well."[37]

At this time in her preaching career, Woodworth took a rigid position for divine healing and against medicine and doctors. Because she herself had been healed, was in good health, and had seen others marvelously healed, she saw no reason everyone with faith could not be healed. Bar none.

Healing was in the atonement, and was no less available than salvation. She would later alter the extreme position on healing, but in Springfield in 1888-89, she taught that healing was for all and for every case.

In a newspaper article published during the first tent meeting in Springfield, Woodworth gave advice, which characterized her critical views on the value of medicine. It occurred when a woman testified she had come to Springfield to see doctors about her asthma and "general debility." But she heard about the tent meetings, and instead of going to the doctors, attended the services. "Now I don't need no doctor," she told the crowd, "for I am cured, bless the Lord."[38]

Woodworth responded to the testimony, advising the crowd, "Just throw physic to the dogs ... and take the standard prescription which acts with power and glory.[39]

Today animal rights advocates would take issue with Woodworth and support the poor dogs, but her 19th century crowd seemed to accept her advice without question.

An Impromptu Springfield, Illinois, Performance
Woodworth saw the usual number of trances, healings, gifts of the Spirit, visions, and other emotional responses in the 1888-89 Springfield, Illinois, meetings—not all of which received her blessing. One embarrassing moment came when a Catholic convert, Annie Matthews, put on a performance in July 1889 that prompted a negative report in the *Springfield Journal*.

Annie's conversion came during the previous winter meetings, and she had been "under the power" several times. According to the reporter—probably C. E. Kalb—Annie monopolized the meeting to such an extent it "almost made Mrs. Woodworth sick."[40] The woman's actions and the crowd's responses make the story well worth including in this Springfield report.

"Annie stood for a while near the platform with eyes and arms raised heavenward. Then she hurried through the crowd for a distance of fifteen feet, and stopped. She seemed to gaze intently at something in the top of the tent, as she swayed backward, forward and sideways. Presently she took another sudden start over chairs and the rough plank seats, the crowd giving away and scattering in every direction. Those behind watched intently lest she should step between the seats while she was looking upward and apparently giving no heed to her foot steps. The anxious spectators were not disappointed, for before she reached the edge of the tent she made a misstep and took a fearful fall among the rough board seats. Then the excitement increased, people gathered around her by the score to see if she had killed herself. Her clothing was of course disarranged and she presented a pitiable aspect, at which the ungodly giggled. A number of those present assisted in arranging her garments, placed two planks together and got her laid out.

"Suddenly, Annie sprang up again and made a start for the open air. Out she went into the darkness, men, women and children fleeing as if she were some mad person. This nearly broke up the meeting, as fully three-fourths of the audience gathered around Annie to see what she would do next. The men folks were especially "leary" of her and were determined to keep out of her clutches. While she was out in the park, there was more hilarity than was becoming a religious body. Once she tried to sing, but as a songstress, it cannot be said that Annie is a sweet warbler.

"After a half hour of this green-sward entertainment, during which Mrs. Woodworth had to labor hard to preserve the meeting, Annie took a spasmodic whirl and started back for the stand. Occasionally she would stop and, with arms raised, would lean backward until her head came within a foot or two of the ground. After remaining in that position a full minute she would raise gracefully, with apparent ease, proving herself an accomplished contortionist, as well as an expert powerist. Two young men, who seemed to have become satisfied that she was tame and harmless, accompanied her on the return trip through the benches, as body guards. Occasionally she whirled gracefully round and round, proving that at some time in the sweet gone by and by, she had indulged in the wicked waltz. When she got back to the stand, the crowd was with her, but the hour had grown late. Mrs. Woodworth looked discouraged, probably from the fact that Annie had monopolized the meeting, and she dismissed the audience with the announcement that there will be services this afternoon and evening."[41]

For obvious reasons, Woodworth chose to leave Annie's performance out of her Springfield reports.

The small tent crowd, which Woodworth welcomed to her meeting in June 1888, rapidly grew, and this nucleus became the Church of God in Springfield. In July 1889 she returned to the city in a triumphal entry to help dedicate a new church building at 3rd and Dodge Streets. The man Woodworth placed in charge of the congregation during her absence, a Mr. Bechtel, drew up plans for the building and was in charge of its construction.

In writing of the dedication service, the *Journal* reporter described the building as being 40 by 78 feet and seating over 600; the auditorium was carpeted and furnished with chairs while the platform was covered with Brussels carpet and furnished with a sofa; the windows were of cathedral glass, and over the pulpit were the words, "Welcome, Church of God." The building was constructed in two months at a cost of $3,000—most of which was raised before the dedication service, July 28, 1889.[42]

Obviously, Woodworth was pleased that God had helped perform an impossible feat in such a short period.

"The house was crowded with the best citizens of the city and surrounding country. God poured out his Spirit in showers of blessings. Our enemies, the enemies of the Lord who had done everything they could against the church as a body, and against the individual members, driving them from one building to another, causing them to pass through fiery trials and bitter persecutions—looked back one year to the time when we first came to the city strangers, not knowing one person there, not a member of the Church of God in or about the city, and when they saw amidst all these difficulties how the Lord had blessed and prospered the church, and gave them a house to dedicate to God, had to confess that this was the work of God."[43]

During her travels across the country, Woodworth often found time to stop for visits with the Springfield congregation. She held extended meetings later, but none would equal the meetings she conducted in 1888-89—for that was the time for Springfield's spiritual visitation.

Evangelist Maria B. Woodworth's Gospel blitz during the 1880s was extremely effective. As C.H. Forney, one of Woodworth's sharpest critics, admitted, "Mrs. Woodworth was a revivalist of remarkable power."

She had gained a huge following since she left the farm near Lisbon, Ohio. Churches were planted, thousands of converts testified of their changed lives, men and women were called into full-time Christian service, and hundreds of sick people testified that their bodies had been healed.

They chalked up many mistakes—just as people do a century later. Woodworth made some enemies and often got by with unorthodox means and practices. But the positive results of the blitz seem to far outnumber the mistakes. The victories totaled far more than the defeats.[44]

Now the scene shifts from the Midwest. Late in 1889, Woodworth felt a tugging from California, and she responded with plans to conduct meetings in Oakland. Little could she know this next series of meetings would go down as probably the lowest point in her travels on the sawdust trail.

ENDNOTES

1.   Maria Beulah Woodworth, *Life, Work and Experience* (St. Louis: Commercial Printing Co., revised edition, 1894), p. 242.

2.   The modern Pentecostal revival is usually associated with two American cities that experienced Holy Spirit baptism accompanied with speaking in tongues: Topeka, Kansas, in 1901, under the ministry of Charles F. Parham; and Los Angeles, in 1906, under the ministry of William J. Seymour.

3.   "Camp Meeting in Indiana," *The Church Advocate.* June 9, 1886.

4.   *Acts of the Holy Ghost*, p. 302. See more on O.W. Looker in chapter 8.

5.   Reprinted June 9, 1885, in the Kokomo *Gazette Tribune* from the *Xenia Journal.* The Kokomo editor's reaction was predicable, he called the *Journal* "a crossroad's publication that ekes out a sickly existence in the obscure town of Xenia."

6.   Editorial, Kokomo *Gazette Tribune*, June 9, 1885.

7.   Ibid.

8.   *Kokomo Dispatch*, May 28, 1885. The *Dispatch* claimed the editors of their rival *Gazette Tribune* were condemning the trances in private but didn't have the courage to put it in writing like they (the *Dispatch*) often did. The *Gazette Tribune* countered that the *Dispatch* often put down country people as

unintelligent because many of these people went into trances. The war of words between the papers went on for several days even after the meetings closed.

9. Ibid.

10. *Gazette Tribune*, June 9, 1885.

11. Ibid. A few days later after the meetings had closed, the *Gazette Tribune*—with an obvious shot at the *Dispatch*—said, "Thus far the writer has heard nothing but good, sound Gospel preached in these meetings, strongly backed up by 'thus saith the Lord.' .... We have heard of no evil report, and until such is reported and proven the *Gazette Tribune* will find no fault with them" (June 16, 1885).

12. *Kokomo Dispatch*, June 18, 1885.

13. Ibid. This issue contained two letters from readers who argued against the trance as having biblical precedent.

14. Kokomo *Gazette Tribune*, June 16, 1885. Hile remained at Kokomo for at least a year to lead the new congregation formed as a result of the Woodworth meeting.

15. *Gazette Tribune*, June 23, 1885. Woodworth stated the aims of the Daniel's Band were interdenominational; it was not organized to antagonize the churches but to give religious guidance for people who couldn't find what they wanted in their own churches. The idea was to have the believers attend their own churches and then meet with the Daniel's Band at other times. However, the Kokomo group started its own church. Two churches actually started as a result of the meeting. The Hile Church, which Woodworth supported, was formed without a creed; another group wanted a creed so they formed the St. Paul's Christian Church (*Dispatch*, July 2, 1885). There is a possibility the two groups worked out a compromise and consolidated their efforts.

16. *Life, Work and Experience*, pp. 226-27.

17. Ibid. , p. 202.

18. Ibid. Woodworth does not say these people spoke in tongues, but in later reports she mentions people did speak in tongues early in her ministry. Based on what is common in the 20th century among Pentecostals and Charismatics, it is not difficult to imagine people speaking in tongues in the environment Woodworth describes in this 1885 Alexandria meeting.

19. *Muncie Daily News*, Sept. 21, 1885.

20. Anderson *Weekly Review,* April 24, 1885.

21. *History of Madison County*, p. 808. Judge West attended Woodworth's meeting at Greensburg, Indiana, the next year and testified he had been healed of consumption (*Life, Work and Experience*, p. 256). He also represented Woodworth in her divorce from P. H. Woodworth in 1891 (see Chapter 6).

22. *Life, Work and Experience*, p. 238.

23. Ibid., p. 240.

24. Ibid., p. 242. Building a pier into the water evidently was a common practice for baptismal services. The St. Louis *Republic* (Sept. 1,1890) published an artist's drawing of Woodworth's baptismal service in the Mississippi, which also shows a pier.

25. Ibid., pp. 242, 268. Participating in the dedication service were Elder Lachshaw, president of Findlay College, Findlay, Ohio (The Churches of God school), and Elder R. H. Bolton, also of Findlay. The new building was crowded and hundreds were turned away. During the service $1,400 was raised which cleared the indebtedness. In recent years the brick building had been used by a Oneness Pentecostal congregation. It was razed in the late 1970s to make room for a street.

26. *St. Louis Post-Dispatch*, Jan. 4, 1891. For a report of P. H. Woodworth's attempted confrontation with Woodworth in this same 1891 Anderson meeting, see Ch. 6.

27. *History of Madison County*, p. 808. Newspaper files for Anderson during this period are incomplete, and the county

clerk's office was unable to find records of a suit involving Woodworth.

28. Forney, History of the Churches of God, p. 244. In this same report, Forney—who certainly was no Woodworth protagonist— wrote that the church Woodworth founded at Muncie also went into a tailspin and the building was sold to the United Brethren in 1897. In an article appearing in the Feb. 11, 1903, issue of *The Church Advocate*, an Indiana pastor, W. R. Covert, criticized certain people who looked at Woodworth as a "patron saint" and "Virgin Maria." Covert claimed Woodworth "had visions to destroy the church at St. Louis and Anderson and the Eldership" (a district). The Covert criticism is quoted in "Maria B. Woodworth-Etter and the Churches of God," by Jon R. Neely, and published in *The Church Advocate*, Aug. 1975, p. 5.

29. *The Church Advocate*, May 29, 1889, as quoted by Jon Neely, p. 6.

30. Now, more than a hundred years later, Springfield has grown to around 111,000 in population. The biggest church in the city is an Assemblies of God congregation, Calvary Temple, whose pastor is Mark Johnson who succeeded his father, Mitchell M. Johnson. The pastor's grandfather, the late Thomas Paino, Sr., was converted in one of Mrs. Woodworth's meetings in 1919; Paino later traveled with Woodworth's evangelistic party and then became pastor of the Woodworth-Etter Tabernacle in Indianapolis a few years after Woodworth's death. See Ch. 13 for more about the Paino association with Woodworth.

31. *Life, Work and Experience*, p. 288.

32. Although Kalb's name did not appear on the several stories published in the *Journal* during the 1888-89 meetings, I discovered his identify while researching a meeting Woodworth conducted in another capital city, Salem, Oregon, in 1892. Kalb wrote a letter to the editor of the Salem *Statesman* (May 26, 1892), stating he had written the Springfield meetings "up in good style." Then he recommended Woodworth and her coworkers to Christians in the Salem area "who love the Lord

and the salvation of souls." Kalb had a closing word for the *Statesman* editor: "I hope you will give the cause such assistance as you can in printers' ink, whether you are a Christian or not." Kalb's effort in Salem fell on deaf ears, for the staff wrote several negative articles and editorials about the 1892 meetings.

33. *Life, Work and Experience*, p. 314. Woodworth had Briney pegged as a "great theologian and champion debater." Today John B. Briney (1839-1927) is viewed as one of the Restoration Movement's brightest defenders.

34. Ibid., p. 315. Failing to find the paper Briney wrote, I have relied on Woodworth's report in her book and the newspaper accounts.

35. Ibid.

36. Ibid., p. 296.

37. Ibid., p. 310. Ingersoll, "The Great Agnostic," died in 1899, about nine years after Wood's death.

38. *Springfield Journal*, July 28, 1888.

39. Ibid. The headline on this article read, "Throw Physic to the Dogs."

40. "Annie Had the Power and Made the Faith-Cure Meeting Rather Lively," *Springfield Journal*, July 2, 1889.

41. Ibid.

42. Ibid., July 29, 1889.

43. *Life, Work and Experience*, pp. 328-29. Woodworth refers to the Winebrenner Churches of God, of which she was a member at this time.

44. Richard F. Lovelace, in *Dynamics of Spiritual Life*, p. 239, reminds his readers that not everything accompanying a revival is necessarily healthy, productive and purely of the Holy Spirit: "Almost every major revival recorded, in fact, has been surrounded by an aura of irregular religious activity and has also

been centrally affected by elements of weakness and sin. As a result, successive eras of church leaders have found it easy to immunize themselves and their followers against awakening movements by applying caricatures stressing the worst features of past revivals." On the other hand, later revival proponents often look back on the 19th century and see people barking like dogs or climbing light poles and justify it or use for models in their own meetings.

CHAPTER 5

Here Comes the Tidal Wave

"God had revealed to her, Woodworth warned the people who
sat in her tent in Oakland on that January night in 1890,
that the cities of Alameda, Oakland, and San Francisco
would be destroyed by an earthquake and tidal wave in
80 days or on April 14."[1]

California has had more than its share of prophets who
have stood on her sunny shores and shouted doom
and destruction. Most of the prophets are accepted as an
integral part of California, as native as grapes and oranges,
but the masses steer clear of them. Perhaps the most common
prediction is that a large chunk of southern California will
some day drop off into the Pacific Ocean. Geologists who
have studied the faults lacing California's terrain do believe
"the big one" will hit someday, but predicting the exact time
is another matter.

When the prophecies fall short, the wanna-be prophets
revise their prophecies or move to greener pastures, and the
dismayed flock scatters, ever searching for another prophet
who dares to stand against the world to foretell earthquakes,
wars, tidal waves, plagues, and lesser calamities.

Even in California, though, prophets of doom get little
notice unless they put details into their predictions. That's
why both skeptics and believers took notice when Maria B.

Woodworth predicted that an earthquake and tidal wave would strike the San Francisco-Oakland area on a specific date—April 14, 1890—and destroy three cities in four minutes.[2]

God had revealed to her, Woodworth warned the people who sat in her tent in Oakland on that January night in 1890, that the cities of Alameda, Oakland, and San Francisco would be destroyed by an earthquake and tidal wave in 80 days or on April 14. Many of the people who heard the prophecy that fateful night had heard Woodworth tell of previous prophecies that she claimed came to pass in the Midwest. Many panicked. Others who read about it the next day accepted the prophecy as being from God. And during the next several weeks, they sold their furniture and their homes, they quit their jobs, they warned their neighbors, and then they fled into the hills to escape the cities that Woodworth saw being swept away like sandcastles at high tide.

Soon other prophets joined in and added details to what Woodworth had seen. George Erickson, one of Woodworth's converts, got most of the headlines during the 80-day period of grace, but they were usually written in a blatant derogatory tone. Erickson also found a place high and dry—a padded cell at Stockton's insane asylum.[3]

Part 1: The Battle Under The Big Top

The First Cannon Blast in Oakland

Throughout her long ministry criss-crossing the country, Woodworth described her work in colorful battle terms—regardless of whether she was in church buildings, under tents, in the open air, in skating rinks, or in other improvised cathedrals. The battle lines could be drawn any place, and they always pitted God's soldiers against the devil's, good against evil. And often in Woodworth's method of viewing the battlefield, she could see the enemy troops and their big guns made up of preachers, hoodlums, and newspaper reporters.

She came by the use of the battle imagery honestly, from scriptural metaphors such as believers using the whole armor (Ephesians 6), mighty weapons (2 Corinthians 10:4), tapping supernatural strength and using the shield (Psalm 28:7). Her prayer asked God to "fight against them that fight against me" (Psalm 35:1). And her testimony of God's help came from King David's shout, "For by thee I have run through a troop; by my God have I leaped over a wall" (2 Samuel 22: 30). And hymn writers provided emotional ammunition with "The Battle Hymn of the Republic," "Stand Up for Jesus," "Onward Christian Soldiers," and other inspiring militant themes.

Woodworth needed all the high-powered spiritual weapons she could find once she set foot on a soggy lot at 26th and San Pablo in Oakland, October 28, 1889. A comparative unknown on the West Coast, Woodworth's opening service could hardly have called for a happy Jericho March, what with only 23 people daring to brave the cold rain to see what the new tent offered.

But Woodworth, true to the grit and determination that characterized her ministry, was undaunted by the weather, which was one of the wettest on record. She confidently told the small, curious crowd that God had sent them there, and a great work would be accomplished, that hundreds would be saved.[4]

Maybe those 23 people had doubts about a great work being accomplished in Oakland as they hurried through the flapping tent exit and into the downpour, but within a few days, the doubts disappeared. The small crowd had soon multiplied to hundreds, and the tent was jammed to capacity.

When a larger tent, seating over 8,000, was purchased and set up at 7th and Market, attendance simply boomed. You couldn't expect to take your time getting to the meetings and still get a seat, because thousands of people were braving the rainy weather to see trances, and hear of visions and other Charismatic phenomena that had made Woodworth famous throughout the Midwest.[5]

The crowds, the excitement, the trances, the conversions, the healings—and yes, even the hoodlums—made Woodworth feel right at home, even though she was 2,500 miles away from the area that established her fame during the 1880s. She knew within a few days that the city was ready for her type of meetings. She knew the West could be won with the same methods that had given her so many victories in Hartford City, Muncie, Kokomo, Devil's Den, and dozens of other places throughout the Midwest. She knew that, in spite of the weather, Oakland could be revived and that this meeting would be only the beginning of large crusades in the West.

If she could have seen the future, however, maybe Woodworth would have closed the meeting and ordered the tent taken down after the first few nights. For here in Oakland, she would experience the most difficult meeting of her ministry, one that would have shattered the average evangelist at the end of the nineteenth century. This would be her husband's last crusade. Here the couple would separate under a scandal. Here the critics would launch their greatest offensive thrust. Here a predicted tidal wave-earthquake would plummet Woodworth's credibility to the bottom of the Bay.

Only the courage, faith, and determination of the little general from the obscure village of Lisbon, Ohio, kept the crusade from being the Waterloo for the Woodworth evangelistic party.

Newspapers Take Notice

Newspapers in the Bay area made Maria B. Woodworth a household name, even though they were seldom sympathetic in their coverage. One bright note came from a paper that described the meetings as "a series of the most remarkable revival meetings ever held in Oakland."[6] The meetings were even described as orderly after the tent had been moved to Market Street and away from a rowdy neighborhood. Orderly, yes, "although not exactly quiet in the ordinary sense of religious meetings."[7] And there seemed to be no prejudice, no racial bias, and the rich and poor sat side-by-side on the same rustic benches.

With free publicity from the Bay area's three leading newspapers—San Francisco's *Examiner* and *Chronicle*, and Oakland's *Tribune*—there was no need for paid advertisements. Rather, the biggest concern for the Woodworth party was to find enough benches to seat the thousands who were jamming the tent nightly.

The *Examiner* regularly covered the meetings being held in their sister city across the bay, and they gave their readers a vivid description of Woodworth: "She is a woman of fine presence, much intelligence, some education, is on the easy side of middle life and talks with thrilling force. Her gestures are few but forcible, and her most noticeable characteristic is the sweet and winning smile which wreathes her face during the greater portion of her discourses."[8]

It was claimed that no other evangelist anywhere had a tent as large as the one Woodworth's friends purchased for her during the 1889-90 Oakland meeting. Unfortunately, the three men who were responsible for its purchase later became disenchanted with Woodworth over what they termed excessive physical manifestations and visions—the very reason the *Examiner* credited for the huge crowds.[9] The three men asked Woodworth to stop the manifestations that threatened to, in their opinions, ruin the good that was being accomplished. Woodworth listened to her friends, but turned a deaf ear to their counsel. "These manifestations," she replied, "are the way of the power."

About 200 people from Woodworth's flock were in sympathy with the trio, and they quietly left the tent to form a local church.[10]

In spite of a number of minor conflicts in the early weeks of the meetings, there were unquestioned results. A sea captain and his wife and 12 seamen came to the meetings and were all converted. Another ship's first and second mates, infidels, skeptics, drunkards, church members, and ministers had "also been led in the right way."[11]

After a critical report of the early meetings, the Oakland *Tribune* revised their estimate of Woodworth and her meetings in a Dec. 24 story, stating that without a doubt, Woodworth was a revivalist of "remarkable power." A gang of hoodlums looking for a fight, they added, created the unfortunate early impression.[12]

Before the meetings closed in Oakland, the editor would wish a thousand times that he had published a less positive analysis.

Several people reported they were healed after Woodworth and her workers prayed for them. And as was her policy throughout her ministry, Woodworth attributed the healing to God's power. "I have no power to heal or convert. God does it. We preach the word and pray. God backs up the work [probably "word"] by signs and wonders."[13]

One of Woodworth's visitors, a world traveler who was visiting Oakland, experienced a life-changing conversion of at least a three-year duration, disputing Woodworth's critics who often claimed the conversions were not lasting. Before attending the meetings, the man claimed no religious inclination and was there only out of curiosity. When he saw a particular manifestation near the front of the tent, he made a critical remark and started toward the platform to investigate.

But before he reached the platform, he was struck to the ground and lay there for over two hours. Because seeing people in trances was a common occurrence in the tent, few of the crowd nearby paid any attention to him. They couldn't know that there on the ground the man saw a vision of heaven and hell and that God spoke to him about making his choice of the two places. He called upon the Lord to save him and then came out of the trance, praising God and realizing that he was saved and filled with the Holy Spirit.[14]

Three years later, this man attended Woodworth's meeting in Portland and told of his conversion, saying that he had been kept by the power of God and was active in His work. Evidence seems to support the claim that this man's conversion was not an isolated case and that many were testifying of God's delivering power manifested in their lives.

Ministers Are Divided

Although Woodworth was an ordained minister with the Churches of God from 1884 to 1904, she operated independently in her evangelistic crusades. Cooperation from the denominational ministers varied from full acceptance by a few, qualified acceptance by others, and total repudiation from the majority. Oakland was no exception.

Charles W. Wendte, pastor of the Oakland Unitarian Church, wrote a scathing letter to an editor in which he called for the authorities to put an end to the "disgraceful exhibition" at the tent. He argued,

"These physical manifestations are of the same low order which characterizes the African Voodoo, the frenzied leaps and gushings of the Mohammedian Dervishes, and the delirium of the Indian Medicine Man." He believed that Woodworth probably "superinduced" the manifestations by some hypnotic power. He added critically, "Its continuance is a greater discredit to the fair fame of our city for intelligence and order than a score of opium joints and a hundred additional saloons."[15]

Wendte wasn't the only one to associate the demonstrations with Voodoo, for in the same issue of the newspaper, an editorial writer called Woodworth "The Voodoo Priestess." A second editorial supported Wendte in his concern and warned parents that their children could "have their nervous system shattered" by attending the meetings. The editorial added that the meetings produced "mental debauchery," and the people who attend must "do so at their own risk."[16]

W. C. Potter, an Oakland citizen, read Wendte's letter and quickly penned his own long and well-written rebuttal, reminding readers that Woodworth's followers were entitled to the protection of law. "Their only crime seems to be that of having the jerks, nervous hysterics, etc. … If there was a little more of this power which makes this tent resound with the shouts of 'Glory to God for my salvation,' scattered around Oakland there would be a grand religious revival in less than a week that would rival the outpouring of the Pentecost."[17]

Potter closed his letter by stating that he was in the tent one night when a former alcoholic from a wealthy and highly respected family in San Francisco gave his testimony. For years the man had lived only for drink, but was drawn to the tent by an irresistible power. He told the tent crowd that he had "gone under the power" and awoke to a new life, with all desire for whiskey and tobacco gone. Potter said the testimony was "a temperance lecture worth more than the condensed virtue of 10,000 saloons and opium joints … Cure the appetite and we abolish the saloons."[18]

But Potter's defense was only a Daisy® Air Rifle shooting at a tank. In addition to the many ministers in the Bay area who opposed Woodworth, the well-known Evangelist John Alexander Dowie jumped into the fray.

Dowie, who later founded Zion City, Illinois, and became the self-styled "reincarnated Elijah," had come to San Francisco in 1888 from Australia, where he had a reputation as a man of faith. Because of his success in praying for the sick and his Charismatic leadership, Dowie commanded a tremendous following. He had previously supported Woodworth—probably in this same Oakland meeting—but later they had a public falling out, and the satirical newspapers enjoyed every minute of the squabble. Dowie told of casting a devil out of a young girl in Melbourne and implied that Woodworth needed the same attention.[19] Dowie attacked Woodworth's teachings on salvation, water baptism, divine healing, and the trances—labeling them as "anti-Christian error coming in the guise of Christian teaching."[20]

Woodworth usually tried to avoid fights, but she was certain she had God on her side in this one. In the Oakland meeting, she took off her kid gloves and dealt Dowie a few blows. He had been preaching divine healing in California, she said, but his people had lost confidence in him. After the people left him and attended her meetings, "he became mad with jealousy." She added, "I always told the people that I would leave him in the hands of God, and that I would go right on with the Master. I told them to watch and see how we would come out, and they would see that he would go down in disgrace; and that I would be living when he was dead."[21]

Did Woodworth ever confront the formidable Dowie after the Oakland meeting in 1889-90? If she did, she does not mention it in her books, only preferring to "leave him in the hands of God."

Unlike the critical Dowie, several ministers cooperated with Woodworth in her Oakland crusade, including two influential pastors in the black community, D. E. Johnson and J. E. Currin. When a local pastor, Dr. Bothwell, used a newspaper to call Woodworth a "pious fraud," Johnson quickly responded. Woodworth had been opposed by the devil, saloonkeepers, and ministers, he answered, "yet draws greater audiences than any minister in town without the aid of a fine choir and organ."[22] Pastor Johnson added that he thought Bothwell had spoken against the Holy Spirit.

Pastor Currin wrote a strong letter in support of Woodworth, defending her calling from Acts 1:5-8 and 2:4.[23] Pentecostals, through the decades since that Oakland meeting, have used these same passages to defend their Pentecostal experience and speaking with other tongues.

A well-known New York minister, Carrie Judd Montgomery, who had enjoyed success in a healing ministry before going to the West, entered Oakland to conduct meetings. But there she found that Woodworth was already drawing huge crowds to her tent. Montgomery met Woodworth, and it was the beginning of a lifelong friendship. In her autobiography, *Under His Wings*, Carrie gives a positive report of the Oakland meetings, marveling at the huge crowds, and the "people who were intent on the Lord Himself."[24]

Even the severest critics would admit that some good had been accomplished under the preaching of Woodworth during the early weeks of the four-month Oakland campaign. The corroboration of Christian magazines, the three major daily newspapers in the Bay area, and Woodworth's own books are testimony that the meetings were more than circus sideshows.

But all was not well in the crusade, and the courageous little general at the pulpit knew this better than anyone else.

A Series of Crises

One crisis after another brought increased public pressure and threatened to destroy any positive results of the meetings. In spite of the crusade's early successes, the press predicted that the tent meeting faced chaos just around the corner. Men in the pulpit continued to hammer away at Woodworth's theology, and citizens repeatedly called for the authorities to close the meetings. It seemed as if the entire area focused its attention on the tent and its Midwestern invasion force.

As the battle heated up in and around the cold, damp Gospel tent, another famous woman, Julia Ward Howe, came to Oakland in behalf of women's rights. One of the points Mrs. Howe made during her speech was to make an appeal to denominations to permit women to enter the ministry. Ironically, a few blocks away, one woman was already in the ministry and fighting to keep her tent open so she could continue preaching the Gospel.

Because of the socioeconomic extremes, the racial mixture, the weather, the religious conspiracy, and Woodworth's own particular form of pre-Pentecostalism, more unsolvable problems popped up in this one meeting than most evangelists face in a lifetime. Perhaps if Julia Ward Howe had had a chance to see what Woodworth faced in her tent crusade, she would have either commended her for her courage or advised her to forget evangelistic work and return to the quiet countryside of Columbiana County, Ohio.

Woodworth had no control over the rainy weather and a gang of hoodlums that plagued the Oakland meeting, and these two elements figured in a disturbance early in the crusade.

Heating stoves had been set up in the big tent and the nearby smaller tents that the Woodworth party used for living quarters. One night, two boys thought that putting explosives in one of the stoves in the big tent would add more excitement to the meeting. They were right. Noble Davis and Lyle McKay, the two culprits, slipped the explosives into the stove during a rare moment of silent prayer. The resulting explosion blew the doors off of the stove and caused a near panic. Davis and McKay were arrested on the spot by one of the ushers; a judge convicted them of disturbing a religious service and fined each $5.[25]

The stoves rattled again during a service one stormy January night. That's when the wind knocked the stovepipe down, interrupting the service and creating a problem for the men who tried to repair it. They replaced the pipe, but it would not stay up. Finally, an exasperated Woodworth put the blame squarely on the devil: "That's it," she cried, "the devil will get into the stovepipe if he can't get anywhere else."[26]

An earlier storm victimized the Gospel tent that the Woodworths had shipped from the Midwest when a sudden gust of wind ripped it apart, crashing the canvas down on about 1,000 terrified worshipers. Fortunately nobody was seriously hurt in the mishap, and the usually critical *Tribune* complimented Woodworth and her flock for their "admirable self-control" during the storm and resulting tragedy.[27] A short time later, the new and much larger tent was ready for services.

Another severe blow to Woodworth during the Oakland meeting came from her own husband and co-worker, P. H. Woodworth, whom she accused of adultery. Fortunately for Mrs. Woodworth and her efforts in Oakland, her husband's alleged marital infidelity was not aired in the local press and only came to light in St. Louis during another tent meeting the following summer. The public was unaware of the reason he suddenly left Oakland, but it must have been a difficult cross for the evangelist to bear on a frame that was already bent under a heavy load.[28]

Just as they were attracted to Jesus and the Disciples, the mentally challenged—and those whom Woodworth believed were demon-possessed—poured out of the woodwork and into the tent, causing no little embarrassment to her and the team. Some of their publicized actions only added to the poor impression that the press and townspeople already had of Woodworth's efforts. The press and some area ministers blamed the meetings for driving people insane, but more than likely, they were mentally challenged before they ever saw the Gospel tent.

Take Albertson Smith, for example. He said he was born again at the tent and then learned that he was the only son of Jesus Christ, and that like his father, he had come to save the world. "I can do everything that my father did in Jerusalem 1800 years ago. I am the smartest man in the world....My father has chosen the *Examiner* to be his paper and it is to be changed to the *Morning Smith*." The *Morning Smith* would become so popular, Smith added, that one third of the population of the world would subcribe.[29]

Smith received his first taste of publicity at the Oakland waterfront shortly after his conversion and his "ordination." Thinking that he could fly, he leaped from the upper deck of a ferry as it slipped into the Oakland dock. After his crash landing on the dock—apparently unhurt, except for his pride—Smith was taken to the police station where he summarily appointed Chief Tompkins, Captain Wilson, and Jailer Quackenbush as his disciples. He was committed to the Stockton Asylum for the Insane following his attack on the deputy district attorney, calling on the Lord to drive him out of the Kingdom.[30]

In all fairness to Woodworth, there was no way she could possibly control the types of people who attended the meetings. The nature of the tent meetings, much to

Woodworth's dismay, gave an opportunity for a crossection of the people to express themselves in a variety of ways.

Woodworth Bouncers Flex Their Muscles
When the mobs gained the upper hand in the early days of the tent meetings, the Oakland police department deputized some of Woodworth's followers for special duty in the tent. This move relieved the police department of providing manpower at the tent, but it served to embarrass Woodworth and her followers on several occasions.

The *Tribune* reprinted a well-written editorial from their competition across the Bay, the *Examiner*, in which the writer recognized that some people had been attracted to the meetings and had been reformed. Some good had been accomplished, but the editorial called for an end to the special police commission because the men were "entirely lacking in tack [*sic*] and almost so in sense." The police power should be taken from these fanatics, they added, "and cool headed, firm, regular officers stationed in the tent to quell disturbances."[31]

The editorial also called for the meetings to be closed to the young. "Such scenes of excitement are not fit for children whether they result from preaching or pugilism."[32] Years later, Woodworth would hear the same argument in Topeka, Kansas, when the city council enforced an apparent existing law that prevented children under 16 from participating in the meetings.

What Woodworth regarded as a valid New Testament experience, the medical profession now challenged as bordering on hysteria and insanity. Little did she realize here in 1890 that the spiritual experiences she promoted, and that were challenged by outsiders, were setting a precedent for the Pentecostal movement, which would begin within a decade.

Meanwhile, residents in the area of the tent, who had been annoyed at the constant turmoil created by the meetings, circulated a petition addressed to the city council, asking "that the nuisance caused by these meetings be abated."[33] The Oakland Police Department hardly had time to consider pulling the commissions of the special tent police when another altercation threatened to turn the tent into a battlefield.

An Oakland artist, John Alexander Massie, and his aged mother stepped inside the tent out of curiosity. Woodworth was conducting a service with a crowd of some 1,500 to 2,000 people in attendance. One of the special tent policemen noticed Massie and his mother and ordered them to sit down, but Massie explained that they would be there only for a moment and then they would leave.

Unsatisfied with Massie's reply, the bouncer grabbed the artist and began pushing him toward the tent exit, dragging Massie's mother with him. Massie managed to pull loose and then began grappling with the special officer. Three more tent policemen came to the aid of the first one. But then a crowd of men—already upset by previous nasty incidents and perhaps looking for an opportunity to put the tent police in their place—rushed to Massie's aid.

Soon a battle royal erupted in the rear of the tent, with the tent police using their clubs and the crowd swinging canes and broken benches.

All this time, Woodworth tried in vain to maintain control of the crowd, thinking the tent police could handle the ruckus in the rear of the tent. How wrong she was! It was a hopeless situation. The crowd paid little attention to Woodworth's efforts to maintain order, and surged toward the rear of the tent to see the full-blown riot in progress. Out of desperation Woodworth turned to the choir and ordered them to sing.

A reporter wrote, "Above the music of five hundred voices there came to the throng about the altar the sound of benches being broken and smashed and the hoarse cries of men, maddened by conflict."[34] Finally someone called the riot squad—the first call in Oakland's history—which quickly dispersed the crowd, or as the reporter described the crowd's flight, "they scattered like chaff in the wind."[35]

Throughout the riot, Woodworth and her choir sang at the top of their voices. When it was all over and a relative calm settled over the crowd, Woodworth tried to talk, blaming the ministers of the city for inciting riots. "You know what that minister wrote. It was all lies. They, the ministers, have given the hoodlums of this town license to come here and disturb these meetings."[36] She confessed to the crowd that it was the worst situation that she had ever faced in her ministry. The crowd believed her. Anything worse than what they had just seen would have been a declared war.

But what happened to the Massies? After the mob rescued them, the Massies quietly walked away, probably wondering if tent meetings always ended in riots.

In the evening service the next day, an unruly mob created yet another disturbance, driving Woodworth to despair. She had stood before crowds of 25,000 people, she told them, but had never seen anything like the unruly Oakland mob.

Her friend, the ever-present Dr. Sidney Smith, summed up the evening's frustrations in his judgmental benediction. Going to the pulpit, Smith yelled in a somewhat less than charitable spirit, "May Jesus be with those who love Him tonight, and may He curse with eternal damnation all those who mock Him and who do not love Him."[37]

The manner in which the special tent police mishandled several incidents put an end to their authority. Oakland authorities revoked the commissions and ordered the regular police to the scene with the hope that some semblance of order could be maintained.

Things did quiet down for a few days. But it was only the calm before the storm, for within three weeks a tidal wave prediction for the Bay area would make the problems of the past fade into insignificance.

Part 2: Destruction on the Way

Few of us in the 21st century take seriously the words of self-proclaimed prophets. We are too sophisticated for the most part to even stop on a sidewalk while a prophet screams of coming judgment, not even if they were to predict that a tidal wave-earthquake would decimate our city or county on a given date within a couple of months. Not even bad memories of the October 1989 quake in the same San Francisco Bay area would make believers out of very many of us.

Too many prophets crying "wolf" have left us skeptical at best. But it was a far different story when Maria Woodworth thundered in Oakland a hundred years ago. Then a tidal wave-earthquake prophecy—which Woodworth initiated based on a so-called vision—sent possibly a thousand wild-eyed people scurrying out of the Bay area into Santa Rosa, Vacaville, St. Helena, and even higher ground. Many of the believers—who were members of the tent revival group and lampooned as "doom-sealers"—sold or gave away their possessions and fled the judgment scheduled for Monday, April 14, 1890. Epicenter Oakland and San Francisco had disaster written all over them.[38]

Oakland's Lake Merritt would be sucked into the sky and cascaded all over the east Bay area; water from the Bay would drown San Francisco; and for the coup de grace, a giant earthquake—probably a 10 at least—would level everything in sight.

Reporters filed almost daily accounts of the doomsday antics—usually ridiculing the most visible prophets, Woodworth and layman George Erickson, on front pages in the Bay area. And national papers took up the judgment countdown as April 14 drew near.

A day before the judgment was to fall, the New York *Tribune* reported in a column that "several hundred deluded people" had headed for the California hills. About a hundred others, according to the *Tribune*, were camped in the hills near Oakland "prayerfully awaiting the doom that will fall on a stiffnecked generation."[39]

In faraway London, a religious magazine, which thrived on end-time messages, published two long reports from one of the participants in the Oakland revival meeting. The bad press, according to the informant, Elizabeth Sisson, resulted in Woodworth's ability to draw people away from the churches and saloons.

Unfortunately for the prophets and their followers, April 14 came and went with not even a tremor. Lake Merritt and the Bay waters lapped their placid shores all day long, singing and sharing reality with the unbelievers who went to work just as they always had. Weather reports called it one of the nicest days of the spring.

Unbelieving Oakland *Tribune* editors rolled out some of their biggest type with a cynical headline: "WE ARE STILL HERE. ERICKSON'S DOOM WAVE MISSES CONNECTION."

The *Examiner* reminded its readers across the Bay that "SAN FRANCISCO SHOULD NOW BE BENEATH THE WAVES." And the *Chronicle* summed up the state of the ridiculed doom-sealers in their mountain retreats with a page one finis to the three-month scare: "WAITED IN VAIN." Up north, the Portland *Oregonian* titled their account of the scare as "FOOLS AND THE FLOOD."

Locked up in the Stockon State Hospital by April 14, Prophet George Erickson reasoned that God either made a mistake or that He was extending mercy for a few more hours. Woodworth was unavailable for comment as she had left for St. Louis the week before.

This strange flight to the hills more than a century ago remains a part of California's long-forgotten past, but only in newspapers and diaries of the period. Nobody is alive who witnessed what must have been one of the area's most embarrassing days. The prophecy is not so unusual, but it is unusual to have a thousand people fall for it. They were not dealing with terrorists and a 747—whose plans of destruction could leak—but unpredictable Mother Nature and a strong presumption that they knew God's calendar of events and judgments.

The Oakland doomsday episode actually got its start when the revival for which Woodworth prayed did not come and strong opposition continued to mount against her non-traditional church efforts. She then resorted to other means out of frustration and an urge to teach her persecutors a lesson. On January 27 she told the audience that God had shown her huge waves rolling over the Bay area cities, a devastating earthquake, and a warning that the people were to flee to the mountains.[40] Soon several of Woodworth's followers agreed that they had seen the same vision. One of these was a Norwegian emigrant, 29-year-old George Erickson, who had recently moved to town from the northern coastal county of Humboldt.

If we can accept the newspaper accounts about Erickson, he, paradoxically, was hardly one to command a following. And as it later turned out, he was suffering from mental illness. In typical, insensitive 19th century editorializing, the

Chronicle viewed Erickson as stupid and as one "whose conceit is as colossal as his ignorance." The *Tribune's* tone was no less sympathetic, rating Erickson not only as an unsuccessful prophet, but "as a fool he ranks with Yosemite and the Pyramids."[41]

Erickson titled his written version of the judgment, "The Doom of the Cities. Woe! Woe! Woe!" and proudly presented it to Woodworth and the revival party. One reporter characterized it as containing much "unintelligible matter," but the Woodworth's camp decided that with a fair amount of editing, the document would become credible and useful to scare the devil out of the Bay area's ungodly. Edited versions later appeared in tract form and in the newspapers.

To add to the Bay area woes, Erickson said he saw the cities destroyed in only four minutes. A new city would rise near the Golden Gate and be called San Francisco Fall. A new city called San Pablo would replace Oakland and Berkeley. As could be expected, Erickson's version received mixed reviews—from total repudiation to blind acceptance.[42]

About two weeks after the first report of a doomsday, Woodworth said that she had heard from God again. She was to take down the tent and open a crusade in Santa Rosa. In noting the Woodworth departure, the *Tribune* published a cynical front-page story titled, "UP OUT OF THE WET. Mrs. Woodworth Will Not Go Down With That Wave." In the news account, Woodworth wanted it understood that she in no way set a date for the doomsday. "But many others beside myself," she warned, "have been inspired with the idea that destruction is coming soon."[43]

The Oakland medical doctor, G. Sidney Smith, assumed charge of the tent-meeting remnant after Woodworth moved to Santa Rosa. Although sympathetic with the judgment idea—as can be noted in his prayer in Part 1—Smith stood with

Woodworth on the folly of setting a date. Warn of judgment, he seemed to say, but let God choose His time and place. But the date setters were certain that April 14 was still in God's plan. And because they knew time was short and they would not gain favorable press coverage in their attempts to warn citizens to escape the coming judgment, they took to the streets. It was Jonah's cry to Nineveh. Peter's sermon on Pentecost. It was either escape to higher ground or die.

V. E. Bennett, the most visible street preacher, loudly warned passersby of the coming doomsday from his high-wheeled bicycle. With Bennett leading the way, doom-sealers sounded their warnings from strategic Oakland street corners and in other Bay area cities. Wherever the 19th century Jonahs met, however, antagonists tried to shout them down with ribald heckling in a running battle for the minds of the people.

Several business leaders quickly tired of the bedlam and petitioned the city council to put an end to the daily circus on their doorsteps. It hurt their business, they argued, and the council agreed. Police then stepped in and jailed a Salvation Army boy preacher—who may or may not have been a doom-sealer—for obstructing a street. It would be only the beginning of many arrests, doom-sealers were warned, unless they took their act away from the business area.

The most shocking event for the doom-sealers came about a month before the scheduled doomsday when the police picked up Prophet George Erickson for a sanity hearing. Nobody outside the doom-sealer camp was surprised when Erickson was committed to the Stockton State Hospital. But even around the Stockton cell, Erickson's followers on the outside hung on to every doomsday word he uttered. They needed a spark of hope that they had not believed in vain and that God still wanted them to head for the hills.[44]

The Doomsday Clock Down to 30 Ticks

Humorous accounts of doom-sealer antics appeared almost daily in area newspapers. Judge Thomas Milliard tested the faith of the derided minority by offering to trade his inexpensive piece of property in the hills for property in Oakland or San Francisco. It isn't known whether or not he had any takers.

An open letter to Woodworth invited doom-sealers to relocate in Nevada City, east of Marysville. Mines had closed there, the writer explained, and rental houses were available for only $6-10 a month. A display ad in the *Tribune* urged Bay area residents to "Flee to the Hills," more specifically to the Napa Soda Springs Resort—"a first-class watering hole." With tongue in-cheek, the ad offered a place of safety 1,000 feet above the tidal wave: "It behooves all those who do not feel good enough to die so soon...to betake themselves to the elevated heights until after the deluge."[45]

The famous New York syndicated columnist, Bill Nye, got into the act with a satirical piece. Nye claimed that he had bought some corner lots in Oakland at 10 percent of their value. "I am putting my limited powers as a prophet," he wrote, "against those of ... the bicycle prophet of the Pacific Slope."[46]

As the day of doom approached, Nye's satire was not far off. Reports circulated that bargains were indeed available from people who took the advice of the doom-sealers. Many of them, who might not have been "good enough to die," quit their jobs, sold their homes at sacrifices, and almost gave away their possessions to others who chose to ride out the wave.

Of all the methods the doom-sealers used to "save" the Bay area, none was more convincing of their sincerity than a petition they sent to Governor Waterman about two weeks before doomsday. Call a day of prayer, they urged the governor, so the doom might be averted. (Earlier prophecies offered no hope that God would change His mind about the destruction.) The petition also urged Waterman, if he chose not to call a day of prayer, to remove all Bay area prison inmates and money to safe places. As usual, the newspapers and citizens took delight in ridiculing the latest doom-sealer effort.

In Berkeley, an editorial writer for the *Advocate*, noting that April 14 had been scheduled for spring vacation at the University of California, hinted that the university faculty was "under the power" by scheduling a day off so students could escape the destruction.

By April 1, doom-sealers began streaming out of the doomed area by train, on foot, or in horse-drawn wagons. Their destination was generally one of three higher elevations of refuge—St. Helena, Santa Rosa, or Vacaville. In a more serious and ironic note, a Chicago family moved to the city during the upheaval and hurriedly returned to the Midwest because of the scare, only to lose two family members in a Kentucky tornado.

On the eve of the doomsday, the *Examiner* looked across the Bay and defended San Francisco's honor by stating their polls showed most of the people leaving were from Oakland. The *Tribune* countered that probably half the people leaving were from San Francisco and probably not more than 200 would leave Oakland. One thing on which the competing newspapers could agree came from an *Examiner* writer who summed up the scare: "No stranger spectacle has ever been seen in the history of fanatical movements."[47]

When the long-awaited day of wrath finally arrived, believers, tucked safely in the hills, looked toward the Bay area for any sign of a giant waterspout. They saw nothing.

They listened for the big rumble that would level the cities. They heard nothing. As the day wore on, doom-sealers began to have doubts about the prophecy. Before nightfall, some of them probably agreed with the New York *World*, which stated that Woodworth and Erickson had no more skill at predicting calamities than brute beasts.

A Prophet Johnson of St. Helena reasoned that the date had been misunderstood or that "the good God has willed it otherwise." Sacramento believers who had climbed the dome of the capitol building for safety, believed that the Lord had relented in His wrath—as He had done with Nineveh in Jonah's day—an explanation that was as equally easy to defend as it was to deny.

Meanwhile on that day in Stockton, George Erickson held out that the prophecy would come to pass, even giving God the freedom to wait until midnight. The next morning, he still had faith in the prophecy, but decided "God made a mistake in the date." He asserted, "The cities named will be destroyed in time." Erickson would probably never again see his doomed cities, for he would spend the rest of his life at the Stockton mental facility. His death came in January 1941, 51 years after he associated with Woodworth, and his name became a rather infamous household word.

Evangelist Maria B. Woodworth would survive the Bay area fiasco and continue preaching to huge crowds almost to her dying day in 1924 at the age of 80. In later years, almost predictably, she looked at the 1906 San Francisco earthquake as a fulfillment of her 1890 prophecy. Obviously it was prudent that she not mention the fact that her 1890 prophecy also mentioned a killer tidal wave—a little of which San Francisco firemen could have used in 1906 to quell the raging fires.

Today in many circles, Woodworth is highly regarded as an important Christian evangelist, healer, and church planter.

Her contribution to women's rights in the pulpit and integrated meetings even before the turn of the century should never be underestimated. But pressed by critics and violent mobs in Oakland in 1890, she yielded momentarily to frustration and revenge, uttering what she thought to be divine retribution.

The result was personal disaster to many people and possibly the Bay area's—and Woodworth's—most embarrassing day, April 14, 1890.

ENDNOTES

1.   Although the newspapers quoted Woodworth "80-day warning," she later denied adding a date to her prophecy. Readers will notice that I rely heavily on daily newspaper reports as sources in this chapter. The primary sources are the Oakland *Daily Evening Tribune*, the San Francisco *Chronicle*, and San Francisco's *The Examiner*. They will be referred to as *Tribune*, *Chronicle*, and *Examiner*.

2.   *Tribune*, Jan. 28, 1890. The sarcastic front-page article was titled "Flee to the Mountains."

3.   *Tribune*, March 12, 1890.

4.   *Life, Work and Experience of Maria Beulah Woodworth*, p. 333.

5.   *Examiner*, Jan. 9, 1890.

6.   *Chronicle*, Dec. 2, 1889.

7.   *Tribune*, Dec.24, 1889. The *Examiner* in its Jan. 11, 1890, edition attempted to describe a typical prayer session in the tent: "There is nothing which approaches this dissonance in intensity except that weird jumble of jangling voices which greets the ears of a visitor approaching the female ward of an insane asylum."

8. *Examiner*, Jan. 9, 1890.

9. Ibid., April 13, 1890. The newspaper identified the three men as George Montgomery, a "capitalist"; J. S. Higgins, a retired sea captain; and Clarence Tripp, an Oakland attorney. George Montgomery became the husband of Evangelist Carrie Judd on May 14, 1890 (see note 24). They founded Home of Peace of Oakland in 1893 and were later well known in the Pentecostal Movement. The Assemblies of God recognized Mrs. Montgomery's ordination in 1914. Through the years George and Carrie Montgomery remained close to Woodworth. They frequently published accounts of her meetings in their magazine *Triumphs of Faith*. In an interview I conducted with their only child, Faith Montgomery Berry, in 1985, I learned that she too highly regarded the ministry of Woodworth.

10. Ibid.

11. Ibid., Jan. 9, 1890.

12. *Tribune*, Dec. 24, 1889.

13. *Examiner*, Jan. 9, 1890.

14. *Life, Work, and Experience of Maria Beulah Woodworth* , pp. 336-37. It is interesting to Pentecostals who trace the Pentecostal Movement to Charles Parham's 1901 meeting in Topeka, Kansas, that Woodworth, as did other preachers and writers of her generation, picked up Pentecostal terms in her book above, which was published in 1894. Other terms in use were "Pentecostal power," "the power," "baptized in the Spirit," "slain in the Spirit," and synonymous terms. She does not mention speaking in tongues in her early books, but she does report in the 1922 *Marvels and Miracles* (p. 68) that a woman attending her St. Louis meeting in 1890 spoke in several languages and then went to foreign countries preaching with her gift of tongues. It is anybody's guess why Woodworth failed to mention such a miraculous experience in her *Life, Work and Experience*, which was published just four years after the St. Louis meeting.

15. *Tribune*, Nov. 30, 1889.

16. Ibid., Dec. 2, 1889.

17. Ibid.

18. Ibid.

19. Ibid., Feb. 1, 1890.

20. "Trance Evangelism," by John Alexander Dowie, *Leaves of Healing*, March 8, 1895, p. 382. Reprinted from *Leaves of Healing* (labeled "old issue"), p. 98.

21. *Acts of the Holy Ghost*, pp. 384-85. After Dowie founded Zion City, Illinois, he suffered financial ruin and rejection by his followers and even by his family. He had rejected the Pentecostal message, but ironically many of his followers at Zion City embraced the message. Dowie died in 1907, 17 years before Woodworth's death.

22. Ibid., Dec. 9, 1889. Woodworth rewarded Johnson, pastor of the African Methodist Church in Oakland, for his support by asking him to pray the dedicatory prayer for the new tent.

23. Ibid., Feb. 13, 1890. Woodworth evidently survived an earlier threatened black boycott of her meetings following the death of a black woman who had attended one of the meetings. The *Tribune* of Jan. 13, 1890, reported that the woman, a Mrs. Rice, suffering from paralysis, attended one of the early meetings and asked for prayer. She went under the influence of the power and then claimed she was healed. "The cure was not lasting, however, Mrs. Rice going to bed a day after her trance. She rapidly grew worse until yesterday, when she died. The woman's relatives say that her death is due to the evangelist's influence, and the colored population is turning against the evangelist as rapidly as it flocked to her standard."

24. Carrie Judd Montgomery, *Under His Wings*, pp. 130-31. In defending the practice of falling under the power, Woodworth told an *Examiner* reporter that "Sister Judd, the great divine healer, who came out here from New York, has been under the

power several times since these meetings began" (*Examiner*, Jan. 9, 1890). Carrie Judd was associated with the Christian and Missionary Alliance (C.M.A.) and had served as the organization's first recording secretary. A break in the Judd-Woodworth harmony is revealed in Carrie Judd's Sept. 1890 *Triumphs of Faith*, page 213, "The Work and The Workers." She viewed the Oakland meeting as taking a different shape from the opening meetings late in 1889, and she said the devil wrought havoc through false prophecies and Woodworth's mistake of "exalting of 'the power' above *Jesus Himself*." She added that Woodworth's teachings "create a tendency on the part of people to seek to obtain 'power' as an abstract thing, instead of seeking Jesus Himself as the power for service." Many had been bruised, she said, but the Lord was gathering them after the disaster.

25. *Tribune*, Nov. 21, 1889.

26. *Examiner*, Jan. 13, 1890.

27. *Tribune*, Dec. 24, 1889. At least two other tents fell during Woodworth's ministry, proving the vulnerability of canvas cathedrals.

28. *St. Louis Post-Dispatch*, Sept. 11, 1890. See Chapter 6 for a closer look at P. H. Woodworth.

29. *Tribune*, Dec. 26, 1889. No doubt the owners of the *Examiner* would have gladly renamed the paper if Smith could guarantee that one third of the world would subscribe. At this time they advertised that 250,000 people read their paper.

30. Ibid., Dec. 27, 1889.

31. Ibid., Jan. 13, 1890.

32. Ibid. See Topeka meeting (Ch.12) for a legal ban against children participating in the meetings.

33. *Examiner*, Jan. 10, 1890. The newspaper held little hope that the petition would be effective. For another month the meetings continued, and then Woodworth felt that God wanted

her to move to Santa Rosa, about 50 miles north of Oakland (see Part 2).

34. Ibid., Jan. 9, 1890.

35. Ibid.

36. Ibid. Woodworth probably referred to Charles W. Wendte, pastor of Oakland's Unitarian Church, although he was only one of many Oakland ministers to oppose her meetings. The day after the riot, several of Woodworth's supporters were on the platform to speak in her behalf, including Dr. Sidney Smith, the Rev. D. E. Johnson, Dr. Morgan (a Methodist minister from Indiana), Elizabeth Sisson, and a Dr. Greenwell. The latter told the crowd that a deputy sheriff had come into the tent drunk and had threatened to tear down the tent.

37. Ibid., Jan. 10, 1890. (See Part 2 for more on this early Pentecostal medical doctor, Sidney Smith.) An editorial reprinted in the *Tribune*, Jan. 13, 1890, from the *Alta*, with tongue-in-cheek, said that since Woodworth claims people can be struck dead if they touch people who are in trances, "she misses a golden opportunity to make herself the most popular person in the State by doing some of this striking dead on some of the hoodlums and blackguards who resort to her tent. If she will administer a whack at them and kill them good and dead she will fill a long felt want." Woodworth did claim that evildoers were struck down in earlier meetings; the *Examiner* of Jan. 11, 1890, reported that she told the Oakland believers: "If you would all unite in prayer when one of these disturbances occurs, we would have no need of the police. God would strike the disturber to the floor where he stood. That is how we used to do in Indiana." At least a few newspaper reports in Indiana supported her claim.

38. *Tribune*, Jan. 28, 1890.About three weeks before Woodworth gave her famous prophecy, she told an *Examiner* reporter (Jan. 9, 1890) that a young girl had seen a vision with the figure "9," shining with "a wondrous radiance" over the platform of the tent. The figure rotated to make the figure "6," and then a short time later turned back to make the figure "9,"

and then back to "6." The girl also saw a harp with broken strings. Woodworth could not understand the significance of the harp but understood the figures "9" and "6" to mean that Christ would return in 1896 "according to prophecy." S. J. Yahn, a minister in the Churches of God and later editor of that group's periodical, *The Church Advocate*, stated in the June 15, 1904, issue that Woodworth "repeatedly stated the belief now common among a certain class that the Lord will come in 1914" (quoted by Jon Neely in "Maria B. Woodworth-Etter and The Churches of God," *The Church Advocate*, Aug. 1975.

39. "Beyond the Sierras," New York *Tribune*, April 8, 1890.

40. "Flee to the Mountains," Oakland *Tribune*, Jan. 28, 1890.

41. Ibid, April 15, 1890.

42. *Examiner.* The March 11, 1890, issue of the *Tribune* printed a condensed version of the prophecy, "The Doom of the Cities," which prompted Oakland officials to arrest Erickson and order him to appear before a sanity board. The board ordered his confinement at the insane asylum at Stockton. In addition to what Woodworth had already related concerning the prophecy, Erickson said he saw pestilences in Africa, Russia defeating England and France, war in Europe until Christ's return, a great famine in China, floods and great heat in Australia, and great earthquakes in North America. The Bay cities would be destroyed in four minutes, according to the prophecy. San Francisco would be rebuilt and renamed San Francisco Fall. Oakland and Berkeley "shall be no more." Chicago would never be rebuilt because the world was too close to the end (Erickson, too, had accepted the 1896 date for the return of Christ). The remainder of the prophecy was an emotional plea for the believers to flee to the mountains where they would be spared from the coming judgment.

43. *Tribune*, Feb. 10, 1890. In their usual humorous treatment of the prophecy, the editors titled the article concerning Woodworth's leaving Oakland "Up Out of the Wet."

44. Ibid, March 11, 1890. "WHOA, WOE! Prophet Erickson Will

Go to Jail."

45. Ibid., April 7, 1890.

46. Ibid. Reprinted from the *Examiner*. The bicycle prophet was V. E. Bennett. *Examiner*, April 13, 1890.

CHAPTER 6

A Thorn in the Flesh: P. H. Woodworth

"The husband of the evangelist is of a thrifty turn, and while the meetings are in progress he and two assistants operate a peanut, candy and lemonade stand within sixty feet of the pulpit. The other day, as men and women were shouting and going into trances, old Woodworth sat beside an ice cream freezer and cranked it unconcernedly."—Wabash Weekly Courier[1]

W hen young Maria Underwood felt called to the ministry, she determined that if she ever married, her choice would be "an earnest Christian," so they could enter the ministry together.[2] Her first husband, red-bearded Philo H. Woodworth, was hardly an earnest Christian, and he was hardly anxious to leave the farm and haul tents around the country. Driving tent stakes and listening to his wife preach was not his idea for a mid-life career change.

Woodworth came courting after being injured in a Civil War battle, and he swept the impressionable young woman off her feet with his romantic interests and his eyewitness accounts of danger and adventure and other tales of which Civil War novels are made. Perhaps Maria Woodworth believed that Philo would share the same burden to evangelize as she had held for several years. No doubt if Woodworth had told Philo during their one-month courtship that she felt impelled to go into the ministry whenever the opportunity came, the walk to the altar would never have happened.

Years later, when Philo did yield to his wife's pleas and agreed to accompany her on an itinerant ministry, they did not make an ideal team for evangelizing. For one thing, Philo's mind and health had been affected in the war, which explains some of his actions and speech, and which frequently embarrassed his wife and the cooperating pastors.

Even though Philo traveled with his wife during the big campaigns in the 1880s and was in charge of erecting the tents and operating the food and book stands, he was simply not cut out as an associate evangelist or campaign manager. He belonged on the farm, and the more deeply Maria and Philo became involved in this pioneer evangelism effort, the more they both knew that he should have remained tilling the soil of Columbiana County.

But Maria found herself in a perplexing situation. She held that marriage was ordained of God, and she would never consider separating from Philo because he lacked dedication and social skills. Next to her ministry, Maria's marriage—with all of its defects and problems—was sacred. She honored the relationship and her husband, as evidenced by her reluctance to enter the evangelistic field without his approval and willingness to go with her.

Maria never publicly criticized Philo. Whenever she mentioned him in her books published prior to their separation in Oakland in 1889, it was always positive— admittedly it was with a guarded tone, but still positive. No newspaper reporter would ever hear her defame her husband. She locked horns with pastors, editors, and local officials on controversial matters, but she kept her marital relationship confidential. She was a high profile person, but Philo Woodworth's shortcomings were not aired publicly.

Newspaper reporters reserved no such loyalties. Some of them, even though they knew about Philo's war injury, would have fun at his expense. Other reporters would criticize him mercilessly.

Philo's lack of charity is seen during the 1885 Hartford City, Indiana, revival, when the people were slow to respond to an offering appeal in one of the services. He took matters into his own hands, according to an always-watching reporter. "The other half of Sister Woodworth—and, by the way, much the lesser half—was so disgusted with the proceedings on the part of the church that he arose in his place and made some observations that were untimely, and most certainly did not come from a peaceful heart."[3]

When Maria conducted a meeting in Indianapolis in December 1886, she invited penitents and those who wanted the power to the altar. A reporter pushed his way through the crowd near the front to get a better view of the praying followers and Philo, whom he described as the center of attraction. In contrast, he wrote, "Her husband ... does not attract, but rather repels."[4] He sat on a bench, taking no part in the meetings and seemed uninterested in the prayer service until the crowd pressed too close to those seeking the power. Then, like a sergeant at arms, he would stand and order the people back.

A few days earlier, the reporter had given Maria high marks, but was unimpressed with her "grim spouse" and the crowd that was attracted to the meetings. Mrs. Woodworth seemed out of place in the meeting, he wrote, and is much superior to the crowd following her. "Indeed she appeared displeased with the absurd buffonery [sic], and during her husband' s loudest yelping she was noticed to punch him in such a manner that he became quiet.[6]

Another reporter, covering the same meeting in Indianapolis, described P. H. Woodworth as having a face "as severe as a Roman senator."[7] The report likened Philo's meeting announcements as given "in tones of a circus ring master advertising the grand concert.[8] The criticism of P. H. Woodworth in these instances is typical of the news coverage he received from Ohio to California.

Because the meetings everywhere attracted hundreds and thousands of people and because many were receiving the power and going into trances, reporters frequently delved for answers to Maria's extraordinary charisma. A reporter cornered Philo in the Indianapolis meeting and asked him how he accounted for his wife's power. He answered that it was beyond human power, not of her own. Then he went into a brief discourse on the two spirits in the world: "One of these is the devil and the other is God. This [his wife's power] must be one or the other, and it's fair to assume that it's God. I held off from this thing for a year, but now I accept it fully."[9]

Within five years, about a year after the couple separated, he would repudiate everything his wife preached, especially what he called the "trance business, " which in his opinion was a "great money-making scheme."[10]

Philo said Maria had two young women who were well trained in what he called the trance act. "I tell you they have got it down pretty fine." He summarized his view with a statement that must have made his former wife shudder: "The whole business, I tell you is a d—d fraud."[11]

While Philo traveled with his wife, his main duties were handling the business operation. He was soon tagged with a reputation of being involved only for the money he could make in his various related enterprises. In an obvious attempt to draw a contrast between Maria and Philo, a Decatur, Illinois, newspaper viewed his role as having "great faith in the power of dimes."[12]

At this 1887 meeting, Philo sold songbooks, pictures, and his wife's books.[13] In a meeting conducted in Xenia, Indiana, in 1885, the *Indianapolis Times* said Philo "turned an honest penny selling peanuts and circus lemonade to the crowd."[14] A writer for the Wabash *Weekly Courier* who was covering the Xenia meetings was less charitable in his vignette of Philo's commercial enterprises. Describing him as "a thrifty turn," Philo and two assistants operated a peanut, candy, and lemonade stand within 60 feet of the pulpit. "The other day, as men and women were shouting and going into trances," the reporter noted, "old Woodworth sat beside an ice cream freezer and cranked it unconcernedly, preparing a supply of the popular refreshment for the weary, sinsick crowd." When Sunday morning came, Philo "was dispensing cigars and plugging watermelons for the million, and the nickels, dimes and quarters flowed into his till in a steady stream, while the wife was laboring with care-burdened sinners."[15]

The *Courier* writer added that Philo's "mercenary character" had hurt Maria's efforts at Xenia, but the majority of the people were convinced of her sincerity.

Operating a commercial food stand at the meetings was the subject of a long satirical editorial column in the *Indianapolis Journal*. In "A New Revival Feature," the writer claimed that in the winter when people came directly from the supper table to the meetings, Mrs. Woodworth's "success in snatching unsuspecting sinners from the downward path and laying them out cold, so to speak, in the road to glory, was phenomenal."[16]

But later in the summer when people attended camp meetings, the writer explained, the afternoon schedule caused them to miss a meal. "When people are hungry, they are not converted and do not go into trances." Something had to be done, the writer continued, so P. H. Woodworth revived an old-fashioned frontier camp meeting tradition. He made food available on the grounds. "Brother Woodworth, whose services had hitherto not seemed valuable in the evangelistic work, here came out strong. He would be caterer to the crowd; he would feed the hungry—at so much a head—and Mrs. Woodworth [who] encouraged and aided him, would go on conquering Satan and his allies with her aforetime assurance. Gradually, when hungry seekers were filled, the stream to the altar increased."[17]

Because some had criticized the Woodworths for charging prices for the food he dispensed, the writer—with tongue-in-cheek—concluded the long column by defending the couple's commercial operation. "There is no good reason why Sister and Brother Woodworth should feed people and get their souls into shape for salvation for nothing, and criticisms of this sort are unbecoming. Let the bad men of Kokomo go to camp-meeting and be fed with real and spiritual lemonade of the Woodworth brand, and if it profit them, the evangelist and the rest of the community will give thanks.[18]

It is unlikely that the Woodworths clipped this editorial for their scrapbooks.

Other newspapers joined in the food stand criticism and railed on Philo's "mercenary character." Maria, however, failed to mention her husband's company store in any of her books. Rather, she keeps his part of the work "spiritual." This was characteristic of her Christian charity. In her 1886 book *Trials and Triumphs*, published three years before the couple separated—Maria recaps the year 1884 and mentions her husband's ministry: "Mr. Woodworth was with me all the time, doing all he could to take care of my health, and assist in the work of saving souls."[19]

The beginning of the end of the Woodworth marriage happened early in December 1889, during the divisive Oakland meeting. A front-page story in the Oakland *Tribune* told of trouble brewing in the Woodworth family.[20] Later that month, Woodworth would be gone—possibly never seeing his wife again.

As in previous campaigns, Maria preached while Philo took care of the business arrangements in the Oakland meeting. However, a local committee was appointed—presumably by Maria—which took away many of the responsibilities Philo normally handled. His illness, no doubt, played a part in the committee appointment. Naturally he felt threatened and wanted to regain the control he enjoyed in meetings they had conducted in the previous six or seven years.

One of the friction points at Oakland involved the suggestion to enlarge the tent to accommodate the crowds pouring into the Bay Area meetings. Philo got wind that the committee planned to slice the tent in half and add more canvas to give it additional seating capacity. He vetoed that idea, so the committee raised money and later purchased a tent that would seat more than 8,000. It later turned out that a new tent was necessary because a windstorm tore apart the old tent a few days after Philo turned down the idea of enlarging it.

In all fairness to P. H. Woodworth, he did not wish to air their troubles in the newspapers—at least not in Oakland in 1889. When a reporter asked him about the trouble with the committee and the rumor that had him leaving Oakland for St. Louis, he replied, "Now look here, young man, the less you say about our troubles, the better it will be for us."

Saying that it would do little good for their troubles to air in the newspapers, Philo admitted that he might go east, Los Angeles, or elsewhere to sell books. It was beginning to appear that the soggy lot in Oakland was far too small for Philo H. and Maria Woodworth to occupy at the same time.[21]

Philo, though, couldn't resist answering one last question concerning the committee and the tent. "Well, all I've got to say is that no committee or anyone else will touch that tent. That tent belongs to me and I paid for it in Chicago."[22]

With that, he left the reporter standing in the rain and withdrew to his tent living quarters. Although the reporter noted that Philo and Woodworth were living in separate quarters, he didn't know that he was sitting on what could have been one of the biggest stories of the controversial Oakland meeting. That story, an account of Philo's alleged infidelity, would remain covered possibly as late as the following summer, during yet another controversial meeting in St. Louis.

Had the story of his sexual indiscretion hit the Oakland and San Francisco newspapers in December 1889, it is conceivable the meetings would have closed immediately. In hindsight, closing the tent at that time would have avoided the several riots and the doomsday prophecy that sent Woodworth followers fleeing to the hills to get away from the predicted tidal wave and earthquake. Because the adultery story apparently went unpublished until September 1890, it is possible that Oakland residents never learned of the final straw that broke the Woodworth relationship.

Ten days after Philo granted the *Tribune* interview in the rain, he was out of the encampment and on his way east—at the insistence of his wife. The "Combination," as he called their evangelistic group, took on a new look. The face "as severe as a Roman senator" would never be seen again around Woodworth's tent. If worshipers bought peanuts and lemonade on the tent grounds after the Oakland meeting, they would buy them from someone other than the stocky red-bearded Civil War veteran. His alleged breaking of the Seventh Commandment cost him his position, his reputation, his Churches of God exhorter's license, and a part in the free-will offerings (which he always considered too small).

From northern California in April 1890, Maria Woodworth went to St. Louis and later set up her big tent where she conducted meetings until October. Three daily newspapers in St. Louis, the *Post-Dispatch*, the *Republican* and the *Globe-Democrat,* each looked at her meetings as the biggest single event in the city during late summer—if judged by the generous coverage they gave.

One of the reasons the St. Louis meeting gained so much attention from the press was the fact that two doctors tried to have Maria committed to an insane asylum. While this controversy raged in St. Louis, the forgotten Philo Woodworth resurfaced. He wrote at least two uncomplimentary letters to his wife's chief adversaries, a minister and a doctor in St. Louis. In his second letter, he claimed he was compelled to leave his wife on December 15, 1889, in Oakland. He had been sick in Oakland, he wrote, but was forced to leave the camp and was now living in Indiana, almost penniless. "I am broken down, [a] total wreck among strangers," he described his lot. "I need medical aid, but I have not one cent of income."

He wondered whether his wife ever turned her thought toward him when he got "down to a crust of bread and a cup of water." He closed his letter with what sounded like a sincere prayer. "The only thing I desire is for her to repent and make Heaven Her Home. God save my wife from a burning Hell is my prayers."[23]

Maria's helpers in St. Louis, however, judged that Philo was closer to hell than was his wife. They jumped on the *Post-Dispatch* story like a hawk on a chicken. Allegations Philo made in the letter were false, they told the newspaper, and the separation in Oakland was really P. H. Woodworth's fault. People who were in Oakland told the St. Louis reporter that his conduct was so bad that he was ordered away from the tent.

He should have been driven out of town, they said. Two of Mrs. Woodworth's single helpers, Miss Isenberg and Miss Ollie Daggett, accused P. H. Woodworth of making sexual advances toward them. Other very serious charges were brought against him, according to the helpers who were in Oakland. "His wife was advised to sue for a divorce on the ground of infidelity," the story reported, "but she declined to take this extreme step. It is said that she has always been willing to help her husband to reclaim, but that his conduct has rendered a reconciliation impossible."[24]

What had been a closed family affair was now thrown to the public like feathers in the wind. Wags from the tent to the waterfront now knew what had formerly been hidden behind the tent flaps.

The St. Louis article named ministers, a medical doctor, a judge, and others who vouched for Maria's character and who were willing to go to bat for her. Elder H. H. Spiher, a Churches of God leader in Indiana, wrote that Mrs. Woodworth's standing with the church was excellent and that "her name is beyond successful reproach, and farther she is perfectly sane."[25]

Spiher claimed that P. H. Woodworth had proven himself "unworthy of Christian support, and that his name has been erased from said eldership and church." He alledged that Philo was trying to injure his wife's good name and work. He advised "all good men to abstain from him."[26]

Perhaps only a few people knew just how "unworthy of Christian support" Philo Woodworth was. Apparently it did not become public knowledge until December 1890—a year after the separation in Oakland—when Maria filed a divorce complaint. She charged him with repeated instances of adultery with two black women and another woman of "bad repute." Maria claimed Philo was guilty of adultery in June 1889 and that they had not lived together as man and wife since that time. She also claimed in the complaint that Philo had threatened her life with a pistol.[27]

In January 1891, probably after Maria had served him with the divorce complaint, Philo repeatedly tried to see his wife in Anderson, Indiana, where she was conducting a meeting. She refused to see him. Philo didn't want to air his problems and opinions in Oakland in 1889. But in Anderson it was a different story, and the reporter could hardly wait to get his story in print.[28]

• Woodworth suspected Woodworth was having undue intimacy with a St. Louis preacher.

• He called the trance business a fraud.

• His wife's visions were "humbug."

• Their work was a money-making scheme.

• Worshipers were deceived.

• Churches she established did not last.

Judge William R. West, who testified that he was converted and healed in Mrs. Woodworth's Anderson meeting in 1886, represented her in the divorce that was heard in Fulton County at Rochester, Indiana. According to the Rochester *Weekly Republican*, Judge A. C. Capron did not bother even to hear all of the charges Maria leveled against Philo. He granted the divorce February 26, 1891.[29]

Philo was not to remain single long. A month after the judge granted the divorce, Philo H. Woodworth once again became what one newspaper writer called a "matrimonial Mariner." The bride had been previously married and was "just over the border of sweet sixteen."[30]

The abortive confrontation with Maria in Anderson was possibly Philo H. Woodworth's last attempt to see her. The next year in Cleveland, he died of typhoid fever.[31] Thus—without much fanfare and tears—ended the rather strange saga for the husband of one of the most famous woman evangelists in history.

Maria was conducting a meeting in Salem, Oregon, when she heard of Philo's death.[32] Despite the stormy 26 years she spent with Philo, the sentimental and emotional Woodworth must have experienced sorrow. And maybe she even believed that it had been God's will for them to marry. If it was, she could have further reasoned that God could not have picked a more painful thorn in the flesh.

ENDNOTES

1. Wabash (Indiana) *Weekly Courier*, Aug. 21, 1885.

2. Woodworth *Marvels and Miracles*, p. 3.

3. Cincinnati *Enquirer*, Jan. 26, 1885. The previous day's report called Woodworth "a dead weight" to his wife's efforts.

4. Indianapolis *Sentinel*, Dec.17, 1886.

5. Ibid., Dec. 15, 1886.

6. Ibid., Dec. 9, 1886.

7. *Indianapolis Journal*, Dec. 14, 1886.

8. Indianapolis *Sentinel*, Dec. 15, 1886.

9. Ibid.

10. Cincinnati *Enquirer*, Jan. 8, 1891.

11. Ibid.

12. Decatur (Illinois) *Daily Republican*, Oct. 3, 1887. Mrs. Woodworth conducted the meetings in Decatur's Oakland Park. Unusual but not unique was an admission charge of ten cents set to help cover the rental fee of the park. The famous Brooklyn Tabernacle pastor, T. DeWitt Talmadge (1832-1902), was known to charge admission to hear his sermons while on tour.

13. Ibid.

14. *Indianapolis Times*, Aug. 18, 1895.

15. Wabash (Indiana) *Weekly Courier*, Aug. 21, 1885.

16. *Indianapolis Journal*, Aug. 23, 1885.

17. Ibid.

18. Ibid.

19. *Trials and Triumphs*, p. 157.

20. Oakland *Tribune*, Dec. 5, 1889.

21. Ibid.

22. Ibid. Woodworth added that he owned property and money in the East that needed his attention. He was probably referring to their small farm near Rochester, Indiana.

23. *St. Louis Post-Dispatch*, Sept. 11, 1890.

24. Ibid., Sept. 12 , 1890.

25. Ibid. Spiher wrote the letter in response to Philo Woodworth's earlier letter and the insanity charges made by medical doctors in St. Louis.

26. Ibid. Vouching for her sanity, Spiher apparently answered charges the doctors had leveled against Mrs. Woodworth.

27. Maria B. Woodworth vs. Philo H. Woodworth, divorce complaint, Fulton County, Indiana, Dec. 27, 1890.

28. Cincinnati *Enquirer*, Jan. 8, 1891.

29. Rochester (Indiana) *Weekly Republican*, March 5, 1891.

30. Ibid., March 26, 1891.

31. Records of Deaths, Cuyahoga County, Ohio. The record is unclear on his age. It appears that he was either 54 or 64. Maria was 48 when Philo died June 21, 1892. Evidently Maria interrupted her Salem, Oregon, meeting to attend his funeral in Cleveland (the Salem meeting ran from May 13 through August 14). Although she does not mention going to Cleveland in her Salem report, her *Marvels and Miracles* (p. 71) leads us to believe that she not only attended the funeral but also perhaps directed the service. In this reference, which is about her daughter Elizabeth, Maria wrote, "Her father I had buried at Cleveland, Ohio."

CHAPTER 7

In the Vanguard of the Pentecostal Movement

"The people were hungry for the word of God. They sat during the sermon, which was an hour or more long, and paid the best of attention. The city was wonderfully stirred. ... All classes of sinners came home to God. A number of bodies were healed of different diseases, and a number laid out as dead under the power of God."[1]—*Topeka, 1891*

"While we stood between the living and the dead, preaching the Gospel on the apostolic line, earnestly contending for the faith once delivered to the saints, proving to the people that Christ is the same yesterday, today and forever, according to the Lord's promise, he was with us, confirming his word with mighty signs and wonders following."[2]—*Los Angeles, 1893-94*

By 1915 many rural communities, as well as small and large cities across America, had strong Pentecostal congregations. Enthusiastic believers had received what they were calling the baptism in the Holy Spirit as a result of the ministries of Charles F. Parham at Topeka, Kansas (1901), William J. Seymour at the Azusa Street outpouring in Los Angeles (1906), and other ministries. From Los Angeles and Topeka, enthusiastic believers scattered everywhere, establishing missions wherever they could find empty stores or abandoned church buildings. They believed they had been touched by the fire of a new Pentecost and that flame was soon spread throughout the world.

Church history records several occurrences of speaking in tongues through the centuries following the Apostolic Age,[3] but it wasn't until the 20th century that the experience was widely accepted as being the initial physical evidence of the baptism in the Holy Spirit.[4]

The decade before Charles F. Parham's small Bible school was formed at Topeka (and where Agnes Ozman first spoke in tongues) was known as the Gay Nineties. But despite the happy and carefree attitudes that prevailed for most of the decade, the Holiness movement with its anti-worldly attitudes was gaining momentum. They took literally the command to separate from what they perceived worldly appearances, actions, and certainly steered away from alcohol and tobacco in any form. A close look at the Pentecostal movement of the 20th century shows some striking similarities to the Holiness counterpart of the 19th century.

These Holiness leaders were staunch defenders of orthodox Christianity, but they were seeing higher criticism infiltrating the pulpits and classrooms. They prayed for the sick while opponents claimed the gifts ended with the Apostles. They believed in a subsequent experience to salvation, which they called sanctification (some believed in a third crisis experience which often had a blurred theological definition), but often simply called "the power"—the position Maria Woodworth rigidly held and practiced. To the secular world and the Christian church in general, the Holiness people appeared clannish and, above all, promoted an extremely strict lifestyle.

Five well-known preachers of this era, who were successful in praying for the sick, were John Alexander Dowie, A. B. Simpson, A. J. Gordon, Charles Cullis, and Maria B. Woodworth. Of the five, only Woodworth embraced the Pentecostal experience with speaking in tongues. As a result of her many years of experience on the evangelistic field and her acceptance of the Pentecostal teachings, she became one of the leading Pentecostal evangelists after the turn of the century.

To understand better the early happenings of the Pentecostal movement in this century, it is important to look into the 1890s at the ground that was being prepared. Certainly Woodworth was not the only person who had an impact during this period, and she was the least among the preachers when it came to preaching a well-defined theology. However, she relentlessly crisscrossed the nation with her simple but powerful preaching that helped prepare the world for something more from the church—either a great revival or the Second Coming of Christ, or both.

Although some of his Pentecostal friends might disagree with him, Holiness historian Donald W. Dayton believes 19th century Holiness thought and life contained every significant feature of Pentecostalism. His argument is that the Holiness movement laid the groundwork for the Pentecostal movement.[5]

Woodworth's ministry, prior to the 20th century revival, would certainly qualify as one example of Dayton's case. Reading her own literature and that of friends and critics alike, which was published in the 1880s and 1890s, is ample proof of her contribution. George R. Stotts even feels Woodworth perhaps should receive more credit for preparing the church for the Pentecostal revival than others such as Charles F. Parham, William J. Seymour, and Aimee Semple McPherson.[6]

Ample evidence exists that people who attended Woodworth's meetings were encouraged to seek for a more powerful Christian experience. A. P. Dennis was one. Dennis wrote that he attended one of Woodworth's meetings in 1886 where he received "a wonderful anointing and enduement of power." Then two years later in another meeting where several people were "slain in the Spirit," Dennis said he began to stutter "and then suddenly began speaking in other tongues." It wasn't until 1912, while attending a camp meeting G. T. Haywood conducted, that Dennis realized that what he had received a quarter of a century earlier was the baptism in the Holy Spirit with speaking in tongues.[7]

It is probable that Dennis was one of hundreds and maybe even thousands who received the Pentecostal experience before Agnes Ozman received it at Parham's school in Topeka in 1901.

American church historian Grant Wacker acknowledges that many reports exist for speaking in tongues before Parham's 1901 oft-told account at Topeka, as in the 1886 experience above, for example. But Wacker says he cannot find evidence that, 1) the person speaking in tongues viewed the experience as the baptism in the Holy Spirit at the time— as Parham did; and 2) there is documentation at the time— as in published report.

Even though Woodworth at the time did not associate speaking in tongues with the "power" that she urged her hearers to receive, her terminology prior to 1900 was similar to what Pentecostals used after 1900. Obviously the reports she gave were intended to inspire readers and lay groundwork for similar experiences, wherever they were.

Her book, *The Life, Work and Experience of Maria Beulah Woodworth,* was published in 1894, but if readers are unaware of the publication date, they would think it was published sometime after the turn of the century. Much of the terminology used is Pentecostal. For example, take a meeting she conducted in Fairview, Ohio, in 1883 (and which is also mentioned in Chapter 2). She wrote that the people confessed sin and "prayed for a baptism of the Holy Ghost and of fire."[8]

What were the results of the meeting in Fairview? Woodworth wrote that 15 people came to the altar screaming for mercy and fell over in trances. It was something new for Woodworth, but she believed it was of God. The people at Fairview called the experience "the Pentecost power," and Woodworth added that "these outpourings of the Holy Ghost were always followed by hundreds coming to Christ."[9]

Keep in mind that the meeting in Fairview took place in 1883—some 18 years before the Pentecostal revival at Topeka and 23 years before the outpouring in Los Angeles. Also keep in mind that Woodworth wrote this report as early as 1894, so could not tap into 20th century reports and terminology.

In Chambersburg, Pennsylvania, in 1885, Woodworth described one of her meetings as a "Pentecost meeting from the beginning." Ministers, church workers, unbelievers, and all classes of men and women were pricked in their hearts and cried out, "What shall we do?" Woodworth reported in her 1894 book what happened next:

"[They] went down by the mighty wind power of the Holy Ghost. He sat upon the children of God til their faces shone like Stephen's when his enemies said he looked like an angel. Many received gifts; some for the ministry, some as evangelists, some of healing, and hundreds of sinners received the gift of eternal life."[10]

In September 1885 Woodworth conducted her largest meeting ever near Alexandria, Indiana, when an estimated 25,000 people jammed into a field and wooded area.[11] In one of the services she preached on the Holy Ghost power, and God took control of about 500, and "many fell to the ground. Others stood with their face and hands raised to heaven. The Holy Ghost sat upon them. Sinners were converted, and began to testify and praise God. I was overpowered, and carried to my tent."[12]

In this meeting, a Mrs. Sarah A. Dilts was raised from an invalid's bed at home in the same hour Woodworth prayed for her while riding in a buggy some distance away. Mrs. Dilts went into the ministry as an evangelist and was still preaching as late as 1921.[13]

Proving that every generation sees past events through rose-colored glasses, Woodworth—while conducting an 1887 camp meeting at Boiling Springs, Illinois—criticized the church because many did not believe in healings as they once did. A nearby Decatur newspaper covered the meeting and highlighted Woodworth's views: "The power which was given to the Apostles in their day had never been taken from the church. The trouble was, the churches had sunk to the level of the world and were without the unlimited faith that will heal the sick and make the lame to walk. She prayed for the return of the old days and more faith in Christ among the people."[14]

Woodworth accepted certain popular dispensational views, but not when it came to the Pentecostal experience. One wonders if back in 1894 she foresaw the Pentecostal movement when she cried out with this call for renewal: "If we were ready to meet God's conditions we would have the same results, and a mighty revival would break out that would shake the world, and thousands of souls would be saved."[15]

Trying to encourage 19th century believers that their age was no different from the 1st Century, she added: "The displays of God's power on the day of Pentecost were only a sample of what God designed should follow through the ages. Instead of looking back to Pentecost, let us always be expecting it to come, especially in these last days." The full impact of her influence on others with preaching like this is impossible to measure. Certainly she influenced many who later became leaders in the Pentecostal movement.

The San Francisco *Examiner* interviewed her during the 1889-90 Oakland meeting, demonstrating that she was preaching something besides judgment, typhoons, and earthquakes. After telling the reporter that Carrie Judd and Elizabeth Sisson, two ministers, had been under the power several times, she told of a candidate for the experience: "Brother Curry, the Scotch Evangelist, has not received the baptism of power, but he writes that God has shown him that he ought to receive it."[16]

A few days later, the same newspaper described one of Woodworth's sermons in which she explained that the experience people were receiving under the Oakland tent was nothing new; it was just something that the church had lost. "The evangelist described in a fervid manner the 'day of Pentecost,' and claimed that the power that caused her converts to act as drunken men was the same today as in that wonderful day."[17]

Following the Oakland crusade, Woodworth moved to new territory in St. Louis. While preaching under the tent in St. Louis, she invited people to receive the "power," and many went into trances. One newspaper artist illustrated the platform which showed people stretched out on the floor, totally caught up in a spiritual experience.[18] Later when a building was secured for the new congregation, a reporter described a service:

"The mysterious power pronounced as that of the 'Holy Ghost' is visible among the people who attend, as that seen when the Woodworth revivals first begun. The ones who are overcome usually extend and raise their arms, but are not overcome with a faint. As they stretch out their arms, they reach into the air with a movement that evidently seems to be in the act of raising them from their feet. Several felt the power last night, and one convert said he felt the effect so strongly that he became as light as air, and indeed had a sensation as though being wafted in air."[19]

Another St. Louis paper editorialized in their September 3, 1890, edition regarding the critics in St. Louis who said Woodworth was insane and that she was hypnotizing the people. The writer said the experiences occurred frequently wherever "old-fashioned revivals are held." The paper criticized a Dr. Dudley of the St. Louis health department for interfering with the meetings; the *Republic* said he could best earn his salary in the city by "seeing that the watermelon rinds are kept out of the alleys."[20]

Needless to say, Woodworth had many contemporaries— both religious and secular—who attributed the "mysterious power" to something other than the Holy Spirit.

One of her high profile critics was John Alexander Dowie, who had clashed with Woodworth in the San Francisco Bay area in 1889.[21] In answering a question whether divine healing was the same as Christian Science and mind healing, Dowie said the two forms of healing were "seductive forms of Spiritualism." He added that "trance evangelism is also a more recent form of this delusion, and it deceives many."[22] It is obvious that he had Woodworth in mind when he spoke of trance evangelism as this experience was one of his points of criticism of her meetings which he attended in Oakland.

Another contemporary, A. B. Simpson, would probably have felt as out of place in Woodworth's meetings as she did in his in 1885.[23] This spiritual giant who founded the Christian & Missionary Alliance often prayed for the sick in the privacy of his own home, but abhorred emotional camp meeting styles that were associated with many healing services. As early as 1883 he was cautioning ministers about the "solemn ground" in praying for the sick and avoiding making it a "public parade." "Its mightiest victims," he wrote, "will always be silent and out of sight, and its power will keep pace with our humility and holiness ... We greatly deprecate the indiscriminate anointing of all who come forward." He added, "We hope the wonder-seeking spirit will not be allowed to take the place of practical godliness and humble work for the salvation of men."[24]

Woodworth would often pray for the sick in their homes and in her own residence, whether she was on the road or at home in Indianapolis. But it is clear that Simpson's advice against a "public parade" had little effect on how she conducted her patented mass meetings.

The editor of *The Christian Advocate*, a Methodist publication, while visiting churches in the Midwest in 1891, attended one of Woodworth's meetings in St. Louis. He believed the trances common in Woodworth's meeting were not of divine origin, but similar to what was going on in early Methodism and which were then occurring "among the colored people and among Baptists and Methodists in some parts of the world, Adventists, and other sects holding camp meetings."[25]

The Advocate editor in his long editorial reasoned that the trances came as a result of continuous and contagious excitement and could occur to people not at all under the influence of the Holy Spirit.

Despite her often vocal and written critics, Woodworth paid little attention. She continued determinedly, altering her message and practices very little during her preaching career. As can be seen by studying her sermons, her revival reports, and the many newspaper accounts, Woodworth's 1890s preaching contained many of the elements that marked the Day of Pentecost: prophetic preaching, praying for the sick, speaking in tongues, an experience of power subsequent to salvation, people under the influence and conviction of the Spirit, water baptism, churches established, wide publicity, persecution—but always evangelism.

For Woodworth, the bottom line of everything she did was evangelism. Her first sermon was evangelistic, and she had seen hundreds of conversions in her early meetings, long before the Charismatic elements were added. She simply had a passion to convert the sinners from the broad path of sin. And she was extremely successful at it both before and after she began to pray for the sick and for believers to be anointed with the Holy Spirit.

The 1890 St. Louis meeting was in many ways a diamond in the rough. In spite of the opposition and at times Woodworth's unusual theology, the results were rewarding. While doctors were trying to put a stop to the meetings, Woodworth led a baptismal service one Sunday afternoon within a stone's throw of the Eads Bridge—right in the Mississippi River. And it was no small affair. A front-page story in the St. Louis *Republic* estimated the crowd at 10,000.[26] True, not everyone who came to watch 54 people baptized in the Mississippi was in sympathy with the bold evangelist and her followers. The two-column illustration and the generous news story treated the service with ridicule.

But a nucleus established a strong church in St. Louis and erected a new building. In 1895, Woodworth turned over this church and its 500 members to the Churches of God.[27]

Many other meetings in the 1890s could be cited, showing Woodworth in what she firmly believed was her calling to awaken believers and call sinners to repentance. And the success she enjoyed in St. Louis was repeated in such widely scattered places as Los Angeles, Oregon, Washington, Topeka, Louisville, Indiana, Illinois, Ohio, Florida, Missouri, and Iowa.

Beginning in 1894, Iowa—while not everyone liked it—received a strong dose of Woodworth's apostolic preaching. And from all indications, the meetings paved the way for later Pentecostal groups such as *the Apostolic Faith* from Topeka, the Assemblies of God, Aimee Semple McPherson's International Church of the Foursquare Gospel, the Open Bible Standard Churches, and other Pentecostal groups after the turn of the century.

One of the outstanding meetings conducted in the 1890s was in Woodworth's native state of Ohio. During the winter of 1896-97 she preached a series of meetings at the Church of God in Fostoria. Even her strongest critic, C. H. Forney, had praise for this meeting as he reported over 400 people were converted, 200 healed, and 26 received into the church as members.[28]

Woodworth didn't understand everything that theologians tossed around in seminary classes. She couldn't explain how God worked. But she reduced the Gospel to very simple patterns, believed God for signs and wonders, and offered herself to Him for service. Her voice could be heard in villages and cities from the Atlantic to the Pacific, calling for a return to New Testament Christianity. And as the Pentecostal train came rolling by in the 20th century, she grabbed a handle and swung aboard.

ENDNOTES

1. *Life, Work and Experience of Maria Beulah Woodworth*. Rev. edition, 1894, p. 364.

2. Ibid., p. 428. This meeting in Los Angeles in 1893 lasted more than five months.

3. See chapter 2 of *The Promise Fulfilled*, by Klaude Kendrick .

4. J. Roswell Flower, an early leader in the Assemblies of God, believed Parham's acceptance of speaking in tongues as the initial physical evidence gave birth to the modern Pentecostal movement. J. Roswell Flower, "Birth of the Pentecostal

Movement, " The *Pentecostal Evangel*, Nov. 26, 1950, p. 3.
Ironically, Flower tossed a curve at later Pentecostals by
describing his own experience as what one writer called a
"delayed evidence." He was baptized in the Spirit, he said, but
spoke in tongues later.

5.   Donald W. Dayton, "Christian Perfection to the baptism of
the Holy Spirit," *Aspects of Pentecostal Charismatic Origins*,
Vinson Synan, ed. (Plainfield, N.J.:Logos, International, 1975), p.
51. See also Vinson Synan's *The Holiness-Pentecostal Movement*.

6.   George R. Stotts, "Mary Woodworth-Etter: A Forgotten
Feminine Figure in the Late 19th and Early 20th Century
Charismatic Revival," a paper presented at The American
Academy of Religion, Washington, D.C., Oct. 26, 1974, p. 31.

7.   *The Weekly Evangel*, May 20, 1916, p. 4. The Indianapolis
Sentinel, Dec. 9, 1886, described one of Woodworth's converts
in a meeting conducted in Indianapolis: a woman by the name
of Mary went into a trance after someone started a song, and
she "staggered about in a dazed way, alternately swinging her
arms and shaking hands, all the while yelling something
unintelligible, which sounded like maniacal ravings."
Pentecostals today would hesitate to accept this experience as
reported by the *Sentinel* as a Pentecostal experience. But one
must remember that newspaper reporters at Topeka and Los
Angeles after the turn of the century made those Pentecostal
believers look insane with their extremely critical reporting.

8.   The *Life, Work and Experience*, p. 54.

9.   Ibid., p. 55.

10. Ibid., p. 211. The entire area around Chambersburg was
stirred and some 8,000 people turned out to watch a baptismal
service.

11. See Chapter 3.

12. *The Life, Work and Experience*, p. 202.

13. *The Pentecostal Evangel*, Oct. 1, 1921, p. 14. The

Indianapolis Journal in their Sept. 9, 1885, edition published a lengthy feature on the Dilts healing, "The So-Called Faith Cure of a Madison County Lady," in which they describe the illness as a "paralysis of the will" and the cure based on "psychological principles."

14. Decatur *Daily Republican*, Sept. 10, 1887. Numerous other examples of Woodworth's Pentecostal preaching before 1900 could be cited. The following two are typical: When Woodworth held a meeting in Louisville, Kentucky, during the summer and fall of 1888, the *Courier-Journal* for Aug. 24 reported that "Fifteen persons asked to be prayed for preparatory to fully receiving the Holy Spirit"; and in commenting on a meeting she conducted in Indianapolis in 1891, Woodworth wrote, "A number of God's children received the anointing for service. They obeyed the command of Jesus, 'Tarry ye in the city of Jerusalem, until ye shall be endued with power from on high'" (*The Life, Work and Experience*, p. 359). From the latter quotation, and others written in this 1894 book, it is evident that Woodworth looked at the experience—subsequent to salvation—as preparing people for service.

15. *The Life, Work and Experience*, pp. 437- 38. See Appendix C for the complete sermon, "The Glory of the Lord."

16. San Francisco *Examiner*, Jan. 9, 1890. This Carrie Judd [Montgomery] and Elizabeth Sission both became well-known Pentecostals and members of the Assemblies of God. Woodworth added in this interview, "Ministers who fall into line with the meetings are led out to seek more power."

17. Ibid., Jan. 13, 1890. In their April 13, 1890, edition, the *Examiner* told of people seeking the power, "fervently praying to be baptized in it."

18. The newspaper artist shows people "under the power" on the platform of Woodworth's tent in a St. Louis meeting during the summer of 1890 (see p.169). The woman standing with her hands raised is probably Woodworth, a common scene in her meetings, *St. Louis Post-Dispatch*, Aug. 21, 1890. Woodworth looked at the trances happening in her meetings (which was

"receiving the power") as what the Apostle Paul experienced in the Temple (Acts 22: 17) . She also viewed a trance and a vision as the same experience (*The Life, Work and Experience*, p. 91).

19. Ibid, Nov. 9, 1890. By this time, Woodworth had left St. Louis, placing a minister in charge of the new church.

20. St. Louis *Republic*, Sept. 3, 1890.

21. See Chapter 5.

22. John Alexander Dowie, *A Voice from Zion* (Chicago: Press of Zion Printing Works , Aug. 1900), p . 25.

23. Woodworth, *Acts of the Holy Ghost*, p. 118. After attending one of Simpson's meetings in 1885, Woodworth wrote that she "was surprised to see it so cold. Not one saved or healed, and no signs of the Holy Ghost baptism." It is anybody's guess at this point why Woodworth did not express the same critical remark in her 1894 book, The *Life, Work and Experience*.

24. A. E. Thompson, *A. B. Simpson, His Life and Work*, revised edition (Harrisburg, Penn.: Christian Publications, Inc., 1960) p. 140.

25. *The Christian Advocate*, April 30, 1891, p. 2. Although the editorial was unsigned, the author could have been J. M. Buckley, editor of the New York *Advocate*, a Methodist publication. (Magazine also had regional editions.)

26. St. Louis *Republic*, Sept. 1, 1890.

27. Forney, *The History of the Churches of God in the United States of America*, p. 241. Incidentally, this same building at 2929 Montgomery Street was the first permanent home for the Assemblies of God congregation in 1915 (*The Weekly Evangel*, Jan. 15, 1916).

28. Ibid., p. 237.

CHAPTER 8

Born for Such a Time as This

"Nearly twenty years ago the great outpouring of Pentecost came ... And suddenly the Holy Ghost came on a band of saints in Los Angeles. The fire fell and there were many signs of the presence of the Lord ... There never has been any religious movement that has grown or spread over the world so quickly or done so much for the salvation of souls and the glory of God."—*Maria B. Woodworth-Etter, 1921*[1]

What started as small prayer meetings and Bible studies in Topeka, Los Angeles, and other places at the turn of the 20th century, quickly grew into a network of Pentecostal groups around the world. Their passion was to seek God for a repeat, or restoration, of the Day of Pentecost that would shake the world and bring a great harvest of converts into the Kingdom.

As these believers saw the Pentecostal revival blaze across the land like a prairie fire, they united their hearts and groups in a common bond. But much to their dismay, few of the organized church leaders shared their enthusiasm for the new movement. The established church leaders looked at the new groups as being a divisive coalition, and they soon began dismissing the new "Pentecostal fanatics" from their churches.

The outcast Pentecostals—or "disinherited," as author Robert Mapes Anderson called them—locked arms for self-preservation, fellowship, and evangelization of the world. But despite their admirable goals, despite the new power they had received, and a new social entity, they soon realized they were still human and subject to many of the same failings and weaknesses of the past.

Some began to emphasize certain pet doctrines that carried over from their former denominations. Others promoted what they believed were revelations or visions. A strong leader could promote certain new teachings, which were often unscriptural, and quickly gain a following among new Pentecostals.

As a result, the Pentecostal movement soon broke into innumerable groups, emphasizing any number of doctrinal positions and practices, with speaking in tongues as the glue that gave what little bond they had.[2]

If anyone could have worked within the fledgling Pentecostal movement without harping on any of the pet doctrines, it was Maria B. Woodworth-Etter. In some respects she was like Queen Esther, raised "for such a time as this."

But before Woodworth began to minister within the Pentecostal movement, an important event took place in her life. This was her marriage to Samuel Etter. P. H. Woodworth and Maria had divorced in 1891, and then he died in 1892. For more than ten years, Woodworth had traveled without a husband. Then a gentle man from Hot Springs, Arkansas, came into her life. From Woodworth' s comments concerning his ministry, the reader is quick to see that no one would confuse the two. Samuel Etter was as different from the often crude P. H. Woodworth as a dove is from a hawk. Contemporary preachers and newspaper reporters of the day would appreciate the difference.

Etter believed in his wife's ministry. There was always a confirmation. He had no jealousy when he saw his wife in the pulpit and receiving accolations from the Pentecostal movement, which began about the time of their marriage. He believed she was being used of the Holy Spirit to convict sinners, heal the sick, and to lead believers into a Spirit-filled life. He believed in her healing ministry, even though he himself often suffered from illness.[3]

Woodworth viewed Samuel Etter as God's gift to her. He would "defend the word, and all the gifts, and operations of the Holy Ghost, but does not want fanaticism, or foolishness." And perhaps thinking about the trials she had suffered with P. H. Woodworth, she wrote that Etter took care of her in and out of the meetings. "It makes no difference what I call on him to do. He will pray, and preach, and sing, and is very good around the altar." Although little is known of Etter's background, he evidently was educated, because Woodworth added that he did most of her writing, helped publish her books, and supervisesd the meetings. She added, "The Lord knew what I needed and it was brought about by the Lord, through his love and care for me and the work.[4]

Woodworth was blessed with her husband's devoted support for 12 years. But then during a meeting she was conducting in Philadelphia in 1914, word came that this 71-year-old gift of God had finished his course. Woodworth returned to Indianapolis where she buried her husband and then boarded the train for the return trip to Philadelphia where she resumed her meetings.[5] Kind-hearted, devout Samuel Etter would want it no other way.

It isn't known just when Woodworth found her place in the Pentecostal movement. What is known is that she did find acceptance, and by 1912, began to take a prominent role.

During the early years of the Pentecostal movement, she withheld her cooperation because of what she felt was false teaching among certain leaders, and apparently she had little impact on early Pentecostals. Some of these went overboard on tongues, which turned Woodworth and others away from the movement. She said she "could not do much with the movement at first."[6] Without naming individuals, Woodworth complained that some wanted the Holy Ghost to work their way, not His. Her rule was simple: "Let the Holy Ghost work in any way that agrees with the word of God."[7]

Roscoe Russell, who was a teen-ager attending the Woodworth-Etter Tabernacle in Indianapolis in about 1920, said she told them when she began to hear people speak in tongues—presumably after 1901—she recognized it as the same experience she had received years before. Russell said, in her earlier years, she used the gift in her private devotions; however, when the Pentecostal outpouring began early in the 20th century, she accepted it as a genuine gift for the congregation and as the initial physical evidence of the baptism in the Spirit.[8]

Woodworth's first recorded meetings after the turn of the century were conducted in the Quad Cities area of Illinois and Iowa, beginning in 1902 a year after the first reported incident of speaking in tongues at Topeka, which was associated with the baptism in the Holy Spirit. She chose the Mississippi River town of Muscatine as her first stop, but she was no stranger to Muscatine, as she had held two successful meetings here during the 1890s. And success seemed to crown this 1902 meeting as well, for we read that she preached for seven weeks at the fair grounds. Then she moved up the Mississippi to Andalusia, Illinois, from there to Moline, back to Andalusia, and then back to Moline.

The Moline meetings in the fall of 1902 were especially remarkable, even by Woodworth's standard. Although she does not mention speaking in tongues in her reports at Moline, she does emphasize healing and apostolic power necessary to perform healings. A reporter for the *Moline*

Daily Dispatch quoted Woodworth as saying she experienced "the baptism of power such as was possessed of the Apostles of old."[9] And the reporter added that she claimed to do the same work they did.

One of the numerous healings reported during the Moline meeting received considerable newspaper coverage and corroboration by a physician in the city, Dr. O. W. Looker.

The patient, Mrs. John Kisor, had suffered from rheumatism for more than 20 years. She was unable to walk but a few blocks and could do very little of her housework because of a frequent severe pain in her neck and shoulders. Before her healing she could not wash more than three pieces of clothing before suffering excruciating pain; now she joyfully testified she was able to do a three-weeks' washing without trouble.

One day Dr. Looker saw Mrs. Kisor walk by his office, but he hardly recognized his patient. She looked as strong as a young woman. Looker called her into his office and asked what she had done to cure herself. Her answer was that Mrs. Woodworth had prayed for her and that she had been healed. Looker knew something beyond his help had intervened. But he discovered it wasn't limited to Mrs. Kisor. He told reporters that several others whom he could not help had been healed in the same manner. And even Looker got in on the healings. The story stated, "He himself had had a bronchial [affliction] for many years and had been healed so that he had been able to attend the meetings and sing for an hour or more at a time without resting his voice."[10]

Ten years later, Woodworth, in reporting the Moline meetings in her book, refers to Dr. Looker, calling him "one of the finest men in the city."[11] The churches, Woodworth added, could not make an impression on him, but then "he saw so many of his patients healed, was converted and became an earnest worker."

Based on newspaper reports and Woodworth's books, the Moline meetings attracted people from all walks of life and from every church. Even Jews were in attendance and came to Woodworth for prayer. She recalls that the wife of a rabbi came and asked if she could be healed without accepting Jesus. Woodworth tells what happened. "I told her no, she could not. She said she did not want anything to do with Jesus. She was badly afflicted, and had suffered much for many years. I talked some to her, and then she went away; but she came back in a few days, was saved and healed, and confessed Christ in public, praising Him for His wonderful works."[12]

Realizing that good soil should be reseeded, Woodworth returned to Moline and then to Rock Island during the summer of 1903. Again the healings and trances are reported, but Woodworth fails to take note of people speaking in tongues—if it actually happened.

She reported that people spoke in tongues in her St. Louis meeting held during the World's Fair in 1904.[13] As usual, numerous healing testimonies were given, but the significant part of the report came from a reprint of a story that first appeared in *Apostolic Light*, a paper published in Salem, Oregon.

A writer for the Salem paper attended the meetings and reported hundreds were saved, a great number healed, and others spoke in tongues: "The Lord was there in great power; there were wondrous miracles of healing and the Holy Ghost power was manifested in many signs and wonders, and in speaking in other tongues with the interpretation, and with heavenly songs."[14]

A Swedish woman "was entirely under the power of God and spake in many different languages and gave the interpretation.... Another sister was wonderfully baptized and sang an anthem in Greek and one in Latin.... Another young lady received her baptism and spoke in eight different languages."

The writer adds that while he (or she) was preaching and explaining that people who receive Pentecost speak in tongues, "the power of God took possession of me and I began to speak as the Spirit gave utterance in other tongues."[15]

As often happened in early Pentecostal revivals, an apparent big-time legend is associated with the St. Louis meeting in 1904. Woodworth supposedly went into a trance and stood like a statue for three days. Thousands of people who were visiting the fair heard about Woodworth's experience and came by to see her, the story goes, to give it redeeming value.[16] However, even though it was not uncommon for Woodworth to go into a statue-like trance for an hour or so, it seems unlikely that the trance lasted for three days.

If Woodworth went into a three-day trance and it, in fact, testified of the power of God to the many foreigners who were in the city for the World's Fair, the story more than likely would have been reported in her next book. The Salem report, which is reprinted in *Acts of the Holy Ghost*, refers to a trance Woodworth experienced on Mar. 24, 1904, in which she "had to be laid on the platform for over an hour."[17]

Embellishing evangelistic stories is not limited to Pentecostal revivalists, but because miracles are associated with the movement, the stories somehow get "stretched" with the telling. The exploits of Englishman Smith Wigglesworth are examples of this. He supposedly told a man with no legs to go to a shoe store, buy a pair of shoes, and press them against his stumps. As the man obeyed, his legs immediately snapped to normal size and his new feet went into the shoes. A perfect fit. But, as usually is the case, the man's name is not given and nobody knows the shoe salesman or the location of the store. And the story—which even Wigglesworth does not tell in his books or give as a sermon illustration—is related after Wigglesworth's death.

Documented? No, but it does make interesting and inspiring literature. And it sells books.

Beginning with the 1904 St. Louis campaign, the emphasis seemed to shift from trances to speaking in tongues—but always evangelism and physical healings. This included meetings she conducted in Indiana, Colorado, and Arizona. During a meeting in Arizona in 1904, Woodworth wrote, "There were many manifestations of the Holy Ghost, some spake in new tongues, and sang like it came from heaven, as the Spirit gave utterance."[18]

In the fall of 1904, Woodworth set up her tent in the southern part of Indianapolis, possibly her first revival meeting in the city in 15 years. Here many healings were reported along with the testimonies of people speaking in tongues. One woman, Woodworth wrote, "spake in unknown tongues all night." And Woodworth made it clear that this was almost two years before the outpouring of the Holy Spirit at Azusa Street in Los Angeles.[19]

Woodworth returned to Indianapolis in the summer of 1905 and pitched her tent on the same lot, and the meetings picked up where she left off the previous year.

A rather strange period in the life of Evangelist Maria B. Woodworth-Etter came from about 1905 to 1912. Compared with her previous all-out campaigns and thorough reporting in her books, this several-year period could almost be called her "silent" years. Her *Acts of the Holy Ghost*, which was published in 1912, jumps from the Indianapolis meeting of 1905 to another meeting in the same city in the spring of 1912.

Is this the period in which Woodworth was having trouble relating to the Pentecostal people? Was she experiencing physical problems? Did she feel she had done enough in the Kingdom and that a woman her age—she had reached 60 in 1904—ought to take it easy? Did she feel there were enough gifted evangelists to take her mantle?

Two sources that came to light after I published my first biography on Woodworth fill a few of the gaps during the early years of the 20th century. After obtaining her 1904 book, I discovered that she and her husband bought an Illinois farm, about a hundred miles east of St. Louis. Here, near the town of Cisne, she set up a home base for her evangelistic efforts. She had also planned to operate what might be termed a faith home in that day, where followers could come for prayer and teaching. Samuel Etter, in addition to raising sheep and farming, brought in an oil drilling company, which searched, apparently unsuccessfully, for oil. A local newspaper thought the operation was newsworthy enough to publish brief stories on the farm activity from time to time.

The second book, an autobiography of a pastor, follows the Woodworth narrative to Denver in 1907 and then to Phoenix. S. S. Scull was head of a holiness mission in Phoenix when he heard some of the reports from the Azusa Mission in Los Angeles. In 1907 he and his family attended a summer camp meeting that the Azusa people sponsored at Arroyo Seco in Los Angeles.

Scull was convinced that the Pentecostal revival was genuine and returned to Phoenix and told the holiness people where he stood. But he had not yet become a Pentecostal in experience. Later he went to Denver and met Woodworth, who was preaching in a small mission. "We are here stranded and broke with no opening," she told Scull. Her ministry would go well in Phoenix, Scull reasoned, and agreed to sponsor a series of meetings in a skating rink beginning in January, 1908.

"The situation was peculiar," Scull wrote, "the pastor had not received the Pentecostal baptism, [and] neither had the evangelist, and yet we were holding a Pentecostal meeting." According to Scull's report, the meetings met his expectations. Crowds packed the skating rink and spilled into the street. Scull triumphantly recorded nearly a hundred conversions and about the same number who received the Pentecostal experience. At the close of the 8-week meeting, a group of about 150 people called Scull to pastor a church, which he did for six years.[20]

Whatever the reason for the silent—or slow-down—years, she put them behind her in 1912. And for the next 12 years, and until her death in 1924, she remained active in the Pentecostal movement and hit the sawdust trail with the vigor she demonstrated in her mid-western blitz during the 1880s. Pentecostals were calling her from all over the country to conduct meetings in their cities. Woodworth believed without a wavering of her faith that she had been raised "for such a time as this!"

One of the calls she accepted came from a young Pentecostal pastor in Dallas, Texas, in 1912. The young man had attended Woodworth's meeting in Indianapolis in the spring of that year, and he was certain she could stir Dallas with her powerful charismatic preaching. Fred F. Bosworth, the young pastor, would within a decade become a well-known evangelist who specialized in city-wide salvation and healing campaigns.[21]

Despite the fact that this five-month Dallas campaign proved to be a key Pentecostal rendezvous, the Dallas newspapers for the most part ignored the thousands who were meeting daily and nightly. During this time they published an editorial marking the 15th anniversary of the legendary Baptist George W. Truett's pastorate at First Baptist. Generous coverage marked the death and funeral of General William Booth, founder of the Salvation Army. Locally, the now famous Neiman-Marcus department store was celebrating its fifth anniversary. And the national election that gave the voters three major presidential candidates—Wilson, Roosevelt, and Taft—was heating up.

But the media gave very little space—or sympathy—for the rousing high octane Pentecostal camp meeting going on in a tent, and later in a big wooden tabernacle, which commanded attention at the intersections of Parry and Fletcher streets.

So it was left up to the writers friendly to the Pentecostal movement to chronicle the meeting for their contemporaries in other parts of the country. And the one best suited for the writing task seemed to be the host pastor, Fred Bosworth.

Historian David Reed called the 1913 Los Angeles World-Wide Camp Meeting, which also featured Woodworth, "probably the high-water mark in the early Pentecostal revival."[22] If this is an accurate assessment, the Dallas meeting certainly could be called a close second in importance. For the success of this meeting in the summer and fall of 1912, in part at least, gained publicity for the Arroyo Seco meeting at Los Angeles the following spring.

Pentecostal editors around the world picked up Bosworth's Dallas reports, and then other writers relayed to their constituency the exciting happenings in Dallas. The list of influential Pentecostals who flocked to Dallas reads like a

"Who's Who" of early Pentecostalism: R. J. Scott, Frank J. Ewart, and Harry Van Loon represented Los Angeles; Andrew D. Urshan, a disciple of William Durham, was there from Chicago; representing Winnipeg, Canada, were Archdeacon Phair and 12 others; Carrie Judd Montgomery and her husband George, who traced their friendship with Woodworth back to 1889, were there from Oakland; M. M. Pinson, who would in 1914 preach the keynote sermon at the organizational meeting of the Assemblies of God, was there from Austin; A. P. Collins, who three years later became the second general chairman of the Assemblies of God, was there from his pastorate in nearby Fort Worth; a group visiting from England included Arthur Little, Miss Anna Barrett, and Stanley Frodsham and Mrs. Frodsham (Frodsham would later become the well-known editor of the *Pentecostal Evangel* and biographer of Smith Wigglesworth).[23] Because the meetings continued from July to December, it seems reasonable to think that the above Pentecostal notables were joined by many others well known in the movement. In one of the few stories the Dallas *Morning News* published on Woodworth's campaign, the first meeting, it reported that a crowd of 300 was present and "many went forward to plead for the visitation of the tongues."[24]

Woodworth quotes a glowing report of the meetings from the Dallas *Daily Times Herald*: "Every night at the Woodworth-Etter meetings God continues to display His power, bearing witness to the preaching of the Gospel 'both with divers miracles and gifts of the Holy Ghost.'"[25] However, no newspaper reporter wrote that copy. Fred Bosworth signed the story and from all appearances it was a paid advertisement.[26] In another report Bosworth wrote for a Christian periodical, "The God of All Earth Working at Dallas," the meetings were acclaimed as one of the high points of the Pentecostal movement.[27]

From reports that are now available, it appears that hundreds and maybe thousands accepted the new Pentecostal message as a result of this Dallas meeting. And to say that Dallas became a strong Pentecostal center following the meeting is to understate the case.

One man who said he was convinced of the reality of the Pentecostal revival was a minister of the Christian Church, Elder Henry C. Mears. He had just returned to Dallas from a pastorate in Corsicana, Texas, and decided he would attend the "show" and find fault with the Pentecostal activities.

After the first service he went away surprised at the way Woodworth ministered. She called on the congregation to believe the word of God, and she preached with power that simply amazed Mears. Yet Mears knew from his own training that Woodworth could not defend speaking in tongues, for that had ended with the Apostles. She could not defend healing, because that too had ended with the Apostles. When someone asked him about the meetings, he replied that Woodworth was mesmerizing the people. Mears, however, would soon change his mind.

For the next three weeks, Mears attended the meetings, checking everything he heard with his own Bible. It was getting more difficult each night to disprove what was happening, and each service, he moved a little closer to the front of the tent. Slowly but surely this Christian Church minister was being backed into a corner with the same Bible that he had used to argue against the claims that Jesus Christ was working in the 20th century as He did in the 1st.

One day, despite what he knew the Christian Church would think of him, Mears went to Woodworth and confessed that he needed what others were getting in this revival. Woodworth answered, "Come to the altar, and I will pray for you and ask God to send the Spirit upon you."[28] Mears accepted the invitation, and Woodworth and another woman prayed for him. "God baptized me with the Holy Ghost," he wrote. "I at once began to speak in another tongue. I have been blessed greatly since then."[29]

Later, Mears' preacher brother in Arkansas heard about Henry's Pentecostal capitulation and sped to the Dallas meeting to get his brother back on track. Bosworth described the scene for the *Word and Witness*:

"He [the brother] is a large man, weighing about 225 pounds. God's power came upon him and he was so violently shaken until convinced, yielded and wonderfully baptized in the Spirit, speaking in tongues and interpreting. While in a standing attitude the power of God lifted him clear from the ground. He is now acquainted with the power as well as the form of godliness."[30]

The Mears brothers were not the only ministers to become acquainted with the power. Howard A. Goss, an early Pentecostal leader, wrote that three very dignified ministers in clerical dress walked into a Dallas service late one night. Since there were no empty seats, three people who were seated on the altar gave up their place to the ministers. It was the wrong place for three proper ministers to maintain their dignity.

Goss said after the service "got well under way with the power of God as strong as usual," one of the clergymen suddenly tumbled off the altar rail and into the sawdust where he lay motionless. The other two ministers paid no attention to their comrade. But within about five minutes. a second minister joined the first in the sawdust. It wasn't long before the third minister also toppled into the sawdust, where he. too. lay motionless.

There they remained, oblivious to all the excitement around the altar, for the next three or four hours. Then simultaneously the ministers arose, brushed off the sawdust, and sheepishly walked to an exit.[31]

Reports of divine healing almost seemed common in Dallas, if divine healings can be called common. And the reports came from others besides Woodworth and Bosworth. Eyewitnesses from many states verified the accounts. Even the medical profession took note of the healings. One of these was Arthur C. Bell, M.D., who had a practice in Dallas and was dean of the College of Physicians and Surgeons.[32]

After describing all types of ailments that were healed in the meetings—from the healing of the deaf to those afflicted with cancer—Bell wrote, "Yes, Jesus can heal while I write a prescription. It is true, and I stand for the truth. No doctor would wish any of the cases I have reported in this report. They are all beyond them. The Lord has been good to send to us our beloved sister, Mrs. Woodworth-Etter. She is a chosen vessel."[33]

Bell added he had seen doctors enraged over the healings and that the doctors had called several meetings in an attempt to suppress the campaign.

Maria B. Woodworth-Etter no doubt arrived in the Pentecostal movement, as Queen Esther did in Persia, "for such a time as this" (Esther 4:14). Fortunately, the Pentecostal leaders recognized her gifts and the timing in this 1912 Dallas meeting, for she would remain a leading evangelist the rest of her life.

ENDNOTES

1.   Woodworth-Etter, *Spirit filled Sermons*, pp. 38-39. It is interesting to note that when Woodworth published these comments in the early 1920s, she referred to the Azusa Street revival in Los Angeles (1906), but overlooked the earlier Topeka

revival of 1901. Why would she ignore the Topeka revival? Did Woodworth ever meet Charles F. Parham, the leader of the Topeka revival? Had she heard about the morals charge brought against Parham in 1907? Did she meet William J. Seymour and Frank Bartleman of the 1906 Los Angeles revival? I have uncovered no evidence to answer these questions. However, since Woodworth and the above three men traveled a great deal in those early revivals, they possibly met, and it seems probable that Woodworth heard about the charges leveled against Parham. Seymour attended the 1913 World-Wide Camp Meeting in Los Angeles in which Woodworth was the main speaker.

2.   Some emphasized a second definite work of grace for their sanctification, others accepted the "finished work." A few took Mark 16: 8 ("they shall take up serpents") as a command to practice in their churches. Some baptized with a triple immersion, a dip for each member of the Trinity; others baptized in Jesus' name only; while the mainstream of Pentecostals baptized in the orthodox Trinitarian manner. Many refused to have any type of organization; others shunned the preparation of sermons in favor of the theory that if they would open their mouths, God would fill them with words to speak. Education for many early Pentecostals was of the devil and would lead them back into formalism. The legalistic and strict standards enforced by many Pentecostals boggles the mind: some refused to eat pork and other forbidden foods of the Old Testament; some believed that visiting a doctor or taking medicine was a lack of faith; wearing any type of jewelry was strictly forbidden by many. Lawrence Catley, an eyewitness at the Azusa Street revival, told a 1974 gathering of the Society of Pentecostal Studies that members of the mission would hide newspapers in the home if someone from the mission visited; he added that they were forbidden to consult a commentary, believing the Holy Spirit would give them the interpretation (See Catley tape, #A016, oral history, Flower Pentecostal Heritage Center, Springfield, Missouri).

3.   When reporters backed Woodworth into a corner and asked how she could claim people in her meetings were being healed

while her own husband was an invalid and unable to attend her meetings, she answered that her husband lacked faith for healing. Unfortunately, this teaching placed an awesome responsibility and guilt on Samuel Etter, and thousands more who couldn't generate enough faith to "claim their healing." It also, argued many, in a certain measure, limited the sovereignty of God.

4. Woodworth-Etter, *Acts of the Holy Ghost*, p. 339.

5. Woodworth-Etter, *Signs and Wonders*, pp. 384, 396-98. This report states Etter suffered from tuberculosis of the bone and stomach . His death certificate (Indiana State Board of Health, no. 2876, Aug. 19, 1914), gave the cause of death as arteriosclerosis.

6. Woodworth-Etter, *Marvels and Miracles*, p. 500.

7. Ibid. Some who disagreed with her interpretations of Scripture would find this rule too simplistic to be effective.

8. Roscoe Russell, from taped interview, 1978. See also *Marvels and Miracles*, p. 500.

9. "Faith Cures by Mrs. Woodworth-Etter. Claims Apostolic Power," The *Moline Daily Dispatch*, Nov. 28, 1902. This same story calls the meeting "the most remarkable series of meetings ever held in this city." In reporting the earlier meetings in Muscatine, the *Muscatine Journal* (Aug. 7, 1894) called the meetings "one of the most sensational if not one of the best (and on this point there will be some differences of opinion) series of religious meetings ever held in Muscatine." The report continued, saying "Mrs. M. B. Woodworth, who well deserves the title of priestess of the doctrine of 'divine healing,' came suddenly in our midst—almost like the flash of a meteour—from the west."

10. The *Moline Daily Dispatch*, Nov. 28, 1902.

11. *Acts of the Holy Ghost*, p. 302. Dr. Looker gives his testimony in the same book, p. 307. Mrs. Sarah E. Kisor's testimony is given on pp. 308-09. Two years later, during the 1904 Indianapolis meeting, another medical doctor—a Dr. David M.

Bye—testified that his son had been raised from the dead some 35 years earlier (*Indianapolis Star*, Sept. 19, 1904). This Bye report was given only as a testimony of God' s power and was unrelated to Woodworth's ministry. I found a related story about this Dr. Bye. Eight years after he gave this testimony in the 1904 meeting, Dr. Bye personally escorted several missionaries to South Africa, paid the fare, and provided them with other monetary gifts. One of the children who went with his parents was six-year-old John Richards, who told me about this account of the generous Dr. Bye (telephone conversation, Nov. 5, 1981). On the trip to Africa, Richards recalled, the ship was struck by a storm late at night. Richards watched Dr. Bye save the life of the ship's captain as a wave was about to take him overboard. Richards returned to Africa as an adult missionary where he remained for 42 years with the Assemblies of God.

12. *Acts of the Holy Ghost*, p. 303.

13. Ibid., beginning on p. 325. Woodworth fails to mention that during this meeting in St. Louis, the Churches of God requested that she return her certificate of ordination because "some dissatisfaction has been expressed relative to the labors and apparent lack of cooperation...and as she cannot now comply with the rules of association." (*The Church Advocate*, Mar. 30, 1904, quoted in "Maria B. Woodworth-Etter and the Churches of God, " by Jon R. Neely, *The Church Advocate*, Aug. 1975, p. 4.)

14. *Apostolic Light* (Salem, Oregon), quoted in *Acts of the Holy Ghost*, pp. 334-35. Martin L. Ryan, who was pastor of the Apostolic Holiness Church in Salem, published this paper. Florence Crawford visited this church in 1906, just before she founded her Apostolic Faith headquarters in Portland. Apparently no Pentecostal church was established in St. Louis as a result of this 1904 meeting; three years later Seeley D. Kinne started a Pentecostal mission after receiving the baptism at the Azusa Street Mission in Los Angeles (telephone call with Bertha Lawrence Schneider, Detroit, Michigan, 1981; Bertha Schneider received the baptism in Kinne's mission and then several years later traveled with Woodworth).

15. Ibid., p. 335. It isn't clear whether this quotation is a continuation from the *Apostolic Light* or whether Woodworth picks up the report. But according to *The Apostolic Faith*, Ryan received the Pentecostal experience at Los Angeles, presumably at Azusa Street in 1906 ("Another Free Paper," Nov. 1906, p. 4).

16. Kenneth Hagin, "A Commonsense Guide to Fasting" (Tulsa: Hagin Ministries, 1981, pp. 2, 3). Hagin writes that the St. Louis *Globe-Democrat* reported this but offers no date for documentation. The same report states that Woodworth had a tent that would seat 20,000; again no documentation is given. We know she had a tent that would seat 8,000 as early as 1889. Hagin's office later explained that he received the information from the late Texas preacher, Fred Eiting, who Hagin said attended the 1904 meeting. Benny Hinn and others have also used this legendary story.

17. *Acts of the Holy Ghost*, p. 334.

18. Ibid., p. 338.

19. Ibid., p. 342. The *Indianapolis Star* gave generous coverage to the 1904 meetings, including a front-page photo of Woodworth and the tent. One of the news stories, however, Woodworth would never reprint. It was the unfortunate case of a black woman who reportedly was driven insane by the excitement of the revival meetings. She frequently attended the meetings and then would return home to read her Bible aloud and sing so loud that the whole neighborhood heard. One day she went berserk, breaking windows in her house, throwing furniture and dishes into the yard, tearing up plants and flowers—all the time singing and praying. Then she tore her clothing from her body and ran naked through the streets, shouting hymns and quoting Scripture (The *Indianapolis Star*, Sept. 21, 1904). It was later reported that the woman had at one time been an inmate in a state hospital for the insane (*Star*, Sept. 22, 1904). The director of a state hospital was quoted as claiming many inmates at mental hospitals were there because of religious excitement (*Star*, Sept. 23, 1904).

20. S.S. Scull, *My Life Story* (Buckeye, Ariz.: self-published,

1947), pp. 33-35.

21. "Pentecostal Outpouring in Dallas Texas. "*Latter Rain Evangel*, Aug. 1912, pp. 10-11. Bosworth and his co-pastor, E. G. Birdsall, were leading the Pentecostal revival a year before Woodworth arrived on the scene.

22. David Reed, "Aspects of the Origins of Oneness Pentecostalism," p. 145, in *Aspects of Pentecostal-Charismatic Origins*, Vinson Synan, Editor.

23. Faith Frodsham Campbell writes in *Stanley Frodsham: Prophet with a Pen*, pp. 41-43, that her parents read about the Dallas meeting while in England and decided to attend. After arriving in Dallas, Frodsham wrote favorable articles for British readers, adding, "There is no reason why there should not be a similar revival in every Pentecostal center." It should be noted here that in Aug., while the Dallas meeting was peaking and attracting Pentecostal leaders from many parts of the country and at least a few from Canada and England, one of the best known leaders of the movement, William Durham, died in Los Angeles. Frank J. Ewart (who was in attendance at the Dallas meeting) became his successor at the Seventh Street Mission, Los Angeles.

24. Dallas *Morning News*, July 26, 1912.

25. *Acts of the Holy Ghost*, p. 359.

26. Dallas *Daily Times-Herald*, Sept. 7, 1912. The fact that Woodworth or her editor deleted Bosworth's name from the newspaper report reprinted in *Acts of the Holy Ghost* gives the wrong impression—that the *Times-Herald* wrote the copy and totally supported all the claims the Pentecostals were making at the meetings.

27. *Word and Witness*, Dec. 20, 1912.

28. *Acts of the Holy Ghost*, p. 364.

29. Ibid. Actually, the Dallas meeting, according to Mears, was the fulfillment of a vision he saw 45 years earlier when he was

15. In the vision he said he saw a crowd of thousands of people gathered to hear the Word; on the platform was a woman—who turned out to be Woodworth—and himself. (The vision is given in *Acts of the Holy Ghost*, p. 397.) Carrie Judd Montgomery, Woodworth, and F. F. Bosworth all quoted this Christian Church minister. Two years later, in 1914, Mears is listed in the Dallas city directory as pastor of the Apostolic Church of Christ at Peabody and Atlantic.

30. "The God of All the Earth Working at Dallas," by F. F. Bosworth, *Word and Witness*, Dec. 20, 1912.

31. Goss, *Winds of God*, pp.160-61. Goss apparently heard the story from someone else in attendance.

32. The 1911 Dallas City Directory lists Bell with a medical practice at 2700 S. Ervey. A check with the Dallas Medical Association fails to turn up any information on either Bell or his college. The Association spokesman, however, added that it was common for doctors to begin their own medical schools with a handful of students who met in the doctors' offices for their classrooms. Dr. Bell preached his own tent meeting in Dallas the following spring (*Word and Witness*, May 20, 1913, p. 3).

33. *Acts of the Holy Ghost*, p. 362.

Maria Woodworth-Etter
1844 1924

An early portrait of the woman evangelist, Maria Woodworth.

Previous page: *Early portrait taken in Los Angeles.*

A St. Louis Post-Dispatch artist shows people "under the power" on the platform of Maria's tent in a St. Louis Meeting during the summer of 1890. The woman standing with her hands raised is probably Mrs. Woodworth. This was a common scene in Maria's meetings.

M. B. Woodworth.　　　　Evangelist.

Early portrait of Maria.

August Feick, Mrs. Woodworth-Etter's faithful assistant.

Left:*Mrs.
Woodworth-Etter,
with hand raised in
a typical pose, and
August Feick, right.
Other two
unidentified.*

Below:*Maria B.
Woodworth-Etter
and workers. From
the left, Verna
Orendorf, August
Feick, Maria
Woodworth-Etter, J.S.
Saunders and wife,
and I. Hall.*

Throughout the years, this was a typical pose of Mrs. Woodworth-Etter, which appeared in her later books.

Left: *Mrs. Woodworth-Etter's granddaughter, Beulah Clark Stroud, and her son, Earl Clark at Enid, Oklahoma.*

Below: *Mrs. Woodworth-Etter conducted meetings in the resort city of Petosky, Michigan, beginning in 1914. Here is a group of worshipers attending one of her tent meetings. Maria is in the white dress, in the center, second row.*

Louis and Carl Romer. Louis was healed of a serious case of St. Vitus's dance in Mrs. Woodworth-Etter's 1915 Topeka meeting.

Thomas and Lyda Paino, Maria's assistants and later successors at the Indianapolis church she founded in 1918.

Congregation of Mrs. Woodworth-Etter's Indianapolis church about 1920. She is on the right with hand raised.

Above: *In August 1913, The Boston* Daily Globe *published this story and photo of Mrs. Woodworth-Etter and two of her assistants, Earl W. Clark, left, and Cyrus B. Fockler, during a meeting at Framingham, Mass. They were tried and released on charges of obtaining money under false pretenses.*

Maria Woodworth-Etter in later years

Elizabeth Ormsby, Mrs. Woodworth-Etter's daughter. Lizzie died a few weeks before her mother as the result of a street car accident.

Maria B. Woodworth-Etter's tombstone in Memorial Park Cemetery, Indianapolis.

CHAPTER 9

Pentecostal Fire Is Falling

"Like moths drawn to a flame, it was only a matter of time until
Woodworth-Etter and pentecostals would find each other.
Initially she kept her distance, apparently because of
pentecostals' reluctance to ordain women. But when she
finally joined forces with Holy Ghost believers in 1912,
they loved her." —Grant Wacker, *Heaven Below*, 2001 [1]

A Christian businessman and transplanted Canadian living
in Los Angeles, R. J. Scott, heard about Woodworth's
1912 Dallas meetings and decided to see for himself if the
miracle, healing, and Pentecostal epicenter had shifted from
Los Angeles to Texas. And if so, he was anxious to pull it
back to southern California because the movement had
crested and people were crying for a return to the "good old
days."

Before identifying himself in the Woodworth-Etter
campaign in Dallas, Scott attended a service to check out
the doctrine being preached. He happily discovered that it
was the same Pentecostal message that the City of Angels
and many other parts of the world had experienced for the
past dozen years. Scott wrote that he saw numerous people
healed in Dallas, many received the baptism in the Spirit,
and others were converted. One girl who had been blind for
12 years, he wrote, was healed in his presence.

That was enough for Scott. He knew Woodworth was the speaker he wanted for his dream meeting—the World-Wide Camp Meeting—in Los Angeles the following spring. Scott planned the Arroyo Seco meeting to "gather His saints together in one place and deal with them, giving a unity and power that we have not yet known."[2]

Scott, who had seen divisions among Pentecostals since the original Azusa Street revival in 1906, apparently believed that the Arroyo Seco meeting beginning in April 1913 would be the panacea for all the ills the movement had known in just twelve years. He had been to Dallas and witnessed miracles and a unity among Pentecostals there and believed the same thing could happen in Los Angeles on an even wider scale. And he was certain Woodworth was God's person for the hour.[1]

Despite the good intentions Scott had programmed for the landmark gathering, this camp meeting is best remembered for an issue that split the new Pentecostal movement. Today historians invariably remember the meeting as the place the Oneness (or what critics of the movement called the "Jesus Only" teaching) surfaced and gained acceptance among many Pentecostals.

Aside from the Oneness controversy, the Arroyo Seco camp meeting proved very successful. Pentecostals unconcerned about the fine points of theology, such as the Oneness vs. Trinitarian, Organization vs. Free, and the Finished Work vs. Sanctification arguments, had a grand time in this "heaven-on-earth" atmosphere. Pentecostal periodicals around the world published favorable reports about the many who were converted, baptized in the Spirit, and healed.

M. M. Pinson, the well-known Pentecostal preacher and writer, described the camp as a "battlefield," a frequently used metaphor for the embattled Pentecostals of the period. Here at Arroyo Seco, Woodworth and the other ministers, through the power of the Holy Spirit, were at war with Satan—and the good guys were winning the battle. Of the 200 ministers gathered for the meeting, Pinson was especially impressed with Woodworth and her prayers of faith for the sick.

A. C. Valdez , Sr., was a teenager at the time, and when he was in his 80s he fondly looked back to the meeting. He recalled that they lived in a tent city, which had streets named Praise, Glory, Hallelujah, and the like. The Valdez family lived at the intersection of Praise and Glory, and the large tent, which would seat 5,000, was on Hallelujah Avenue.

Woodworth was sickly herself, Valdez noted, and sometimes had to be carried up to the crude, unfinished pine platform. But Valdez added, "There was nothing sickly, pale, or weak about her ministering. Once her equally ill husband joined her, she raised her small hands and the power of the Holy Spirit electrified us all."[4]

Near the large tent was a smaller tent that was set up for the children. Valdez recalls that hundreds of children were saved and received the baptism in the Spirit. Two children, who would never forget Arroyo Seco and the children's tent, later became well-known Pentecostal evangelists, Watson Argue, Sr., and his sister Zelma, who were children of Evangelist A. H. Argue. They were both filled with the Spirit in a children's service, and they learned early what Pentecostal worship was all about. Zelma also remembered how insistent Woodworth was that those who were receiving prayer lift their hands in praise and glory to God. And when they did, "the power came down."[5] Fred D. Griesinger, who later became the real estate commissioner in California, told me that he, too, received the Pentecostal experience at this meeting when he was a boy.

Among the many who claimed to have received healing at Arroyo Seco was Mrs. Stanley Frodsham. The Frodshams, who had come to the United States from England in 1912 and had attended the Dallas meeting, were living in nearby Pasadena when Scott launched the World-Wide meeting. Mrs. Frodsham had suffered almost continuously for seven years with telescoped vertebrae. Her pride kept her from asking anyone to pray for her, but the pain became almost unbearable. Finally, she said, the Lord showed her that Mrs. Woodworth-Etter ought to pray for her.

Following the prayer, she said she came so mightily under the power of God that helpers in the meeting laid her on the floor and moved on to pray for others. There alone, Mrs. Frodsham said, she experienced divine healing: "A hand came and laid hold of the middle of my back, and another hand laid hold of the bottom of my spine, and in one short moment the vertebrae that had been telescopic were put into perfect position."[6]

No formal organization of Pentecostals existed during the Arroyo Seco meetings, but that did not prevent them from organizing a missionary program. Several missionaries were in attendance, some returning from the field while others were on the way for the first time. Later it was reported by a missionary committee that the camp meeting crowd gave more than $4,000 for individual missionary support and to provide a home for Pentecostal missionaries in Hong Kong. The appeal also brought in donations of jewelry and real estate.[7]

Woodworth had to look at the meeting with mixed emotions. On the one hand, she saw it as a direct work of God: He had told her that she should call Pentecostals together in a meeting of unity, and He had provided R. J. Scott with a similar burden; both were impressed that God wanted the meeting orchestrated in Los Angeles. People were saved, healed, and baptized in the Spirit, but Woodworth felt the Los Angeles meeting could have accomplished much more if those in charge had given her more liberty.

Was her self-centered importance coming through? Alice Reynolds Flower was a close observer in Indianapolis early in the 19th century and appreciated her ministry, but she told me that Woodworth would ask in public for a person giving a healing testimony to also name the minister who had offered the healing prayer. And of course it was Woodworth herself.

By the time the Los Angeles meeting convened, Woodworth had been preaching for more than 30 years and had conducted larger meetings than most of the delegates had seen. She was not used to sharing the spotlight with other preachers, and her report of the Los Angeles meeting shows her unhappiness at this arrangement. She was given charge of a 10 A.M. service while others preached in the afternoon and evening. Apparently the decision to limit Woodworth' s ministry to the morning service was made after the camp meeting started.

People had traveled many miles to see and hear her, Woodworth reasoned, and they had been shortchanged. The promoters had announced the meeting widely, and the advertisements billed Woodworth as the one to have charge of the "Spiritual part of the meeting." She groused, "The people came from mostly every state and place to see me and be healed."[8]

With the tone of this statement and others, it is evident that Woodworth felt the leaders were making a mistake. One day, the morning service continued right into the time slot set for the afternoon meeting. As someone was helping Woodworth from the platform, she suddenly had compassion on those who were gathered in the congregation—especially the unconverted. Without thinking of infringing on another service, she stopped, raised her hands, and invited sinners to come to the front to be saved. Scores of people responded to the invitation, a response few had ever seen. In defense of her calling and ministry to these people, Woodworth later wrote that she believed hundreds more would have been converted had she been able to continue with her meeting.[9] G. T. Haywood, an African-American and Indianapolis pastor, probably referred to this same meeting when he wrote, "One afternoon such conviction fell on the sinners that many ran to the platform and were saved at once."[10]

Woodworth could have had Frank J. Ewart in mind as one who limited her ministry to the morning service. Ewart, in his report of the meeting, acknowledged the camp meeting to be an outstanding revival, stating that 364 had received the baptism in the Spirit during the four weeks. But he revealed dissatisfaction with Woodworth's leadership. "The people were restless, inquisitive, and on the tip-toe of expectancy," he wrote. "Early in the meetings the preachers rebelled against turning the meetings over to Mrs. Woodworth-Etter." The crowd wanted to hear others "of God's servants, who might have a new message that would take us forward to the glory and power of the faith once delivered to the saints."[11]

Then Ewart, one of the leading proponents of the Oneness message, added to the well-known story about how that "revelation" came to the ministers at Arroyo Seco—the most important part of the entire month of meetings, in his opinion. The "revelation" came to John G . Scheppe, who had spent a night in prayer at the camp meeting. Early in the morning, he believed he had seen something new in the use of the name of Jesus. He ran through the camp telling others of his new insight, and later people on the West Coast began to baptize in the name of Jesus. Believers who had been baptized in the name of the Trinity were told they must be rebaptized. The divisive teaching was dubbed the New Issue, Oneness, Jesus Only, and Jesus' Name.

So, Arroyo Seco, a meeting that was designed to create unity and happiness, became the launching pad for a doctrine that would split the Pentecostal movement.[12]

Sister Woodworth Finds Wider Acceptance

Even though Woodworth's participation in the Los Angeles meeting was curtailed to a certain degree, she would continue to minister to large Pentecostal gatherings until her death in 1924. Pentecostals from the east to the west and from the north to the south honored her as a "mother in Israel" and as a modern prophetess who had been raised to preach the Pentecostal message. "All that was required to draw a crowd," historian Grant Wacker observed, "was to promise that Woodworth-Etter would be present." Wacker added that she "amply proved that Aimee McPherson was certainly not the first and in some ways not even the most important evangelist to preach down the latter rain."[13]

Woodworth was 69 years of age when she preached the Arroyo Seco camp meeting in 1913, but it appears that she was just getting her second wind. The new revival spirit permeating the young Pentecostal movement seemed to give her a new lease on evangelism. Following the Arroyo Seco arena, she conducted high octane Pentecostal meetings during the next two years in Chicago; Long Hill, Connecticut; Framingham, Massachusetts; Hot Springs, Arkansas; Philadelphia; Atlanta, Georgia; and other key cities.

Throughout these meetings, Woodworth's dynamic ministry continued to generate a tremendous amount of news coverage in the daily presses and the Pentecostal publications. It must be remembered that the secular papers would frequently report her meetings, but seldom would they offer anything but critical reports of the teachings and practices. Despite the negative press—which she seemed to have a gift in ignoring—her influence on individuals and churches continued. A few representative cases are related here.

Following the campaign in Long Hill, Connecticut, during the month of June 1913, the famous Stone Church in Chicago invited Woodworth for a series of meetings. Despite a rather cynical story in *The Chicago Daily Tribune*,[14] the meetings brought several Pentecostal missions together where Woodworth was able to share her experiences and exhort them on one of her favorite topics: being led by the Spirit.

Anna C. Reiff, editor of The *Latter Rain Evangel*, described the meetings as Chicago's "mightiest visitation of the supernatural" she had ever known.[15] A. H. Argue, who had been in the Pentecostal movement from the beginning and had traveled throughout the United States and Canada, exclaimed that the Chicago meeting was the "mightiest visitation from God of these latter days."[16] After two weeks of meetings, the old Stone Church could not hold the crowds. From 1300 to 1500 people were packed into the main auditorium and an overflow room in the basement, and large numbers of people were turned away.

The Stone Church meetings in 1913 marked a turning point in the lives of at least one Chicago Methodist family. And nearly 70 years later, Elizabeth Waters of Los Angeles was still praising the Lord and testifying of what the Lord had done for her mother.

Elizabeth wrote to the *Pentecostal Evangel* that in 1913 her mother had been bedfast for two years. So when someone told Elizabeth about the healing meetings, she immediately thought of her mother. She rented a wheelchair for 50 cents, and with the help of a girlfriend, wheeled her mother about eight blocks to the Stone Church.

"The service started at 7 p.m.," she remembered. "We arrived at 5 p.m. It was crowded, but some strong men rolled the chair with others around the platform." Someone pointed at Elizabeth's mother and others lifted her to the platform. During a time of prayer, Woodworth hit Elizabeth's mother on the chest. "My mother leaped to her feet and ran around," Elizabeth wrote. "She was completely healed!"

In a follow-up letter to Woodworth's great-great-great-grandson, Tom Slevin, Elizabeth described the touch as like a bolt of lightning. She began "jumping for joy, and all the people in the church yelled and screamed."

And the rejoicing didn't stop at the church. When Elizabeth's mother arrived home, the neighbors came in to see what had happened to the woman they knew as an invalid. The former invalid demonstrated her healing by walking up the stairs while the neighbors rejoiced with more yelling and crying. She lived another 23 years and died at age 83.

Elizabeth Waters in 1982 looked back with rejoicing of her own to Chicago's Stone Church and the "beautiful white-haired evangelist" who was instrumental in her mother's healing. "I'm 83 now," she wrote, "but I remember that June day very vividly."[17]

So impressed was Reiff with the summer campaign that she devoted the entire issue of the August 1913 *The Latter Rain Evangel* to the revival meeting. Many healing testimonies and reports of conversions filled its pages, and other Pentecostal papers picked up the stories and echoed the Chicago meeting around the world. Woodworth wanted it understood that there were to be no controversial doctrinal points aired during the Stone Church revival. She knew that certain leaders in the Pentecostal movement were teaching the finished work of sanctification, while others were teaching a separate sanctification experience; she knew that already some Pentecostals were baptizing in "Jesus' name," while the majority would not budge from the Trinitarian formula; some were planning to create organizations, while others boasted of their independence. For these reasons, and other differences of opinion, Woodworth kept the meetings simple and steered away from controversy. And it worked in Chicago.

Wherever Woodworth preached, her congregation knew they would receive a heavy dose of the Pentecostal power and divine healing. Here in the Stone Church, she wove these favorite subjects into her sermon of July 6, 1913.

She underscored the scriptural view of a believer's body as a temple of the Holy Spirit (1 Corinthians 3:16), and she spoke of the power that operates the body. "As great pieces of mechanism are moved by electricity, so our bodies, the most wonderful piece of mechanism ever known, are moved by the power of the Holy Ghost sent down from heaven." On the day of Pentecost, the 120 witnessed for Jesus and healed the sick with the power of the Holy Spirit. And it is no different today, she argued in an era that produced non-Pentecostal leaders who were claiming that the gifts of the Spirit and miracles ended with the Apostles.

Urging her hearers to receive everything to which they were entitled, she said, "If we haven't the power, let us confess it and ask God to give us the power He gave the first disciples." And she promised that the same results would follow: "If those who come to the Lord will be filled as they were on the day of Pentecost, we will have streams of living water rushing through us and flowing to the very ends of the earth."[18]

Because the meetings had attracted pastors, missionaries, evangelists, and other Christian workers like honey attracts bees, two special services were conducted in which hands were laid on these leaders, "that they might receive a fresh anointing of the Spirit and have more power in their ministry."[19]

It is interesting to note that while the editor of *The Latter Rain Evangel* used the terminology just quoted, Woodworth gave the impression that she was imparting gifts to the believers: "God has wonderfully blessed me by imparting gifts, and many have received the baptism when I laid hands on them."[20] Earlier when she described the Los Angeles meeting held the previous spring, she wrote, "Many ministers and evangelists received great power and gifts, by the laying on of my hands."[21] A contemporary Pentecostal, Seeley D. Kinne, wrote that the distinguishing feature of the Stone Church meeting was "the impartation of gifts of healing and faith for their exercise."[22]

With this kind of praise, critics might accuse Woodworth of being the founder of the often extreme New Order of the Latter Rain movement of the late 1940s and early 1950s. To Woodworth's credit, however, look at her use of Paul's admonition to Timothy: "Stir up the gift of God which is in thee." She then clarified her position: "If there is any gift God is showing you you ought to have, you can receive it by the laying on of hands."[23]

It appears then that she didn't mean that all one had to do was to "name the gift and claim it." Rather, she obviously believed that any gift from God was in line with His will. And it should also be remembered that Maria B. Woodworth-Etter was not a theologian, and often it appears she picked up expressions that were being used in the early Pentecostal movement, which seemed to suit her particular ministry. Pentecostal historian, D. William Faupel, doesn't see Woodworth as a significant force in shaping Pentecostal doctrine or ecclesiology, but as "a monumental figure in terms of spreading the Pentecostal message."[24] Faupel added that her gifts were in the salvation-healing ministry, "a true predecessor of [Gordon] Lindsay, [William] Branham, [Oral] Roberts, and company who emerged on the American scene in the late 40s and early 50s."

Here in Chicago in 1913, Woodworth believed her special mission was to create unity and love among Pentecostals: "The Lord showed me last night as I lay awake the most of the night to gather together the ministers as far as I could that we might see eye to eye, preach the same Gospel and have the same signs following."[25] Few would doubt that she accomplished that mission.

But the next meeting, at Framingham, Massachusetts, would prove to be one of the most difficult of her ministry in Pentecostal circles. It all started when she accepted an invitation from the Christian Workers Union, publishers of a widely circulated paper, *Word and Work,* to conduct services in their annual camp meeting. Here she would stand trial on a charge that she obtained money under false pretenses. (See Chapter 11 for an account of this humbling yet important trial.)

One of the significant events that took place at Framingham went unnoticed at the time, for the conversion of a certain man from Woodbury, Connecticut, appeared to be no different from others during the month of August 1913. Yet the salvation and deliverance from alcohol and serious illness of E. H. Garlock not only turned his own life around, but also was instrumental in shaping the future of his ten children—including 13-year-old Henry, who would later distinguish himself as a missionary in Africa.[26]

Our story begins during the spring of 1913. Little happiness could be found in the Garlock farmhouse near Woodbury. E. H. Garlock was addicted to gambling and alcohol, and was suffering from illness. Friends and family persuaded him to seek help from A. B. Simpson at Nyack, New York. Simpson had founded the Christian and Missionary Alliance and had been praying for the sick many years. Garlock took their advice and went to Nyack, but he came away discouraged and without the help he needed. The hope he found on the Nyack search was when he learned of Evangelist Maria Woodworth-Etter, who had just closed a meeting at Long Hill, Connecticut.

When Garlock returned to his home, he carried what would open a bright new chapter in his life of sin and sorrow.

It was a copy of the *Word and Work*, which had a report of the Long Hill meetings and the schedule of her meetings in Framingham. Henry and other members of the family urged their father to attend Woodworth's August meetings. The Nyack trip had been a dissappointment, but finally E. H. Garlock agreed to attend services at Framingham. At the close of the only service he attended, Garlock responded to the altar call Woodworth gave. After Woodworth and others prayed for him, E. H. Garlock found himself in a familiar Pentecostal position: prostrate in the straw, where he remained for more than two hours.

Henry would never forget the next day when his father returned to the farmhouse at Woodbury a completely changed man. He was delivered from alcohol, gambling, and was healed of his physical problems. And in the middle of the night, E. H. Garlock experienced a drama that not only affected his own life—which was happening, it seemed, by the hour—but also his family for generations to follow.

He did not remember hearing anyone speak in tongues at the camp, so had little or no knowledge of the Pentecostal experience. "But the night he reached home and retired," Henry recalled, "he woke the family up in the middle of the night speaking in tongues which continued for several days. Even the farmhouse seemed to be shaken by the Spirit."

As a 13-year-old, Henry had misgivings about what was happening, thinking that the crowd at Framingham had hypnotized his father and wondering whether he would ever speak English again. Henry soon saw that a change had come over his father. "He prayed continually and started to read the book of Acts. I soon saw that his experience was real and started seeking for the baptism in the Spiri,t which I received on Christmas day in 1913."[27]

Woodworth would never learn the full impact the deliverance made on this Connecticut family, which has had well-known ministers and missionaries in each generation since E. H. Garlock was touched by the Holy Spirit's power at Framingham.

Another healing should be related. But in this one—unlike the case involving E. H. Garlock—the person healed never saw Woodworth. In the spring of 1917, doctors told Benjamin Denton in New York that he had tuberculosis. For over a year, he was confined to a reclining chair and then was sent to the Ray Brook State Hospital in the Adirondack Mountains. Here doctors pronounced his case as being in the last stages of the disease, and after three months at the hospital, he was dismissed without a hope that he would survive.

Denton went to live with an aunt in Rochester, where he was again confined to a bed. His lungs were bleeding, and his voice was nothing more than a whisper. There, while he was in this hopeless and weakened condition, he received a book from a friend that was to be the means of inspiring his faith. The book was Woodworth's *Signs and Wonders*. As he read, Denton was amazed at the stories of healings and so began to search the Bible while reading the book. "My eyes were opened," he wrote later, "I found Jesus is the same yesterday, today, and forever, and all things are possible to those who believe in God."[28]

With a new hope singing in his heart, Denton wrote to Woodworth requesting a prayer cloth—a means which the Apostle Paul had used to increase faith for one requesting prayer for illnesses and other needs. After receiving Woodworth's prayer cloth, Denton prayed and believed that God would heal him, and he testified many times later that he was healed. He went to the telephone and called his wife—the first time he had spoken in seven months. Then he went outdoors and sawed up an old apple tree just to test the miracle.

Denton's son Charles, who was associated with the Assemblies of God headquarters for many years, remembers that in 1929—11 years after the healing—his father took the family back to Ray Brook State Hospital, where the medical records were kept. The doctors who had examined him in 1918 were amazed, and called young doctors and nurses to see the man they sent home to die, now in perfect health and doing hard physical labor.[29]

The healings of E. H. Garlock and Benjamin Denton are only two cases of the reported hundreds who received healing in Woodworth's meetings during the early years of the Pentecostal movement. These healings, plus the conversions and the Pentecostal experiences, established Woodworth as an important figure in the movement. It is impossible to measure the influence she had on the movement from 1912 to her death in 1924. Many who were converted, healed or received the Pentecostal blessing would carry the Gospel to unnumbered people around the world.

She indeed found her place in the Pentecostal Movement.

ENDNOTES

1.   Grant Wacker, *Heaven Below: Early Pentecostals and American Culture* (Cambridge, MA and London, England: Harvard University Press, 2001), p. 146.

2.   "World-Wide Apostolic Faith Camp Meeting," by R. J. Scott, *Word and Witness*, Mar. 20, 1913. Scott listed his name along with the name of George B. Studd as contact people. Both Scott and Studd later testified they were healed at this meeting—Scott of a rupture, and Studd of sciatic rheumatism and other diseases (*Signs and Wonders*, pp. 256, 257). The Flower Pentecostal Heritage Center has a copy of the song book R. J. Scott

prepared especially for the meeting.

3.   On Monday, Apr. 14, 1913, the day before the meeting opened, a freak storm hit Arroyo Seco and for half an hour the area experienced thunder, snow, pea-size hail, and darkness (*Los Angeles Times*, Apr. 15, 1913).

4.   A. C. Valdez, *Fire on Azusa Street* (Costa Mesa, Cal.: Gift Publications, 1980), pp. 41, 42.

5.   Zelma Argue, "Act Your Faith," the *Pentecostal Evangel*, pp. 8, 9. July 19, 1959. As a young man A. H. Argue suffered "chronic internal trouble." When A. B. Simpson came to Canada for a meeting, he prayed for Argue. Within 24 hours Argue claimed he was well. (See *What Meaneth This?* by Zelma Argue, published about 1924, p. 6.)

6.   Stanley H . Frodsham, *Jesus Is Victor* (Springfield, Mo.: Gospel Publishing House, 1930), p. 98.

7.   *Word and Witness*, June 20 and Aug. 20, 1913. Editor E. N. Bell, who was a former Baptist, urged his readers to make regular monthly contributions for missions.

8.   Woodworth-Etter, *Signs and Wonders*, p. 251.

9.   Ibid.

10. G. T. Haywood, quoted in *Signs and Wonders*, p. 253.

11. Frank Ewart, *The Phenomenon of Pentecost*, p. 76. Howard A. Goss, an early Assemblies of God leader who withdrew with other Oneness preachers in 1916, wrote about "new messages" in his book, *The Winds of God*; a preacher who did not get some new slant on the Scriptures, or some revelation, was considered "slow, stupid, unspiritual" p. 155).

12. Where did Maria B. Woodworth-Etter stand on the Oneness issue? She was probably resting in her tent when this issue first surfaced at Arroyo Seco. She was not a theologian and probably paid little attention to the discussions until later when congregations were split over the issue. Years later she called the Oneness position "the biggest delusion the devil ever

invented" (*Spirit filled Sermons*, p. 153), which would hardly make her welcome in Oneness pulpits of the day. Today the movement has many separate organizations, including the mostly white United Pentecostal Church (UPC) and the black Pentecostal Assemblies of the World (PAW).

13. Wacker, 146.

14. "Sobs, Shouts; Then 'Miracle,'" The Chicago *Daily Tribune*, July 12, 1913. The reporter wrote, "The Pentecosters [sic] are a comparatively new sect whose head seems to be Mrs.Woodworth-Etter." She was not their "head," but certainly was one of the leading spokespersons.

15. Anna C. Reiff , "The Day of Chicago's Visitation," *The Latter Rain Evangel*, Aug. 1913, p. 2.

16. Ibid., p. 3.

17. "Recalls Mother's Healing," by Elizabeth R. Waters, *Pentecostal Evangel*, April 25, 1982, p. 31; and letter from Elizabeth Waters to Tom Slevin, June 12, 1982.

18. Woodworth-Etter, *Holy Ghost Sermons*, p. 32.

19. Ibid., p. 13. See Appendix D for key points of this exhortation to leaders and young Christian workers in the Pentecostal movement.

20. Ibid.

21. *Signs and Wonders*, pp. 250-51.

22. Ibid., p. 303

23. *The Latter Rain Evangel*, p. 16, Aug. 1913.

24. Letter to author, Jan. 31, 1979.

25. *The Latter Rain Evangel*, p. 15, Aug. 1913. Why didn't Woodworth unite with the Assemblies of God that was formed the next year? Apparently she was more interested in spiritual unity than an organization. Too, the Assemblies of God in its early years had effectively restricted women in leadership

positions; they could not pastor churches; they could not vote at the General Councils; and they were ordained only as evangelists or missionaries. Woodworth knew that some men in the Pentecostal movement believed women belonged behind the scenes with very little authority (still the case in many churches). David Lee Floyd, who attended Woodworth's meeting in Hot Springs, Arkansas, in the fall of 1913, told me the local leaders of the meeting appreciated her ministry but were careful not to "give her too much authority" (oral history tapes, No. A028-30, Flower Pentecostal Heritage Center, Feb. 26, 1981). Even in the 21st century women are not represented on the 200-member General Presbytery—eligible but never elected.

26. H. B. Garlock's story of escaping from cannibals is told in *They Speak with Other Tongues*, by John Sherrill, pp. 97-100, and in his own book *Before We Kill and Eat You*. Seven of E. H. Garlock' s children attended Pentecostal Bible schools; five became ministers or married ministers; and two became missionaries. And generations since have been active in the ministry.

27. Letter from H. B. Garlock, in response to my query, Sept. 14, 1979.

28. "An Apple Tree Tests the Miracle," *Pentecostal Evangel*, June 19, 1977, p. 7, and correspondence with me, 1978.

29. Ibid. Denton' s activities at age 93 included running errands on his bicycle. Denton died in 1983 at the age of 99.

CHAPTER 10

Publishing the Good News

"Today closed the 23rd day of the labors of Mrs. Woodworth at Kokomo, which have been remarkable in the annals of our local history ... Vehicles of all sorts began pouring into the city at an early hour, and by the appointed time for service fully 6,000 people were in the city. Nothing short of a circus or a political rally ever before brought in so large a crowd."
— *1885 Newspaper Coverage*.[1]

"Mrs. Woodworth's books were marvelous! Years ago I used to read her books often for the wonderful inspiration they provided." —*David du Plessis*.[2]

Almost as soon as she began her pulpit ministry, Maria B. Woodworth saw the value of extending her efforts through writing. Writing was nothing new for 19th century evangelists. Before Woodworth came on the scene, Finney, Moody, and other evangelists and pastors established a following through the use of periodicals, tracts, and books. In addition, newspapers and religious periodicals of the period helped publicize the Woodworth meetings—even though many of the reports were extremely unfavorable.

The Book Ministry
Nobody would accuse Woodworth of being a literary genius, despite the fact that she wrote at least 10 books. But she told

her story and preached her sermons in the best medium the times offered—which included the writing and publishing of books—and her efforts were very successful. Even today, more than 80 years after her death, people who know about her ministry—and that includes a huge following in the Pentecostal-Charismatic community—collect her books. In the 1970s, a Kansas City area pastor told me that he would give $100 for one of Mrs. Woodworth's books. Today he might have to pay up to three times that amount for an original—even though reprints are available.[3]

Many who have read Woodworth's books put them next to the Bible in importance. Take the famous evangelist and pastor Fred F. Bosworth, for example. He was the pastor of a Pentecostal congregation in Dallas during the time Woodworth conducted her highly successful 1912 meeting there. His uncritical testimony, which was published in one of Woodworth's books, helped spread her fame and credibility among early Pentecostals. He said he wished all Pentecostals owned a copy of her book because of its encouragement to believe for the miraculous. "There has been no such record written since the 'Acts of the Apostles' recording such continuous victories by the Lord in our day over sin and sickness."[4]

Stanley Smith, a member of the famous British cricket team-turned missionaries, dubbed the Cambridge Seven (one of which was C. T. Studd), wrote a testimonial for Woodworth's *Acts of the Holy Ghost*, which she used also for her later book *Signs and Wonders*. He valued the book next to the Bible. "In special seasons of waiting on God I have found it helpful to have the New Testament on one side of me and Mrs. Woodworth's book on the other." He wrote that her book "is a present-day record of 'The Acts' multiplied." Regarding Woodworth's ministry, Smith wrote, "I venture to think that [it] is unparalleled in the history of the Church, for which I give all the glory to the Lord Jesus Christ, as Mrs. Woodworth would, I know, wish me to do."[5]

With publicity and testimonials such as Bosworth and Smith gave, it is no wonder that early Pentecostals were anxious to hear Mrs. Woodworth and obtain copies of her books.

Accolades concerning Woodworth's books occasionally came even in the secular press. Take the Sherburn (Indiana) *Advance-Standard*, for example. Apparently the publisher of the paper thought so much of Woodworth's book *Marvels and Miracles* that he promoted it in the paper, displayed a copy of the book in his office, and took orders. Sherburn pastors probably took exception to his promotional copy that hinted some of them were preaching "uninspired" sermons and that Woodworth's book was worth a million of theirs: "It is the sweetest piece of literature, next to the Bible," he wrote, "that we have ever read." And he recommended it to anyone desiring something worthwhile to read.[6]

With a little imagination, you can see Woodworth break into a big smile, shout, and take a "Jericho March" around the tent.

When I discussed Woodworth and her ministry with the well-known Pentecostal statesman David du Plessis, he responded, "Mrs.Woodworth's books were marvelous! Years ago I used to read her books often for the wonderful inspiration they provided."[7] Many earlier believers would echo du Plessis' sentiments.

Woodworth's first attempt at writing was a small book she published herself in the early 1880s. She refers to this book in her other writings, stating that it was her testimony of healing, which occurred before she entered the ministry. Her second book, *Life and Experiences* of Maria B. Woodworth, was published in 1885, giving an account of her childhood, marriage, call to preach, and evangelistic efforts through July 1882. She updated the book in 1886 and titled it, *Trials and Triumphs of Mrs. M. B. Woodworth.*

Always keeping a living journal, Woodworth updated *Trials and Triumphs* in 1888 and retitled it, *Life and Experiences of Maria B. Woodworth.* In 1894 she added more material and titled it, The *Life, Work and Experience of Maria B. Woodworth.* After the turn of the century, and her marriage, another updated version appeared as *Life and Experience of Mrs. M. B. Woodworth-Etter.* This fourth volume also included sermons and visions.

This energetic evangelist—a local pastor's dream come true—published *Acts of the Holy Ghost* in 1912. Still another revision in 1916 appeared as *Signs and Wonders.* Supporting believers in Great Britain, during World War I, published an abridgement of the 1916 edition. And possibly the last revision was the 1922 *Marvels and Miracles.* These last three American editions are substantial volumes—each running close to 600 pages. In addition to the journal-type books above, Woodworth published hymnals, sermon books, and *Questions and Answers on Divine Healing.*[8]

August Feick, Woodworth's assistant pastor, campaign manager, and successor at the Woodworth-Etter Tabernacle in Indianapolis, published a book in 1925 following Woodworth's death. This book, titled *Life and Testimony of Mrs. M. B. Woodworth-Etter*, is divided into three parts: 1) excerpts from *Life, Work and Experience*, and five sermons from *Acts of the Holy Ghost*; 2) an account of Mrs. Woodworth's last three years of ministry; 3) and—possibly to connect Mrs. Woodworth-Etter's followers with himself as her appointed successor—Feick updated the work at the Woodworth-Etter Tabernacle in Indianapolis and published his sermons.

Because all of the several books that Woodworth wrote were self-published and distributed, she did not have to worry about finding a publisher or of being a polished writer. There was no question that the books found a market. W. J. Mortlock, a minister and editor for Woodworth, wrote in *Marvels and Miracles* that the big books had sold 25,000 copies from about 1912 to 1921.[9]

In addition to this distribution, abridged editions and other book portions were published in French, Italian, Danish, Swedish, Egyptian, Hindustani, other dialects of India and South Africa, and probably other languages known by Pentecostals. It is certain that some of the books were still in circulation as late as the 1970s (before the new English editions appreared), because readers in foreign countries occasionally addressed letters to Woodworth—50 years after her death![10]

A Swiss woman, Mlle. Biolley, translated *Signs and Wonders* into French in 1919. Robert Lebel, a French Pentecostal minister who wrote the preface to the fifth edition of this French translation, commented that the Pentecostal revival in France can be attributed in a certain measure to the ministry of Woodworth's books.[11]

Without a doubt the foreign editions of her other books played an important part in spreading the Pentecostal message and encouraging readers to believe that healing is in the atonement.

Apparently Woodworth's efforts to publish a periodical were short-lived. She published a monthly paper, *The Bible Truth*, during her crusade in Salem, Oregon, in 1892.[12] At that time, the paper was in its third volume, but how many more volumes were published is unknown. It seems logical to assume that she utilized some type of direct mail, because people across the country were aware of her meeting schedule and traveled long distances to attend.

Books, however, seemed to work best for Woodworth to teach her doctrines, promote her ministry, and provide income. So this medium became the most prominent. But it also has a rather shocking disclosure, and the paper trail is self-evident.

A Case for Plagiarism

My 1986 book, *The Woman Evangelist*, revealed that by 1916, Woodworth had picked up a huge selection of questions and answers on the topic of divine healing from an 1899 book and published them as her own. What I overlooked in 1986 is that the same questions and answers also appeared in her 1904 and 1912 books—almost word for word from the 1899 book, with no credit given to the original author.

Let's look at the evidence.

After Woodworth established the tabernacle in Indianapolis in 1918, she began work on another book, *Questions and Answers on Divine Healing*. The book was published in 1919, and she released an enlarged and revised edition some time after January 1922. About half of this revised edition, the question and answer section, appears to be a simple case of plagiarism.

According to the dictionary, a person who plagiarizes can also be called a literary thief, because to plagiarize is "to take and pass off as one's own (the ideas, writings, etc. of another)." The material in *Questions and Answers on Divine Healing* and the person and/or persons responsible for putting it in print seem to fit this definition.

Whether Woodworth knowingly or unknowingly plagiarized *Questions and Answers on Divine Healing* would be difficult to determine now. But obviously no two authors can say the same thing without one seeing the other's work. If the evidence below had been revealed during Woodworth's lifetime, her reputation would have been seriously damaged.[13]

The apparent victim of the plagiarized material is J. W. Byers, a minister with the Church of God (Anderson). Byers was the pastor of a congregation in 1899 when his book *The Grace of Healing* was published by his denomination's Gospel Trumpet Publishing House. He maintained a good reputation with his contemporaries even though some of them thought he took dogmatic positions on divine healing. *The Gospel Trumpet* magazine had previously published most of the text of Byers' book in serial form. One of Byers' chapters, *"Summarized Questions and Answers on Divine Healing,"* was published in its entirety in the October 27 and November 3, 1898, issues—with Byers' name on the articles as author.[14]

Five years later, Woodworth introduced 50 of the questions in her *Life and Experience of Mrs. M. B. Woodworth-Etter.* Then in 1912 and 1916, she reprinted 27 of the questions and answers. Two decades after Byers introduced his book, Woodworth published her 40-page book *Questions and Answers on Divine Healing,* which clearly states on the title page, "By Mrs. M. B. Woodworth-Etter, Evangelist." The *Christian Evangel* introduced the book to their readers June 14, 1919, and again promoted it in the August 9 issue. A second edition of the book was published in 1922, indicating that it had been revised and enlarged. The title of Woodworth's book is identical to Byers' chapter title with the exception of the deleted "Summarized."

Of the 53 questions and answers that Woodworth includes, 52 are in J. W. Byers' *The Grace of Healing* chapter. Not only are they the same questions and answers, almost word for word, but they are also given in the same sequence. Woodworth's book includes one question that is not included in Byers' chapter, and Byers has two questions that are not in Mrs. Woodworth's book.

For an example of the evidence, let's take a closer look at the contents.

Byers quotes a Dr. Jas. B. Bell of Boston in his answer to the 29th question.[15] Woodworth answers the same question, but refers to Bell as "Dr. J. B., of Boston."[16] In her second reference to the doctor in the same answer, she calls him "Dr. Bell."[17] Then in the 32nd question, Mrs. Woodworth again refers to the same doctor as "Dr. B."[18]

Byers also quotes Dr. Oliver Wendell Holmes in the same 29th question.[19] In Woodworth's version, Holmes' name is abbreviated to "Dr. W. H." and "Dr. H."[20]

A common Woodworth practice in handling names should be understood before going farther. In her earlier books, Woodworth used the actual names of people involved in her meetings; but in subsequent editions, when the same stories were reprinted, the names were simply shortened to initials (as shown in the excerpt above). Whether an editor chose to follow this style or whether it was Woodworth's idea is difficult to determine now.

Questions from J. W. Byers, 1899

Q. Do you believe that the Bible teaches divine healing as a redemption blessing?

A. Yes. Do you not see how plain this is made in the prophecies just quoted and in their fulfillment? Jesus worked in every respect, in his life, ministry, death, and resurrection, just according to the redemption plan. His words and deeds are the divine expression of this redemption plan, and we can clearly see that healing for the body is placed upon an equal with healing for the soul. Both are obtained upon the same grounds—obedience and faith.

Q. Can a person possess salvation without healing?

A. Yes; he may. While both are obtained by faith, yet they may not both be obtained by the same act of faith. Jesus will be to us just what our faith takes him for.

Q. Did Jesus heal everybody?

A. Yes; all who came to him in faith. Read Matt. 4:23, 24 and Matt. 12:15.

Q. But they did not seem to have faith, did they?

A. Yes. If you read the references just mentioned, you will notice the people "came to him" for healing, and "followed him." At Nazareth, his own town where he had been brought up, he could do no great work among their unbelief. [This answer is shortened in both examples.]

Questions from Maria B. Woodworth-Etter, 1904
Q. Do you believe that the Bible teaches divine healing as a redemption blessing?

A. Yes. Do you not see how plain this is made in the prophecies just quoted and in their fulfillment? Jesus worked in every respect, in His life, ministry, death and resurrection, according to the redemption plan. His words and deeds are the divine expression of this redemption plan, and we can clearly see that healing for the body is placed upon an equality with healing for the soul. Both are obtained upon the same grounds, obedience and faith.

Q. Can a person possess salvation without healing?

A. Yes; he may. While both are obtained by faith, yet they may not both be obtained by the same act of faith. Jesus will be to us just what our faith takes Him for.

Q. Did Jesus heal everybody?

A. Yes; all who came to Him in faith. Read Matt. 4:23-24 and Matt. 12:15.

Q. But they did not seem to have faith, did they?

A. Yes. If you read the references just mentioned, you will notice the people "came to Him" for healing, and "followed Him." At Nazareth, His own town, where He had been brought up, He could do no great work among them, because of their unbelief. [This answer is shortened in both examples.]

Where does this evidence put Woodworth? Was she aware that putting one's name on another's literary property is stealing? Can we think of her in any better terms than as a plagiarist in handling this material? How could she possibly justify this type of action when she knew the Bible has harsh words against stealing?

In all fairness to Woodworth, and before attempting to reach a verdict in the case, let us look at other possibilities in this question and propose a theory. Is it possible that Woodworth had written the questions and answers in the 1890s and that Byers simply picked them up and published them in *Gospel Trumpet* and *The Grace of Healing*?

Yes, Woodworth could have written the material in the 1890s, because she was publishing books even before this period. And she was praying for the sick as early as 1885. Byers would have taken a high risk, however, to plagiarize something that Woodworth wrote in the 1890s. She was one of the best-known evangelists on the road in the last quarter of the 19th century. The nature of the questions and answers—with the use of personal pronouns and opinions—would have tipped off someone who read Byers' book, or the articles which appeared in the *Gospel Trumpet*, that the material belonged to Woodworth, if indeed it was hers.

Furthermore, if the material belonged to Woodworth in the 1890s, why didn't she advertise it as she did her other books? (The material does not show up in her 1894 book.) Woodworth's 1919 book was introduced as being new: "There has been such a demand lately for information on healing that Sister Woodworth felt led to get out a booklet on Divine Healing." This statement, written by Lillian P. Hardister of Woodworth's church and published in the *Christian Evangel*, June 14, 1919, says nothing about a previous edition or that half of the questions were in *Signs and Wonders*, Woodworth's 1916 book that was more than likely still in print.

Admittedly, it is dangerous for us to speculate on something that happened a century ago, but when there is no way to interview the persons involved, we are limited in our options. With this limitation in mind, here is a theory regarding *Questions and Answers on Divine Healing*, and the earlier use of the materials in Woodworth's books, that possibly could explain what appears to challenge her credibility.

Woodworth decided one day in 1904 that people ought to learn about her interpretations on divine healing, so someone suggested the use of the question and answer format. Perhaps one of the workers was assigned the job of putting together a series of questions and answers that would reflect Woodworth's theological positions and philosophies.[21]

Let's assume that this unknown editor found a copy of J. W. Byers' book *The Grace of Healing*, which already had questions and answers on divine healing. Or perhaps he had never seen Byers' book, but had copies of *The Gospel Trumpet* that had first published the material. Woodworth's editor discovered that the interpretations were similar to what she had preached and taught for years.

The editor returned to Woodworth and presented the newly typed manuscript and told her that he or she had written new questions and answers. Woodworth flipped through the pages, smiled, and told the editor to include it in her forthcoming book. Maybe Woodworth honestly thought her editor had written the material. That would be a simple case of ghost writing.

Rather than accuse her of plagiarism, we would probably be safer in faulting her for selecting an indiscreet ghost writer or editor—who in 1904 could have been her new husband, Samuel Etter. As the years rolled by to 1919, Woodworth was 75 years old, and with as many irons in the fire as she had—her evangelistic meetings, the Tabernacle, her books, her correspondence, praying for the sick—one can understand how she couldn't possibly closely supervise writing projects.

Could she have been sued for using Byers' material? It isn't likely, because Byers' book was not copyrighted and so went into public domain when it was published. (Some of Woodworth's books were published without a copyright notice, as well.)

A closing question might be whether Byers had granted Woodworth permission to incorporate his material in her books. If he did, a fundamental mistake is evident. His name does not appear on Woodworth's publications using his questions and answers.

The 4ᵗʰ Estate—The Secular Press

The 4th Estate—The Secular Press
Vital media for publicizing Woodworth's meetings were the newspapers of the period—even though she often viewed them as earning the "yellow journalism" tags with their sensational muckraking reports of her meetings. Because of the controversial nature of Woodworth's meetings and the huge crowds, newspaper editors sent reporters to cover the services. Few newspapers in the United States that were close to Woodworth's meetings—and that would include many of them over a 40-year period—would miss the opportunity to subjectively describe the meetings in full detail.

As a result, there is an abundance of stories reporting the meetings from about 1883 to 1924. All one has to do is search out the microfilmed and electronically scanned newspapers, and look for stories.[22]

Naturally, there were more negative than positive stories concerning Woodworth's meetings, but even the negative stories gave her publicity she would never have received in any other way.

A good example of negative press coverage serving Woodworth's advantage is the 1890 St. Louis meeting. A *St. Louis Post-Dispatch* reporter attended one of the tent meetings and a four-column story with two line drawings appeared in the August 21 edition. He described the meeting as having "some of the most weird and entirely inexplicable scenes ever witnessed in this or any other city—scenes which puzzle physicians, ministers of the Gospel and cool-headed businessmen, and which seem like miracles to the ignorant."[23]

The story created a sensation. The next night, streetcars going north toward the tent grounds were jammed. And when Woodworth looked across her congregation, she saw that each of the 8,000 seats was taken, and hundreds of curious people milled around outside.

Newspapers everywhere covered the Woodworth meetings: geographically, papers from the Salem (Oregon) *Statesman* to the Boston *Herald*; and in size and reputation from the Muscatine (Iowa) *Journal* to the *New York Times*. If the meetings generated more than the usual controversy, the newspapers covered the services in great detail. Two good examples of detailed coverage were the Oakland and St. Louis meetings of 1890 (see chapters 5 and 7). The tidal wave scare in Oakland, California, and the healing and trance controversy in St. Louis, Missouri, kept major newspapers in the areas always on the alert for further exciting developments.

Woodworth's meetings arguably continued the tradition of the Frontier revivals and the Finney meetings of the first half of the 19th century. But she advanced two other elements on a wide scale, faith healing and the "way of the power"— or a subsequent experience to salvation. The meetings became the prototype of Pentecostal crusades and revivals, combining the Charismatic elements with evangelism. Newspapers, whether they agreed with Woodworth's theology or not, looked at the meetings as worthy of coverage, and many of the major papers gave the meetings front-page attention and discussed her on their editorial pages. The free coverage, of course, simply advertised the meetings and attracted more people.

This is how a few writers described the meetings between 1885-1916:

HARTFORD CITY, INDIANA, 1885. The remarkable religious revival at Hartford City, Blackford County, under Mrs. Woodworth, a lady evangelist, still continues with the most unusual manifestations. It is conducted in the Methodist Church and has set the whole neighborhood in a frenzy. *New York Times*[24]

HARTFORD CITY, INDIANA, 1885. The marvelous outdone, the wonderful outstripped—the magician's wand never produced such startling magical exhibition as were enacted or transpired at the Opera Hall in this city last night. ... Reporters from other cities [another report said 21 states were represented by the news media] were present and each and every one accorded to the evangelist lady a fervency, zeal, earnestness and honesty of purpose as were never seen before by them. *Cincinnati Enquire*[25]

KOKOMO, INDIANA, 1885. Today closed the 23rd day of the labors of Mrs. Woodworth at Kokomo, which have been remarkable in the annals of our local history. . . . Vehicles of all sorts began pouring into the city at an early hour, and by the appointed time for service fully 6,000 people were in the city. Nothing short of a circus or a political rally ever before brought in so large a crowd. *Indianapolis Journal*[26]

WABASH, INDIANA, 1885. Yesterday was a big day in the history of Xenia, south of this city. Fully 12,000 visitors were attracted to the place by the presence of Mrs. Woodworth, the now famous trance medium. *Indianapolis Time.*[27]

SPRINGFIELD, ILLINOIS, 1888. Greater faith can scarcely be found, no, not in Israel, than that manifested by the members of the Christian Union Band. The band is not yet six months old, yet it embraces a larger membership than any church society in the city. ... The meeting in the evening at Electric Light hall was immense in every way. The hall was jammed to suffocation by 7 o'clock and from one to two hundred people, among whom were many ladies, swarmed about the front door until after 10 o'clock vainly seeking to gain admission. After a desperate struggle a *Journal* reporter managed to get through the outside crowd and into the hall just before the meeting was dismissed. *Springfield Journal.*[28]

OAKLAND, CALIFORNIA, 1889. A large tent in the vacant block on Webster and 12th streets has been filled nightly for the past week during a series of the most remarkable revival meetings ever held in Oakland. *San Francisco Chronicle.*[29]

MOLINE, ILLINOIS, 1902. The most remarkable series of meetings ever held in this city are now in progress at Warr Hall. *Moline Dispatch.*[30]

LONG HILL, CONNECTICUT, 1913. Believing they can be cured of ravaging diseases hundreds of people are flocking to the World Wide camp meeting at Long Hill where the Apostolic society is holding daily meetings in Radcliffe's grove. Some have sacrificed their homes and crossed the continent in order to partake of the "divine healing" of Mrs. M. B. Woodworth-Etter, the great Evangelist. *Bridgeport* (Connecticut) *Post.*[31]

SIDNEY, IOWA, 1916. For the first time we can remember, a religious gathering has driven out a good show, and before they went the members of the company which was booked for the whole week before last at the opera house, went over to the campmeeting to see what had taken their crowds. *Fremont County* (Iowa) *Herald.*[32]

Editorial writers got into the act as well. Some criticized or ridiculed Woodworth, while a few treated her favorably or at least fairly. Woodworth could have hardly asked for a fairer treatment than a *St. Louis Republic* writer gave her in 1890 when two medical doctors—Wellington Adams and Theodore Diller—tried to have the evangelist committed for insanity.

Describing the doctors'activities as "meddlesome and mischievous pieces of quackery," an editor claimed the effort would be costly and self-serving, "filling the newspapers with the names of Doctors Clyster and Jalap."

Ordinarily things like this could be treated as a jest, the editorial continued. "But when the effort to obtain free advertising takes the form of cowardly annoyance to a defenseless woman, who, however ignorant and unconventional she may be, is certainly trying to do what good she can, it deserves the unqualified condemnation of all who love fair play."[33]

You can almost imagine Woodworth trotting through the sawdust in another "Jerico March!"

Today the newspaper would no doubt be sued for the slanderous attack on the doctors—especially because of the insulting name-calling.

Editors and reporters used the Woodworth meetings to sharpen their witty and satirical pens, often having fun at the expense of the evangelist, the crowds, and the types of services she conducted. Sometimes the converts who "succumbed to the power" were shocked—or in some cases, thrilled—to find their names in satirically written newspaper stories.

In an article published in the Wabash (Indiana) Weekly *Courier,* a writer called Mrs. Woodworth "The Greatest and Only" in his report of the Kokomo meeting in June 1885. She deserved the title, the writer claimed, because Dr. William Cooper and Attorney Morrison made their way to the mourners' bench in the Kokomo meeting.

With a touch of humor, the writer commented, "We are not so much surprised that a Kokomo doctor has concluded to 'rise, shine, and go to glory,' but it is the conversion of the Kokomo attorney that places Mrs. Woodworth at the very head of religious revivalists."[34]

But then the writer threw out the mother of all challenges to Woodworth. She would be regarded as more than mortal if she could cause "the scales to fall from the eyes of a Kokomo editor."[35]

A Ft. Wayne *Gazette* writer also thought that the conversion of a city editor would be a remarkable feat. After Woodworth closed her Hartford City, Indianapolis, meetings in February, 1885, it was reported that one of her converts was J. M. Ruckman, former editor of the *Hartford City News*. Regarding the conversion of Ft. Wayne's editors, the writer predicted that "Mrs. Woodworth will have poor luck we fear when she strikes Ft. Wayne and attempts to bring the ungodly city editors of our contemporaries from their evil ways."[36]

Obviously editors and reporters were pretty skeptical about the Woodworth results. However, an Indianapolis paper did report that an editor of a Greenfield (Indiana) newspaper was healed in a meeting Woodworth conducted in Indianapolis. His reported healing undoubtedly was an exception for the 4th estate—usually a pragmatic crowd.

The Religious Press

Generally the religious press treated Maria B. Woodworth-Etter as *persona non grata*.

An exception to the treatment the religious press gave her is seen in the Pentecostal periodicals after the turn of the century. Without a doubt, Woodworth, with her many experiences on the sawdust trail, was the favorite evangelist during the early years of the Pentecostal Movement. Such magazines as the *Word and Witness*, The *Pentecostal Herald*, the *Christian Evangel*, the *Pentecostal Evangel*, and *the Latter Rain Evangel* seldom sent reporters to cover the Woodworth meetings, but regularly published reports local pastors and Woodworth's coworkers prepared.

A well-known and influential black Pentecostal leader, G. T. Haywood, consistently supported Woodworth's ministry—at least in the early days of the Pentecostal Movement. After the World-Wide Camp Meeting in Los Angeles in 1913, Haywood wrote that the power of God to heal was evident. "Sick were brought from far and near, and multitudes were touched by the power of God through the instrumentality of His humble servant, Sister Woodworth, whose simple faith brought deliverance to many."

Haywood claimed that the "lame walked, the blind received their sight, the deaf heard, CANCERS were cured, TUMORS and TAPE WORMS passed away and dropsy and CONSUMPTIVES healed." Ascribing an anointing for Woodworth, not unlike the old cricket player Stanley Smith used, Haywood continued: "On one occasion many were healed as Sister Woodworth raised her hands toward heaven, while she was leaving the tent."[37] Haywood, the composer of the moving song "I See a Cleansing Stream," no doubt opened doors for Woodworth in black churches with this glowing endorsement.

When Fred F. Bosworth hosted a six-month Woodworth-Etter meeting in Dallas in 1912, he regularly kept others informed with favorable reports as one that appeared in the *Word and Witness*: "The devil's works are ignored, Jesus magnified, and controverted points of doctrine not mentioned, and the love and unity among the saints is precious. Visitors say they never saw such love and unity. Ministers and others continue to come from great distance."[38]

George C. Brinkman, a layman who edited *The Pentecostal Herald*, frequently published reports of Woodworth's meetings and advertised her books. When Woodworth returned to Muncie, Indiana, in 1920—35 years after her first visit there—Brinkman published an article with this lead paragraph: "Sister Woodworth, a most remarkable old lady is holding a 30 day campaign at Muncie ... Her voice is as strong today as it was more than 40 years ago when she first started in the evangelistic work."[39]

Again from a Pentecostal periodical, M. M. Pinson, an early Assemblies of God leader, stamped his approval on Woodworth's work, but in the same article surprisingly cautioned Pentecostals against a medical doctor who had become a pastor-evangelist, Dr. F. E. Yoakum of Los Angeles.[40] Dr. Yoakum, Pinson wrote, did not take "a real stand for the outpouring of the Spirit according to the book of Acts." Pinson reserved his praise for Woodworth, who was "not trying to build up a 'one-man' or individual affair [which he accused Yoakum of doing], but is trying to spread the full Gospel as recorded in the book of Acts." Striking out against what is a "relative matter," Pinson wrote that Woodworth took her stand "with other leading Pentecostal preachers against false manifestations" (relative because a genuine gift of the Spirit to Pinson and Woodworth could be wildfire to a Pentecostal across town).

Pinson liked Woodworth for another reason. She preached "the real Pentecostal outpouring of the Spirit with the signs following, also healings, etc." [Pinson then cautioned against making claims of healing without testing.] ... "But the fact is, that God is healing people in answer to prayer by this woman."[41]

Another early Pentecostal leader, Robert. J. Craig, a pastor in San Francisco and the founder of Glad Tidings Bible Institute (now Bethany College of the Assemblies of God, Scotts Valley), hosted meetings Woodworth conducted. He wrote a report for the *Weekly Evangel*, urging ministers to use Woodworth's life and ministry as an example: "If the Pentecostal ministry would study her life and count on God, expecting the supernatural to be revealed in each meeting, what a mighty agency ours would be in the hands of God."[42]

Woodworth just took another lap in her "Jericho March."

It isn't any wonder that Pentecostals around the world accepted Woodworth uncritically when they read such positive reports in their periodicals from men like Craig, Haywood, Pinson, Bosworth, Bell, Brinkman, and others.

The printed page served Woodworth well. Her books reached people she would never see, and they were used as "position papers" on conversion, the baptism in the Spirit, the operation of spiritual gifts, praying for the sick, and interpretation of prophecy. The Pentecostal organizations reported her meetings regularly in their periodicals, and both benefited from the cooperation.

It is interesting to speculate how the Pentecostals would have utilized Woodworth's charisma if radio and television were available in those early years—say in 1912 during the big Dallas crusade. No doubt they would have developed a program for her, or Woodworth would have been on the air with her own program.

But these media would be left to others to develop for evangelistic purposes. Radio and television came along too late for Maria B. Woodworth-Etter, but she capably used the available media—books, tracts, magazines, and newspapers—and became a role model for later Pentecostals to follow.[43]

ENDNOTES

1. *Indianapolis Journal*, June 15, 1885. The newspaper reports did not necessarily create the crowds, but they certainly attracted more people, both the spiritually challenged and the mobs.

2. My conversation with David duPlessis, Aug. 17, 1979, Baltimore, Maryland.

3. I had the good fortune to find an excellent copy of *The Life, Work and Experience of Maria Beulah Woodworth* (1894) in an Ohio bookstore. Since 1980 I have seen only two other copies of this book. The Flower Pentecostal Heritage Center has copies of *The Life and Experiences of Maria B. Woodworth* (1885, 1886, and 1888) and *Life and Experience of Mrs. M. B. Woodworth-Etter* (1904)—the only ones I have seen. The center also has scanned copies of her books.

4. *Acts of the Holy Ghost*, p. 351.

5. *Signs and Wonders*, p. 7. This quotation was published previously in *Confidence*, a Pentecostal paper whose editor was A. A. Boddy, Vicar of All Saints Church, Sunderland, England. (A. A. Boddy's wife prayed for the famous Pentecostal evangelist

Smith Wigglesworth when he received the baptism in the Spirit.)
Norman P. Grubb (C. T. Studd's son-in-law), in correspondence
with me, wrote, "Stanley Smith was the predestined successor to
Hudson Taylor." But, Grubb added, Smith came out strongly for
the doctrine of ultimate reconciliation, which caused his
dismissal from the China Inland Mission. Another member of the
Cambridge Seven was George Studd, C. T. Studd's brother.
George Studd was a strong supporter of Mrs.Woodworth-Etter,
but he too later accepted the ultimate reconciliation doctrine,
according to Grubb. He also accepted the "Oneness" position
that divided early Pentecostals.

6.   Sherburn *Advance Standard*, as quoted in *Life and Testimony*,
p. 65; no date on quote but published between 1922-25.

7.   My conversation with him, Aug. 17, 1979, Baltimore, MD.

8.   One of the songbooks is *Revival Hymns as Published and
Used by Mrs. M. B. Woodworth, the Evangelist in her Gospel
Meetings* (1891); a copy is in the Union Theological Seminary
Library, New York. The two sermon books are titled *Spirit filled
Sermons* (1921) and *Holy Ghost Sermons* (1918). Her journal-
type books also contain sermons. *Questions and Answers on
Divine Healing* as a book was published in 1919 and revised
and enlarged in 1922.

9.   *Marvels and Miracles*, p. 113. Mortlock added that
Mrs.Woodworth had published a total of 14 volumes.

10. My 1983 interview with Thomas Paino, Jr., then pastor of
Lakeview Temple, Indianapolis, which is an outgrowth of the
old Woodworth-Etter Tabernacle.

11. George R. Stotts, "Mary Woodworth-Etter: A Forgotten
Feminine Figure in the Late 19th and Early 20th Century
Charismatic Revival," p. 31.

12. Salem (Oregon) *Statesman*, May 29, 1892.

13. The information revealed in my 1986 edition, possibly for
the first time in print, came from *The Grace of Healing*, by J. W.
Byers, and *Questions and Answers on Divine Healing* by Mrs.

Woodworth. Coincidentally, I borrowed the two books from a friend's library on the same day. It should be noted also that 27 of the questions and answers were published in *Acts of the Holy Ghost*, pp. 414-431 (1912), and *Signs and Wonders*, pp. 197-202 (1916). Now we know, after the discovery of Maria's 1904 *Life and Experience of Mrs. M. B. Woodworth-Etter*, that Byers' work was being used only five years after it appeared in his book.

14. Correspondence with John W. V. Smith, Associate Dean, Anderson School of Theology.

15. J. W. Byers, *Grace of Healing*, p. 275.

16. Woodworth-Etter, *Questions and Answers on Divine Healing*, p. 14.

17. Ibid., p. 15.

18. Ibid., p. 16.

19. Byers, *Grace of Healing*, p. 276.

20. Woodworth-Etter, *Questions and Answers on Divine Healing*. p. 15

21. Because it is not uncommon for evangelists and others to employ editors, research writers, and ghost writers, nobody would fault Mrs. Woodworth to this point in our theory. She wrote that her second husband, Samuel P. Etter, was doing most of her writing and book publishing after their marriage in 1902 (*Acts of the Holy Ghost*, p. 339). An Elder A. E. Sidford, edited *Signs and Wonders* (1916), which was published after Samuel P. Etter's death. Another editor, W. J. Mortlock, was responsible for editing *Marvels and Miracles* (1922).

22. Roberts Liardon compliled nearly 300 newspaper stories on Woodworth's meetings in Section Three of his *Maria Woodworth-Etter: The Complete Collection of Her Life and Teachings*. It is reasonable to assume that many more newspapers that contain stories about the Woodworth meetings are available on microfilm in libraries and archives across the country.

23. *St. Louis Post-Dispatch*, Aug. 21, 1890. The St. Louis papers looked at these meetings as one of the most important local stories of the summer and fall 1890.

24. *New York Times*, Jan. 24, 1885.

25. Cincinnati *Enquirer*, Feb. 17, 1885.

26. *Indianapolis Journal*, June 15, 1885.

27. *Indianapolis Times*, Aug. 18, 1885.

28. Springfield (Illinois) *Journal*, Dec. 10, 1888. This article also describes a river baptismal service for 60 candidates, which drew some 2,000 people.

29. San Francisco *Chronicle*, Dec. 2, 1889. See chapter 5.

30. Moline (Illinois) *Dispatch*, Nov. 28, 1902.

31. Bridgeport (Connecticut) *Post*, June 10, 1913.

32. Fremont County (Iowa) *Herald*, Sept. 21, 1916. The report stated the crowds were the largest ever seen in Sidney.

33. St. Louis *Republic*, Sept. 3, 1890. Clyster is a rectal injection, or an enema; jalap is a Mexican plant whose roots are used for a laxative. This editorial was published three days after a rival newspaper, the *Post-Dispatch* (August 31, 1890), published a half-page article titled, "Say She Is Insane." The article was a result of an interview Adams and Diller conducted with Mrs. Woodworth and which a *Post-Dispatch* reporter covered. The judge dismissed the case, declaring he had no authority to judge Mrs.Woodworth's sanity.

34. Wabash (Indiana) *Weekly Courier*, June 12, 1885.

35. Ibid.

36. Ft. Wayne *Gazette*, Feb. 12, 1885.

37. G. T. Haywood, reprinted in *Signs and Wonders*, p. 253. For more about this Los Angeles meeting, which proved to be a launching pad for the Oneness wing of the Pentecostal movement, see Chapter 9. Haywood later embraced the

Oneness doctrine and established Christ Church in Indianapolis. I talked by telephone with Haywood's daughter, Mrs. Rollie Ellis, in 1979. When she was a small girl, Mrs. Ellis attended a few services in the Woodworth-Etter Tabernacle in Indianapolis and remembers seeing crutches, canes, and wheelchairs that were on display as testimonies of physical healings.

38. *Word and Witness*, Dec. 20, 1912. Bosworth named several ministers in attendance, including well-known Pentecostals George and Carrie Judd Montgomery, R. J. Scott, F. J. Ewart, Harry Van Loon, Andrew Urshan, and S. H. Frodsham (see Chapter 8).

39. *The Pentecostal Herald*, June 1920. George C. Brinkman, a printer by trade, edited this paper. He was involved in the formation of what is now the Pentecostal Church of God, Joplin, Missouri (*The Promise Fulfilled*, p. 146). In the spring 1917 issue of the Herald, Brinkman offered a free copy of Woodworth's *Signs and Wonders* to anyone who sent in 10 subscriptions to the *Herald*.

40. Yoakum, while practicing medicine in Denver in 1894, was struck by a buggy operated by a drunken driver. He was seriously injured but later miraculously recovered after 32 doctors pronounced his case as hopeless. His healing testimony was given at the Southern California Christian Alliance in 1897, and excerpts were published in *He Is Just the Same Today*, by P. D. Smith, pp. 119-121 (Gospel Publishing House, 1931).

41. *Word and Witness*, Dec. 20, 1913. E. N. Bell edited this paper, one of the forerunners of the *Pentecostal Evangel*. The *Christian Evangel*, edited by J. Roswell Flower, was the other. Bell published the famous "call" to Hot Springs, Arkansas, which resulted in the founding of the Assemblies of God (published in this same Dec. 20, 1913, issue). Bell was elected first chairman of the Assemblies of God; Flower was named secretary; and Pinson was named as a member of the first executive presbytery. Another member of the first executive presbytery was Cyrus B. Fockler, who had been converted as a result of his mother's healing in one of Mrs. Woodworth's meetings. Fockler

was arrested along with Woodworth in the Framingham, Massachusetts, meeting in August 1913 (see Chapter 11).

42. *The Weekly Evangel*, Dec. 16, 1916.

43. Aimee Semple McPherson is considered to be the first woman to deliver a sermon on radio (April 1922). Mrs.Woodworth-Etter lived another two years, but whether she ever preached on radio is unknown. Mrs. McPherson's own book, *This Is That*, is similar in style to Woodworth's journal-type books. Without a doubt Woodworth was a model for Aimee in the early years of the latter's evangelistic efforts. (See Chapter 13 for more on McPherson and Woodworth.

CHAPTER 11

Facing Down Hell Raisers
and the Law

"The revival meeting conducted at Mount Wait this afternoon
by Mrs. M. B. Woodworth-Etter was interrupted when
Chief of Police William M. Holbrook arose from the audience
in the middle of the session, and, advancing to the pulpit,
arrested Mrs. Woodworth-Etter." — *Boston Herald*[1]

To say Maria B. Woodworth-Etter was controversial is
putting it mildly. She popularized Pentecostal
Charismatic theology and practice, and even though
thousands of church members and unbelievers alike were
attracted to and supported her meetings, she experienced
opposition as soon as she drove the first tent stake or
announced her meetings. To top it off, she was a woman
preacher and—of all things—she usurped authority over men.

As far as can be determined, Woodworth was never
physically abused, as were many early Pentecostals and other
non-conformists such as William Booth and his Salvation
Army. But she was often threatened, and as an evangelist,
received perhaps as much criticism from the press, mobs,
and ministers or anybody else up to the time of the reported
1926 kidnapping of another famous evangelist, Aimee Semple
McPherson.[2]

During Woodworth's controversial Oakland campaign of
1889-90,[3] a San Francisco *Examiner* reporter interviewed her

about nervous reaction in the trances. Woodworth answered that she had "good nerves and good courage," or she would have left Oakland shortly after the first meeting opened, simply because her life had been threatened many times.[4]

Woodworth then told the reporter about a threatening letter she received from the White Caps, a lawless vigilante group similar to the Ku Klux Klan: "At the head [of the letter] was drawn a heart with a dagger sticking into it and the blood dripping down. Then Woodworth said that I must leave the city within 48 hours or die. It was signed 'White Caps.'"

It would take more than that to scare her out of town. "Bless the Lord, I'm here yet," she said. "If God hadn't been with me, I'd been out of the city long ago."[5]

Because Woodworth was obviously well received by a great number of people who appreciated her ministry, why did certain elements of society oppose her? It might sound over simplified, but there are three rather apparent reasons.

She claimed to follow the pattern of the Early Church in her preaching, and as a result she received opposition and persecution not unlike that which the Apostles received. She called people to repentance, prayed for the sick, and sent converts reeling into trances. Other Pentecostals and Holiness pioneers came under the same type of strong condemnation, which continues to this day in certain parts of the world.

A second reason is the company she kept. Although a few professional, educated, and wealthy people attended Woodworth's meetings, she primarily attracted the poor, the uneducated, and socially deprived. In this respect, she set a pattern for later Pentecostals to follow.

She could not embrace everyone everywhere without ostracizing others, she learned. Take her relationship with the black community, for example. In the North and West she frequently invited black singers and preachers to take part in the services—with little opposition. She threw open the tent flaps for all colors and nationalities. Then she discovered an entirely different attitude and a new catalog of rules when, in 1888, she moved her entourage and canvas cathedral across the Ohio River and into Louisville.[6]

The white people assured her that they wanted the meetings in their city, but told her that if she permitted blacks to come under the same tent, they would stay home. Stunned, Woodworth tried a compromise by permitting the blacks to sit in one corner of the tent by themselves. But the whites were still unhappy. The wealthy citizens, ministers, and professing Christians told Woodworth that all evangelists who had been in the city drove the blacks away before they could accomplish anything in Louisville.

That was not Woodworth's style. "I told them God made the whole human family of one blood. Christ had died for all. Christ said, 'Go preach my Gospel to all nations, to every creature.'"

Tragically, millions of blacks would live and die before their descendants would see Martin Luther King and the Civil Rights Movement finally make an impact on the Jim Crow laws Woodworth was trying to circumvent or destroy as early as 1888. "Can we obey God and drive the hungry souls away?" she asked rhetorically. "I thank God we had no desire to drive them away, but felt glad to have the privilege of leading them to Christ."[7]

Despite the opposition in Louisville, Woodworth said God blessed the efforts, and it wasn't long before blacks and whites were seeking for spiritual help together at the crude altar. Not all of her attempts at integration worked as smoothly as this Louisville meeting, and she suffered because of her attempt to reach all classes of people and treat them as equals under her big top.

The third reason Woodworth was opposed simply could not be defended, even by many of her faithful. Despite her sincerity, and that of her followers, she often took dogmatic positions and taught unorthodox scriptural interpretations. Certainly fair-minded people could not support the measures her antagonists took in their opposition, but they were justified in raising a red flag whenever they saw questionable biblical interpretations, fanaticism, false prophecies, and other vagaries that surfaced from time to time. These were the unfortunate incidents that accompanied Woodworth's otherwise highly successful evangelistic meetings.

It would take an entire book to report and analyze the opposition Woodworth received throughout her long preaching career. Therefore, it is necessary in this chapter and the next to limit coverage to only three cases where Woodworth and members of her evangelistic party were arrested: Framingham, Massachusetts (1913), Topeka, Kansas (1915), and Fremont, Nebraska (1920). Only the Massachusetts case, however, would go to trial. In a fourth case, in 1917, Woodworth was arrested in San Jose, California, for disturbing the peace, but these charges were dropped within a few days.

Obtaining Money Under False Pretenses:
The Famous Trial at Framingham

Montwait (now spelled Mount Wayte) is a peaceful residential area of Framingham, a city west of Boston. But it hasn't always been that way. Back in the 1690s, Indians attacked the Thomas Eames family, massacring some and taking others captive. This killing field saw abolitionists in pre-Civil War days gather for their emotion-filled rallies. Later in the 19th century, it became a park, and the New England Chautauquas used it for their famous gatherings, which attracted thousands from miles around.[8]

Staid New Englanders could handle the Chautauqua excitement early in this century, but when Maria B. Woodworth-Etter opened a meeting in their hallowed pavilion at Montwait in August 1913, you would have thought foreigners were trying to overthrow the Middlesex County government. Before the meetings ended in early September, Woodworth had undergone one of the most difficult experiences of her lifetime.

If anybody ever had to hold the fort on the hill at Montwait, it was Woodworth and her followers that hot summer in 1913.

Hundreds of hoodlums tried several times to interrupt the meetings, forcing the police to step in and maintain order. Lawless people of this type were hardly unique to New England, for Woodworth had faced them from the very beginning of her ministry in Ohio. A new experience, however, for Woodworth in Framingham was her arrest and trial in the district court. Here in Framingham, Woodworth—along with two other preachers, Cyrus B. Fockler and Earl W. Clark— was arrested and charged with obtaining money under false pretenses. The prosecution accused the three of misleading the people by promising physical healings that did not happen and then receiving offerings for the alleged deceptions.

The four-day trial—which resulted in charges being dismissed—was unique in early Pentecostal history. During and after the trial, Pentecostals received national publicity as some 35 people testified for the defense that they had received physical and spiritual help through prayer. In addition to the daily coverage in the *Framingham News*, Boston papers sent reporters to the trial and published front page stories and photographs relating to the proceedings.

Woodworth was in Framingham at the invitation of Samuel G. Otis,[9] superintendent of the Christian Workers

Union. This nondenominational group was involved in a variety of para-church ministries, not the least of which was its printing and publishing work. Early Pentecostals were well acquainted with its *Word and Work* magazine, which reported various Pentecostal revival meetings.[10] Evangelist Aimee Semple McPherson became friends with this group in her early years of ministry, and they printed the first issue of her *Bridal Call* magazine which she started in 1917.[11]

In addition to S. G. Otis, several other ministers assisted Woodworth in the Framingham meeting, including Andrew L. Fraser, a former missionary to China and later an executive presbyter of the Assemblies of God; Earl W. Clark, who later married Woodworth's granddaughter; Cyrus B. Fockler, whose mother had been healed in a meeting Woodworth conducted in the 1890s, and who the next year was elected as one of the first executive presbyters at the organizational meeting of the Assemblies of God; Elizabeth Sisson, a well known Pentecostal who had been associated with Woodworth's meetings in Oakland during the tidal wave scare of 1890; and E. W. Kenyon, whose popular "faith" books are used in Charismatic circles today—more than a half century after his death.

During 1912 and 1913, prior to the meeting at Montwait, Woodworth had gained wide publicity and acceptance among Pentecostals in big meetings she conducted at Dallas, San Antonio, Oakland, San Jose, Los Angeles, Long Hill (Connecticut), and in Chicago's Stone Church. She had already established her ministry in the East with the Long Hill meeting in June. Then, after the Chicago meeting, she returned to the East to be with the Christian Workers.[12]

The New England states were slow in hearing and accepting the Pentecostal message at the turn of the 20th century, but the editor of the Framingham *Daily Tribune* offered free news space to publicize the Montwait meeting. He published Andrew L. Fraser's article titled, "Has the Day of Miracles Passed?" in their August 7, 1913, edition, explaining that they were doing so in the "same fairness which is accorded to any religious sect."

Fraser seized the opportunity and made the best of it with a glowing and uncritical report of Woodworth's reputation and track record in the healing movement. Much of his article dealt with the remarkable revival Woodworth conducted in Dallas the previous year.

"Signs and wonders appeared in the heavens. The Shekinah glory covered the Tabernacle," Fraser's uncensored copy claimed. Then Fraser really got caught up in the excitement of his assignment when he thought about the miraculous in Dallas: "Almost every disease known to medical science was represented in the thousands who came seeking healing: tuberculosis, neurasthenia, cancer, goiter, rheumatism, appendicitis, deafness, lameness, Brights' [sic] disease, etc., etc. The lame were made to walk and leap; the deaf were caused to hear and the dumb to speak . . . praise God, nothing is too hard for the Lord."[13]

New Englanders couldn't believe their eyes, that this story appeared in one of their local newspapers. Ministers of the historic old churches must have viewed the invasion as a threat to their survival.

After Fraser emphasized that the experiences in Dallas—continuing right there in Montwait—were simply the "greater things" Jesus promised, he threw open the invitation for everyone to attend the meetings. "Let every needy body come! Let the unsaved come! Let every Christian heart come that is still unsatisfied and reaching out for a closer fellowship with God and deeper experience of his mighty power! Come and see and experience for yourselves that ye be no longer 'faithless but believing!'"[14]

The people did come, not only from the surrounding area, but also from many parts of the country, representing nearly 30 states. A crowd Fraser didn't have in mind in his newspaper invitation came, too. They were the hoodlums. And it didn't take long for them to cause trouble.

The next report published in the newspaper came about a week after Fraser's article appeared: "Police Check Hoodlumism. Pentacostal [sic] Meeting at Montwait Interrupted Many Times Last Evening."[15] Only the arrival of police Chief W. W. Holbrook and other officers stopped the mob from completely breaking up the meetings. During the time given for testimonies, the hoodlums in the back of the building shouted insults. One of the troublemakers brought a rotten egg and saved it for what he must have thought was the right moment.

While a man on the platform spoke in tongues, one of the hoodlums threw the over-ripe egg, which struck a post near the man who was speaking. The broken egg "spilled its contents over the clothing of the man who was laboring under the spell which had overcome him. The victim of the egg throwing was game however and never wavered from his peculiar exhortations."[16]

Another persecutor sneaked around to the platform with a bucket of water that he splashed on several of the workers.

The newspaper called for the authorities to deal with the hoodlums despite what they called the "peculiar traits and manifestations of the meetings." Woodworth's group was being persecuted unfairly, and the editor called for law and order to prevail. *Tribune* readers saw nothing more published about the meetings until Tuesday, August 19. And that story was the big one.

The bold headlines on page one screamed out the news of Woodworth's arrest the day before: "HEALERS APPEAR

IN COURT TODAY." The editor placed in a box bordered with stars the complaint against Woodworth, Fockler, and Clark:

"On the 15th day of August 1913 at Framingham in said county of Middlesex (Mrs. Woodworth), intending to cheat and defraud, falsely pretended to be able to, and to cure and heal persons afflicted with cancer, tuberculosis, deafness, blindness, and leprosy, and pursuant thereto, did pretend to treat various subjects therefore[sic] and through said false and fraudulent acts and representations, did obtain from divers persons, then and there assembled whose names are to complainant unknown, several sums of money amounting to $100."[17]

The Boston *Herald* also gave the arrest front page coverage—right next to a news story about the famous movie actress, Lillian Russell—"WOMAN 'HEALER' IS ARRESTED AT REVIVAL SERVICE."[18] However, the details of the arrest in the two papers disagreed on the details. Woodworth was resting in her room when Chief W. W. Holbrook and some of his officers knocked on the door and announced their mission, according to the *Tribune*. But the Herald reported that Chief Holbrook interrupted Woodworth's afternoon sermon and placed her under arrest.

Regardless, the police made the arrest and took the shocked Woodworth to the Framingham court where she posted $300 bail. Fockler and Clark were out of town on Monday, but Holbrook's men placed them under arrest when they returned Tuesday morning. Ironically, the Pentecostals and local newspaper had been calling for the police to act against the hoodlums, but now—shockingly—the men in blue arrested the leaders of the revival.

With the complaints served on Woodworth, Fockler, and Clark, it appears then the police overstepped their authority by strong-arming the Pentecostals and denying them their freedom to worship as they saw fit. Storming a Monday afternoon service in progress at the pavilion, the police found several people lying about the straw. They rudely awakened the worshipers from their trances and ordered them to move.[19]

On Tuesday, the three defendants appeared in court to answer the charges, but they were not alone. At least 20 followers were there ready to testify in their behalf if they were needed. They were not needed at this hearing except to give moral support. Judge W. A. Kingsbury urged Woodworth to obtain legal counsel, but Woodworth answered that the Lord would provide for her in the predicament. Attorney Maxham E. Nash, however, was later secured to represent the three in court.

And striking changes in news coverage came during Woodworth's stay in Montwait. Before the arrest only the local newspaper carried news of the meetings. After the arrest the Boston *Herald* and Boston *Globe* gave front page coverage during the trial.

Despite the hoodlum element and the arrests, the meetings at Montwait continued to grow in interest. In the evening service after Woodworth and the other two ministers were released on bail, Woodworth walked into the pavilion to the shouts and praises of the crowd. "Praise God!" some shouted. Others joined in with, "Alleluia! Sister Woodworth has arrived."[20] The service continued in the same high energy fashion as it had started. Several people testified of being healed. Others wanted to just praise the Lord and were given opportunity to do so. The Boston reporters could hardly believe this was happening in their staid commonwealth.

Woodworth had her own ideas about who was really behind the arrests. She told the crowd, "I'm not in the least disturbed by my arrest and I've plenty of faith in the Lord straightening out all this trouble. The devil gets in a few pieces of work every now and then. I suppose that he is working now through Chief Holbrook for my annoyance." Role modeling a determination and faith in God for these and coming generations, she added, "For 35 years I've been an enemy of the devil and he's always trying to get me. But the Lord is always stronger, and I'm not afraid."[21]

Gertrude Stevenson, the *Herald* reporter, revealed to her readers that although Woodworth was claiming people were healed in her meetings, her own husband was an invalid who remained in a bedroom at the Otis house. Woodworth argued that healing is for people who have faith, obviously saying that Samuel Etter would continue being a cripple until he could accept his healing by faith.[22] She faced the same questioning concerning Samuel Etter's health and faith while conducting a meeting in Atlanta in 1915.

Unfortunately, say her critics, Mrs. Woodworth's simplistic "name it and claim it" theology had no room for God's sovereignty in Samuel's case nor in the thousands of other cases she faced. Had her faith-equals-healing formula worked for herself, she would never have died at 80 in 1924 and would now be more than 150 years old. Likewise, critics view 21st century faith extremists as burdening themselves and others as Woodworth burdened Samuel Etter.

If the arrest and the hoodlum element were not enough, Woodworth and her workers were threatened with a second legal matter shortly before the trial began. A Joseph Klein told the *Herald* he would file a damage suit against Woodworth, because he claimed she and Earl Clark pushed him from the platform. Cyrus Fockler explained to a reporter that Klein wanted to give a testimony and approached the platform. Woodworth then changed the order of the service, and she and Clark ushered Klein off the platform. Klein later agreed to drop the charges, much to the relief of the beleaguered Pentecostals.[23]

The trial on the charges of obtaining money under false pretenses was scheduled to begin Thursday, August 21, but because the prosecution was unprepared to present their evidence, Judge Kingsbury granted a continuance. So the first day in court was short, and Woodworth returned to the campgrounds, arriving in time for the morning service and a nerve-tingling entrance and ovation. The timing could not have been better, as one of Woodworth's old friends from the 1890 Oakland battleground, Elizabeth Sisson, had been speaking on the trial of faith, which she reminded her hearers is a refining process that brings forth pure gold.[24]

Seemingly the biggest problem facing authorities the day the case actually began in court was controlling the crowd trying to get into the courtroom. The human mass, made up about equally of men and women, made one desperate attempt to force itself inside. A reporter on the scene described the first day that looked more like a carnival than a courtroom: "Women were seized by the officers within and literally pulled out of the entangled crowd into the court room to save them from being crushed to death. Never was a scene like that of this morning witnessed at a session in the local court. Once the room was filled, the doors were again locked effectively barring any overcrowding within the court."[25]

When the crowd settled down, Judge Kingsbury warned them that they could in no way show any sign of approval or disapproval at anything said or done during the proceedings. Obeying that order must have been extremely difficult for some of the believers. They were no doubt tempted to shout now and then during the trial, especially when a defense witness gave a testimony of healing. But the crowd evidently restrained themselves until they got outside or back within the friendly confines of the Montwait pavilion.

Then the courtroom drama began to unfold. David C. Ahearn led the charge for the prosecution while Maxham E.

Nash had the responsibility to defend Woodworth, Fockler, and Clark.

Ahearn's opening plan was most difficult—and would be even today, nearly a century later. He tried to distinguish between faith healing and hypnosis. It was his contention Woodworth was using hypnosis, and the healings had nothing to do with the prayer for the sick, which Jesus commissioned his followers to practice. The witnesses Ahearn called in the opening session of the trial included two doctors and two ministers. In their opinions the healing services at Montwait used hypnotism and that no lasting healing would result, except for those of neurotic or hysterical natures.[26]

Pentecostals and Charismatics have been forced to defend their healing services against the hypnosis charge since the turn of the 20th century. The charge in this Framingham court was nothing new—even though the movement was only about a dozen years old—but it could have been the first case that actually went to trial. And if anything makes Pentecostals and Charismatics defensive, it is when critics charge them with employing emotional tricks and hypnotizing their followers with trances and conditioning them to "fall in the Spirit." The case here in Montwait would bring the battle out in the open.

Dr. Leon W. Jessaman, the medical examiner, and the first witness for the prosecution, testified he believed in the value of praying for the sick. However, in his opinion, the procedure Woodworth and the others used in dealing with the sick was hypnotic or suggestive. He had attended some of the services at Montwait and described to the court how the ministers conducted the healing part of the service. The sick were invited to sit on chairs on the platform, he told the judge. Next the preachers would talk with them, passing their hands over their heads, and then laying their hands on the affliction. "Then the operator would hit the subject's knees," Jessaman stated, "as if a signal to move them, whereupon a movement of the feet and limbs took place."[27]

Later in the trial, a witness for the defense who claimed to have been healed of an ailment of 17 years, Mina L. M. Peck, the wife of a Baptist minister of Petersburg, New York, told the court the Lord revealed to her that the tapping of the feet and the clapping of hands was "the unloosening of the mortal clothes of the body in its spiritual release from suffering."[28] When Cyrus Fockler came to the stand, he didn't offer to explain the tapping of feet and clapping of the hands, but did say the team encouraged it during the time of prayer for the one in need. "While this is going on," he added, "there is generally music going on at the same time."[29] In today's terminology, the physical responses might be called "releasing one's faith," a rallying theme Oral Roberts popularized.

Jessaman said the next step in the process was for the patient to get up, if he was able, and walk off. If the patient was overcome and went into a trance, he was carried away and laid on the floor of the platform. During this time, the doctor testified, the people on the platform clapped continuously and stamped their feet, creating much excitement.

Two other doctors, R. J. Boynton and L. M. Palmer, gave testimonies in support of Jessaman's. The three agreed that the entire process was nothing but hypnotism. Prosecutor Ahearn asked each doctor if hypnotism could cure someone with, say, cancer. Each answered that it could not. When he asked Dr. Palmer if hypnotism could assist in healing at all, Palmer answered, "In cases called functional, it might assist and improve, but where treatment is carried on to a state of rigor, it is not even beneficial, but injurious." He added, "Carried to the extent which I saw it at Montwait, I should say it is dangerous."[30]

A minister, T. J. Gambill, told the court he himself prayed for the sick, but did not employ methods—which he too labeled hypnotic—as Woodworth and others used at Montwait. A layman who had attended most of the meetings, L. S. Roberts, testified that he thought many of those on the platform were hypnotized.[31]

Branding Mrs. Woodworth-Etter a hypnotist was nothing new. From the beginning of her healing ministry in the early 1880s, she frequently heard this charge. And when she later took the stand in Framingham, she denied any knowledge of hypnotism. Before Woodworth could speak in her own behalf, however, her attorney called others in an attempt to prove to the judge that the praying for the sick at Montwait was the same as what the Apostles practiced in the first century.

Eva L. Hearns' 17-year-old daughter had been afflicted with epilepsy and would suffer sometimes as many as 30 attacks in 24 hours. She told the court that leaders at the meetings prayed for her daughter, and she was gradually getting better.[32]

A medical doctor of Cleveland, Ohio, Hanna B. Mulford, who had been a medical missionary in India where she came in contact with Pentecostals, attended the Montwait meetings to investigate the reported cures. The leaders prayed for her on the platform and she went home very much relieved. She told the court she had previously studied hypnotism, and did not believe the people in Woodworth's services were hypnotized.[33]

"If this is hypnotism," a New York funeral home director told the court, "I would like to be hypnotized all my life. I would be a coward not to stand up and say what God has done in my case."[34] Robert G. Lake, a Methodist and a director of the First National Bank, New York City—because of mental stress—decided he and his wife should take a vacation. While on vacation, they saw the Montwait meetings advertised and came out of curiosity. He told the court he had been healed of his mental condition, and his wife had been healed of varicose veins.[35]

Probably the most remarkable testimony of healing given during the trial came from Jessie Van Husen, Knoxville, Pennsylvania. Miss Van Husen had suffered back and stomach pains as a result of a railroad accident. After submitting to three operations, she was a helpless cripple and suffered untold agony. She could get along on level ground, but could not step up or down. Woodworth's book—probably *Acts of the Holy Ghost*—came into her hands, which gave her new hope. She determined she would attend the Montwait meetings despite doctors' objections. Sympathetic friends in Pennsylvania raised money to send her to Montwait, and sent along a trained nurse, Florence Cargil.

In one of the Montwait meetings, Woodworth's helpers carried Miss Van Husen from her wheelchair to the platform and then something miraculous happened, which she described to the court: "God quickened my mortal flesh. For the first time in years my pains left me following my treatment on the platform; my spine and hip are now well, my heart and stomach troubles have left me, and God has given me a spiritual uplift."[36]

The *Herald* reporter added that Miss Van Husen walked to the witness stand without assistance and "to all appearances was in perfect health."[37]

Florence Cargil, the nurse who accompanied Miss Van Husen to Montwait, testified she was a believer, but had been prejudiced against Pentecostals. When she saw what happened to her patient, she yielded her life to the Lord and suddenly became a Pentecostal. "Although I always wanted God to manifest Himself through me in a very quiet way, after I yielded myself to Him," she confessed, "His power came upon me, and I lay under it for an hour." Continuing her testimony, which sounded more and more like it was coming from a midweek church testimony service rather than in a courtroom, she said, "The preciousness of that hour can never be fully explained. I do praise God for taking out all prejudice and making me willing to let Him have His way."[38]

Others paraded to the witness stand for the defense, testifying that they had received both physical and spiritual help during the meetings at Montwait—but without any hypnotic powers in evidence. They also testified that the leaders did not ask patients to pay money for the healings—offerings were taken to support the work, but no pressure was applied.

Almost lost in the Pentecostal parade was E. W. Kenyon, a Bible teacher who founded Bethel Bible Institute at Spencer, Massachusetts. He told the court the leaders depended on God for the healings at Montwait—not on hypnotism.[39] Today Kenyon is remembered as a father of the "Faith" or "Word" teaching common among Charismatics.

Another person who benefited from the Montwait meetings and who could have strengthened the case for the defense had he known about the trial, was a former drunken gambler, E. H. Garlock of Woodbury, Connecticut. Garlock's deliverance not only turned his life around, but also set a standard for his 12 children to follow.[40]

Remember Elizabeth Sisson? Because of her peculiar shaking motion, the California press had dubbed her the "Shaking Matron" during the Oakland tidal wave scare 23 years before this Framingham trial. She became Woodworth's close friend and coworker, but had only seen Woodworth once in the intervening years, and that was the previous June at Long Hill, Connecticut. Here in the Montwait meetings, Woodworth placed her in charge of the morning services, and she was called as a defense witness on the last day of the trial, Friday, August 29.

One of the questions Miss Sisson answered helped focus on who was taking credit for the healings at Montwait. There was no question where she stood on this issue: "I have never heard Mrs.Woodworth or others lay claim to the credit of healing at Montwait. If I had I should have quit the place for it would have been outrageous."[41]

Then it came time for one of the defendants, Cyrus B. Fockler, to take the stand.[42] Fockler, who previously had been associated with John Alexander Dowie, the healing practioner who founded the Christian community at Zion, Illinois, answered questions concerning the healing procedures at Montwait. One of the requirements, he explained, was that the patient become a believer if he had never received Christ by faith. He also stated that he had never studied hypnotism and that he was living on the "faith line" for a salary and had received about $15 a week over and above expenses during the three weeks he had been in Framingham.[43]

When the prosecuting attorney asked Fockler if his power had increased in recent years, Fockler retorted, "I have no power."[44] The questioning also revealed that Fockler believed cancer was caused by evil spirits taking control of the body— still a belief among a certain segment of Christians. In answering a question about hypnotism, Fockler said, "We have stated that if there were any hypnotists present, and if they would come forward in the name of God we would put them out of business."[45]

Following Fockler's turn on the witness stand, the courtroom crowd waited with bated breath. The court had called Maria B. Woodworth-Etter to the front.

Both of the Boston papers covering the trial sensationalized Woodworth's testimony on their front pages.

The *Daily Globe* greeted their readers with a photograph of the defendants and a three-column headline: "SHE FELL WHEN POWER CAME, MRS. WOODWORTH SAYS IN COURT. Montwait Leader Tells Her Story Without Excitement in Courtroom at South Framingham."[46]

Not to be outdone, the *Herald*'s headlines screamed, "SAVED THROUGH FIRE, 'HEALING PRIESTESS' SAYS. Thrills Curious Throng at Trial With Story of Fiery Whirlwind Bringing Salvation."[47]

Woodworth traced her early life in Ohio, including her conversion, call to preach, visions, and her start in the ministry. And as with the other witnesses, attorneys questioned her about using hypnotism in her meetings. The prosecutor was no doubt unprepared for her answer. Hundreds of people had been struck down by the power in her large meetings, she answered. She wanted the court to understand that she had had never studied hypnotism. "Noted hypnotists from Europe have come to my meetings to investigate this wonderful power which has come over me hundreds of times," she said. "Many have said this power is so different from hypnotic power. Some of them have even said, 'If there is a God, this is God.'"[48]

During the course of her testimony, Woodworth gave an interesting, yet rather puzzling answer regarding the complaint that the services were noisy. When the prosecutor asked if the meetings at Montwait differed from other meetings she conducted, she answered, "Since I have been with the Pentecostal people, there has been more of a noisy exhibition in praising the Lord than when I was alone. I tell them to lift up Holy hands; I say, 'Do you know you are a child of God?' I ask, 'Do you know you have been healed of one or more diseases by the Lord Jesus Christ?' I have always done that."

In Chicago, she said, a minister from Canada requested everyone to clap their hands together and make a joyful noise, which she allowed because she felt it was based on scriptural precedents. "The only thing we could do the night the mob came was to stand up, clap our hands, and shout to the Lord."[49]

The answer regarding the noise is puzzling in that previous meetings in Oakland were reported as being "deafening." Another report compared the 1889-90 Oakland meetings to a noisy ward in an insane asylum. If the Montwait meetings were noisier than "deafening," it isn't any wonder the neighbors complained.

On the fourth day of the trial, after the prosecutor and the defense had run out of questions to fire at Woodworth and the other witnesses, the two attorneys presented their closing arguments.

Woodworth's attorney, Maxham E. Nash, reviewed the testimony of the defense and then laid particular stress on the fact the United States was founded on religious liberty: "We come into this hall of Justice, said he . . . recognizing the right of the people to worship God as they see fit. If you draw the line here, you must draw the line against every shrine you have ever heard of where people go seeking spiritual and physical healing."[50]

Then Nash called attention to the tradition of New England's religious liberty, concluding his argument with a dramatic recital of Felicia Hemans' "Landing of the Pilgrims," the last two verses of which answer the poet's questions of why the pilgrims came.[51]

What sought they thus afar?
Bright jewels of the mine?
The wealth of seas, the spoils of war?
They sought a faith's pure shrine!

Ay! Call it holy ground,
The soil where first they trod;
They have left unstained what there they found…
Freedom to worship God!

Prosecutor Ahearn sounded a note of mercy for the defendants and assured the judge that the government was not desirous to punish the defendants nearly as much as it wished a higher court to set its disapproval on the healing and other practices that were common at the Montwait meeting. Ahearn asked Judge Kingsbury to turn the case over to the grand jury; if they returned an indictment, a jury of 12 could decide the fate of the defendants.[52]

The four days of testimony and closing arguments ended on Friday, August 29, 1913.

But nobody would know for sure how the decision would go that day. Judge W. A. Kingsbury told the participants he needed time to review the testimony and would reserve his decision until after the Labor Day weekend.

It is interesting to speculate what went through the minds of the defendants and their supporters as they conducted services over the weekend and wondered and worried about the judge's decision.

No doubt there were much praying and fasting. No doubt it was a long and stress-filled weekend. But it passed. And then came Monday. And it passed. Finally Tuesday, the day the court would rule in this landmark case, rolled around. As expected, the courtroom was filled to capacity and many people waited outside to hear the verdict.

All eyes were turned on Judge W. A. Kingsbury, the man who held the power to convict or set free. Every ear strained to catch his words. Reporters had pencils poised and ready to write.

Then the judge ended the suspense. He was not satisfied that the evidence warranted a guilty verdict and said he was dismissing the case.[53] After defending the police department for inability to quell the violence generated by the mobs, Judge Kingsbury had words of advice to the defendants and a plea for tolerance to those who did not share his decision.

"It is to be remembered that all these defendants are residents of states remote from us, and that they have been in this Commonwealth but a few days, unacquainted with our laws and with the customs of our people. There are sections of the country, perhaps, where these defendants have preached where the laying out in straw on or near a public platform, of a dozen or more persons of both sexes and all ages, in an unconscious state might pass as one of the usual and proper incidents of a meeting intended for the worship of God. But it is repugnant to the general public sentiment of this Commonwealth and these defendants will be wise if they recognize the fact as long as they stay with us."[54]

And so the case involving Maria B. Woodworth-Etter, Cyrus B. Fockler, and Earl Clark came to an end. Naturally, the three were jubilant that their side had won. Woodworth told the *Tribune* that it was "a battle of religion, science arrayed against religion, and we have won the victory through Jesus." She added, "We are so glad to put upon record in this court, so many witnesses who testified to their personal experiences of being healed through the Lord.[55]

Sympathetic Bostonians invited Woodworth to move her campaign into the city where one of the largest theaters would be available.[56] Woodworth no doubt appreciated the offer, but declined. The next day she, her invalid husband, Earl Clark, and Cyrus Fockler took the train to Arkansas by way of Indianapolis, where they would stop for a much needed rest.

One has to wonder what response Woodworth would have received had she accepted the offer to conduct services in Boston. How would the Boston police have handled her "holy roller" style? But that is all we can do—just wonder, because we have no record that she ever returned to this part of the country.[57]

While Woodworth and her workers rejoiced over what they viewed as an overwhelming victory for the Lord in Massachusetts, the critics believed the authorities and justice stopped the Pentecostal invasion in its tracks and drove it back to Arkansas. While the newspapers jostled for sensational stories, the Pentecostal message and divine healing received widespread publicity.

In a front page story of the *Word and Witness*, published in Malvern, Arkansas, Editor E. N. Bell summed up the events of the trial and quoted many of the testimonies given, adding: "The silly claims of unbelievers that people were not healed were disproved by scores of living witnesses under oath and forever set to rest."[58]

The Bridegroom Messenger, another Pentecostal paper, also took note of the Montwait trial and victory: "Satan, the enemy of Jesus Christ, and His power, surely over reached himself when he caused the chief of police of South Framingham, Mass., to issue warrants for the arrest of Mrs. M. B. Woodworth-Etter and her co-laborers, Cyrus B. Fockler and Earl W. Clark for obtaining money under false pretense."[59]

Montwait was the first place Woodworth was arrested. But it would not be the last time the law would step in to put a damper on her enthusiastic Pentecostal meetings. The next interference would come in one of the historic Pentecostal cities, Topeka, Kansas. Then, five years later, Woodworth would face perhaps her most critical charges from a prosecuting attorney in Fremont, Nebraska.

ENDNOTES

1. Boston *Herald*, Aug. 19, 1913.

2. Aimee Semple McPherson claimed she was kidnapped and held against her will for more than a month in 1926. Her critics, including the district attorney, tried to prove it was a lie and that she was having an affair with an employee. The case was finally dropped.

3. See Chapter 5.

4. San Francisco *Examiner*, Jan. 9, 1890.

5. Ibid. In writing about persecution in California (*Acts of the Holy Ghost*, p. 377), Woodworth stated that her friends built a high board fence behind the platform for her protection. An illustration of the tent in the Jan. 9, 1890, *Examiner* shows the protective wall. There was also a barbed wire fence constructed around that part of the tent (Oakland *Tribune*, Jan.13, 1890).

6. See my chapter, "Maria B. Woodworth-Etter: Prophet of Equality." James R. Goff, Jr. and Grant Wacker, eds., *Portraits of a Generation, Early Pentecostal Leaders* (Fayetteville: The University of Arkansas Press, 2002), pp. 199-216.

7. *Marvels and Miracles*, pp. 57, 59. Woodworth used a black barber as a soloist at the 1885 Hartford City, Indiana, meetings. In 1888-89, she used a black woman soloist in the Springfield, Illinois, campaign. In 1904, the *Indianapolis Star* noted it was a black man, Jim Barby, who rescued Samuel Etter from under tons of canvas when a windstorm blew the tent to the ground (*Indianapolis Star*, Sept. 25, 1904). Barby, who was the night watchman at the tent, invited another black, Moses Foreford, who was healed of paralysis ("Paralyzed Negro Becomes Athlete,"*Indianapolis Star*, Sept. 28, 1904). C. E. Cheatham, a black singer, was named in the indictment at Fremont, Nebraska (see next chapter).

8. *The News*, Framingham Natick, May 30, 1970. This is a cynical account of the "Holy Rollers" who gathered to hear

Woodworth.

9. Samuel G. Otis was 70 years of age in 1913 and had been a publisher of Gospel literature for 34 years. He had accepted the Pentecostal message in 1906 and had met Mrs. Woodworth-Etter at Long Hill, Connecticut, in a meeting she conducted in June 1913. He was called to testify in this case (Framingham *Tribune*, Aug. 28, 1913).

10. Stanley H. Frodsham, long time editor of the *Pentecostal Evangel* and author of such well known books as *With Signs Following* and *Smith Wigglesworth: Apostle of Faith*, was associated with this group during 1928-29. Frodsham edited the monthly paper *Word and Work* (not to be confused with E. N. Bell's *Word and Witness*). Fred Corum, whose Springfield, Missouri, roots included growing up in a Pentecostal congregation, edited the *Word and Work* during the 1930s. When this Massachusetts lawyer was a boy in 1907, he witnessed his aunt Rachel Sizelove exploding onto the Springfield scene with the Pentecostal message from the Azusa Street Mission, Los Angeles. Corum's mother, Mrs. Sizelove's sister, received the Pentecostal experience and became the first pastor of the Springfield congregation which later became the historic Central Assembly of God. (My interview with Hazel Corum Bakewell, Springfield, Missouri, Sept. 26, 1980.)

11. McPherson, *The Story of My Life*, p. 95.

12. Otis ran an advertisement in his July *Word and Work* announcing the coming Montwait meetings. And the Aug. 20 issue of *Word and Witness*, which E. N. Bell published in Malvern, Arkansas, publicized the meeting. The latter announcement also stated the music publisher, R. E. Winsett, Chattanooga, Tennessee, would be the song leader. Two days after this *Word and Witness* issue was published, Woodworth, Fockler, and Clark were arrested.

13. Framingham *Daily Tribune*, Aug. 7, 1913.

14. Ibid.

15. Ibid., Aug. 13, 1913. Throughout the Montwait meetings, the *Tribune* misspelled Pentecostal, but it could have been the first time they used the term.

16. Ibid. In the Aug. 19 edition of the *Tribune* an estimate was given that the hoodlums numbered several hundred.

17. Ibid., Aug. 19, 1913.

18. *Herald*, Aug. 19, 1913.

19. *Tribune*, Aug. 19, District court Judge Kingsbury, who tried the case, commented on some criticism the police chief had received for his overzealous actions, but then defended him in what he termed difficult circumstances. These remarks came on the last day of the trial.

20. *Herald*, Aug. 20, 1913. This front page story is headlined, "Healer Calls Arrest 'Work of the Devil.'"

21. Ibid.

22. Healing for Samuel Etter would never come, for he died Aug. 16, 1914—almost a year later—at the age of 71.

23. *Herald*, Aug. 23, 1913.

24. *Tribune*, Aug. 21, 1913.

25. Ibid., Aug. 26, 1913.

26. Ibid.

27. Ibid.

28. Ibid., Aug. 27, 1913.

29. *Tribune*, Aug. 29, 1913.

30. Ibid.

31. Ibid.

32. Ibid., Aug. 27, 1913.

33. Boston *Globe*, Aug. 27, 1913.

34. *Herald* Aug. 28, 1913.

35. Ibid.

36. Ibid. The *Herald* also published a two column photograph of Miss Van Husen. The *Daily Tribune* and the Boston *Globe* also published her testimony in their Aug. 27 editions. The *Word and Work* published a fuller account of the testimony—which is reprinted in Woodworth's *Signs and Wonders*, pp. 319-21.

37. Ibid.

38. Ibid. The *Word and Witness*, Jan. 20, 1914, reprinted excerpts from a follow-up letter Jessie Van Husen wrote to Woodworth, saying that she "continues to rejoice in health."

39. *Globe*, Aug. 28, 1913. Kenyon later moved his Bible school to Providence, Rhode Island. Although Kenyon died in 1948, his books still remain popular among Charismatics.

40. My letter from Henry B. Garlock, Sept. 14, 1979. See Chapter 9 for more on this unusual testimony.

41. *Tribune*, Aug. 29, 1913.

42. Ibid. Fockler was 50 years of age at this time and lived on a farm near Warsaw, Indiana, with his wife and five children. The other defendant, Earl W. Clark, was never called to testify, which puzzled those who watched the trial. Fockler gained wide publicity because of the trial, and it probably didn't hurt his preaching career; a few months later delegates at the organizational meeting of the Assemblies of God elected him as an executive presbyter. He was the pastor of a Pentecostal church in Milwaukee for many years.

43. Ibid.

44. Ibid.

45. Ibid.

46. *Globe*, Aug. 29, 1913.

47. *Herald*, Aug. 30, 1913.

48. Ibid.

49. Testimony as quoted in *Signs and Wonders*, pp. 311-12. Court records in Framingham prior to 1940 were destroyed by authority of the state legislature.

50. *Tribune*, Aug. 29 , 1913.

51. Ibid. "Landing of the Pilgrims," by Felicia Hemans (1793-1835).

52. Ibid. By asking for a grand jury decision in his closing argument, perhaps Ahearn anticipated that Judge Kingsbury would dismiss the case against the defendants .

53. *Tribune*, Sept. 2, 1913.

54. Ibid. Throughout the trial Boston newspapers had given front page coverage, but they stuck the dismissal on page16 in the Sept. 2 issue of the *Globe*, and page 4 in the Sept. 3 *Herald*. A bad train wreck did occupy the front page of the papers, but still the case obviously lost its excitement when the dismissal came.

55. Ibid. That night in the closing service at Montwait, a no hard feelings prayer was offered for the district court, the prosecution and the defense, the Framingham police department, newspaper people, and others connected with the trial.

56. Ibid.

57. A year later Earl Clark returned to Massachusetts where he conducted services in a rented church building in Boston (*Christian Evangel*, July 25, 1914).

58. *Word and Witness*, Oct. 20, 1913. In another article on the same page, Daniel C. O. Opperman wrote concerning the meeting the three Montwait defendants were then conducting in Hot Springs, Arkansas: "God Stretching Out His Hand to Heal."

59. Quoted in *Signs and Wonders*, p. 323.

CHAPTER 12

Midwestern Cops Flex
Their Muscles

"People ask me many times why I do not stick up for my rights more than I do. I have only one answer to these questions, and that is this: 'Jesus Christ has not sent me out to fight the authorities, but to preach the everlasting Gospel of the kingdom.'"—Woodworth, *Marvels and Miracles*.[1]

A 1915 Topeka Shootout

Topeka had been on Woodworth's sawdust trail itinerary through the years since her first meeting there in 1889. So it was not surprising to see her accept the invitation Pastor C. E. Foster offered for a return meeting in August 1915.

As Woodworth returned to Topeka, her thoughts must have gone back to a meeting she conducted there in 1891, when a raging Midwestern storm one night ripped her tent to ribbons just as the people were gathering for a service.[2]

There would be no damaging storm in the 1915 meeting, but city officials would create a storm of opposition that caused Woodworth and her co-workers no end of anxiety. There were threats, arrests, persecution, and finally one night the city officials cut the power to the city park pavilion where they were meeting and ordered the congregation off city property.

Topeka, the capital city of Kansas, is best known in American church history as the birthplace of the modern Pentecostal movement. Here in 1901, in the ornate "Stone's Folly" mansion, Charles Fox Parham's small Bible college experienced a number of baptisms in the Spirit accompanied by speaking in tongues. And from Topeka, the revival movement spread throughout the Midwest, picking up new troops, and then invading South Texas.

But a sexual charge linking Parham and a young man in San Antonio in 1907 effectively put Parham on the outside of the movement's leadership. Because no court records seem to exist—only newspaper and denominational publications' stories—it appears that the case was dismissed after Parham served a few days in jail.[3] But when it comes to sexual sins, Pentecostals usually think in terms of zero tolerance. One strike, and you're out. And often, whether or not the charge is proven doesn't seem to matter.

Although Parham maintained his close following, he would never sway the crowds as he did before 1907. He supervised a few Apostolic Faith Churches and a Bible school in the Midwest. Other Pentecostals, however, a century later still whisper and try to identify his moral failure. It's almost as mysterious as Aimee Semple McPherson's kidnapping claim—except for the way they handled the charges. Aimee wanted hers front page for vindication, and traveled across the country with the same idea in mind. Parham's charge was only whispered behind his back, and then often without mentioning his name.

Parham's biographer, James R. Goff, Jr., summarized his life and death: "He was almost unknown among the developing second generation of the Pentecostal denominations. Yet to no one individual did the movement owe a greater debt."[4]

One person attending Woodworth's 1915 Topeka meeting gave it a touch of a Parham homecoming. In 1901 Agnes Ozman (later LaBerge) was the first to speak in tongues after Parham laid hands on her and prayed that she would receive the baptism in the Holy Spirit. In this 1915 meeting, Mrs. LaBerge, who then lived in Roosevelt, Oklahoma, testified that she was healed of consumption, an affliction of 22 years standing, after Woodworth prayed for her.[5]

Woodworth's services, according to her own reports and the *Daily Capital* reporter, were typical Pentecostal meetings. The reporter described a crowd gathered in Garfield Park participating in spirited singing, dancing, raising of hands, praising God audibly, some speaking in tongues, others "falling in the Spirit," and there was always prayer for the sick. And the crowds came—people from as many as 19 states and Canada were in attendance.[6]

Another player in the 1915 drama was 10-year-old Louis Romer, son of a hardware dealer. Not expected to live through his teen years with the disease chorea, more commonly called St. Vitus's Dance, Romer claimed he was healed in Topeka. And to prove it, friends and family had him around for the next 86 years.

To get Louis Romer's story, one must go back two years to 1913, when he was eight years old. His parents noticed their son was having trouble controlling his arms and hands. His condition grew steadily worse until doctors were asked to diagnose the strange case. The case, however, was not strange to the doctors—although they had no cure for it at the time. The devastating diagnosis and prognosis told the Romers that their son's St. Vitus's Dance would destroy his chances to see adulthood. Today Louis' disease is known as chorea, a serious nervous disease closely associated with rheumatic fever. Children who are afflicted with the disease often lose control of their movements, stumble, and fall easily.

Even though sedatives can combat the disease now, the patient can be afflicted for months.

The illness affected Louis' feet so that his toes drew under, preventing him from wearing shoes. Frequently he would lose control of his hands and fingers. His head, neck, and shoulders would jerk, and the crack could be heard 20 feet away. Louis' condition got so bad that he could no longer feed himself with table utensils. And because there was no effective treatment in those days, doctors had little hope that Louis would live beyond age 13.

When Mary Romer heard that Woodworth was conducting a meeting in Topeka, she took her son from their home in Allen, a small town some 25 miles southwest of the capital city, to Garfield Park where the meetings were attracting a large number of people.

When Louis was 80 and living in Lowell, Oregon, he told me of the Topeka meetings, recalling events as if they happened the day before. "Mrs. Woodworth came over to our quarters and talked to us," he said. "She asked me if I thought God would heal me, and I said I did." Then in the afternoon meeting, Woodworth prayed for Louis while he was standing by his mother who held his hand. "Sister Woodworth laid her hands on my head and I felt a cooling of my nerves as a tingling warmth went through my body. My hands straightened out and I felt so good, I cried." He added that all of this happened in less time than it takes to tell it.[7]

Mary Romer knew it was a miracle. She and Louis went shopping for a new pair of shoes.

But Louis also became the focus of the first major conflict with city officials when he violated a probate court rule forbidding children under 16 years of age from participating in the meetings.[8] The Romer boy, who was kneeling with his mother at the close of one of the services, was forcibly removed while praying to receive the baptism in the Holy Spirit.[9] Earlier that day, Judge Hugh McFarland sent word to Woodworth regarding his rule on the involvement of children in the Pentecostal meetings. Woodworth was not frightened—not even by a probate judge—and challenged the jurist: "God made us to conduct our meetings this way, and we shall keep right on—interfere if you wish."[10]

Judge MacFarland's interference in the meetings followed a visit he made to the pavilion where he saw a 10-year-old girl in what he described as a hysterical condition. MacFarland queried Topeka doctors who warned him that children under such nervous strains frequently lose their minds. That was enough for MacFarland.

Dispatching detective Tom Morgan and probation officer Edward Rooney to the service August 11, the judge ordered them to watch for violations of the order. The two officers soon had 10-year-old Louis Romer in their sights. Louis learned that praying for the baptism in the Holy Spirit wasn't so easy as it might seem, at least in Topeka. And the officers were unprepared for the storm of protest when they picked up Louis to remove him from the meeting. Worshipers crowded around, cheering, singing, clapping their hands and dancing. Louis' mother tried to hold him, but the officer's pull was too strong, and she released her hold when she felt herself going into the officer's arms.

The police took Louis and his mother to a detention home by order of Judge MacFarland who warned Mrs. Romer that they would be sent home if she brought Louis back to the meetings.[11] Mrs. Romer, whose husband was minding the hardware store back home, told a reporter, "Lewis [sic] asked me to take him to the altar so he could be baptized and we were waiting for the blessing when the officers took us away."[12]

To avoid further trouble, Mr. Romer went to the city and took his wife and son back to Allen. But it was not the same Louis who had gone to Garfield Park. Until his death in 2001 at the age of 95, Romer said he never experienced further trouble with the St. Vitus' Dance. He served in the U. S. Navy during World War II, became a rifle marksman, a lapidiarist, and an electrician—all requiring steady hands.

Louis Romer's humiliating removal from the city park pavilion was only the beginning of bans city officials ordered. The next day Mayor Jay E. House issued an ultimatum to Woodworth and her assistants that the meetings would be closed if "any further spectacles were staged."[13] House warned the leaders they would have to put a curb on the "frenzied dances and contortions" or be barred from conducting meetings in the city. The mayor reasoned that the meetings had elements of "immoral spectacles and were detrimental to the people concerned."[14] With House's ultimatum on the line, a Pentecostal woman responded: "[She] prayed fervently in an unintelligible jargon, ending in a request spoken in English, that he think before he took any action."[15]

Showing it makes a difference who is reporting the meetings—Mayor House or Evangelist Woodworth— Woodworth casts a different light on the meeting just with the headline of the report in her book, *Signs and Wonders*: "The Fire Falls At Topeka , Kansas. Enemy Gets Stirred. People Blessed. A Great Victory Won."[16]

The increasing pressure from city officials climaxed on a Saturday night, three days after Louis Romer knelt at the pavilion's altar. A front page headline in the *Capital* told the story: "Cops Drive Holy Rollers From Garfield Pavilion."[17] That night, city officials hardly permitted the meeting to get started when they swooped in and ordered the people to leave the pavilion. When leaders of the meeting, including Woodworth, refused to leave, officers turned out the lights—

leaving the worshipers in the dark. Then sponsoring pastor C. E. Foster told the police chief that the people would resist peacefully, and that if he wanted to, the chief could arrest the entire body of believers.

The chief took the challenge, placing Foster under arrest and calling in a second squad of officers for reinforcements. With Foster's arrest, Mrs. Woodworth—who was a veteran of persecution and pressure from city officials—advised the audience to react peacefully by leaving the pavilion and resume the meeting in a lot across the street that was outside the city limits.[18]

Woodworth and her assistants then went home, leaving the battle to the local people and the city officials. But Woodworth was almost certain she would be the next one arrested: "I went through a martyrdom the next two or three days, looking continually to be arrested. I carried every day a kimono and some things I would need in jail."[19]

After the faithful, now with a martyr's cause, carried benches across the street and set up in the vacant field, the service continued without Foster and Woodworth. Three visiting evangelists led the service and urged the people to bear the persecution meekly and patiently. But the local leaders believed their constitutional rights had been violated. Protesting to city officials was out of the question, so they marched to the state capitol and met with Governor Arthur Capper. The governor, who was reared in a devout Quaker home, said he could see no way he could help in their struggle; but he did suggest the group talk with the attorney general about possible violation of their freedom to worship.[20]

Woodworth looked at the opposition as from the devil, but saw a bright lining in the ominous cloud hanging over Garfield Park and the city. Having to give up the pavilion, they obtained a large tent, and the crowds increased—

underscoring Woodworth's past experiences from the Atlantic to the Pacific, that with increased negative publicity comes a boost in interest and attendance.

As a result of the opposition, Woodworth wrote for her next book, "Many of the best citizens and church members that had taken no part or interest, were very indignant at the way we had been treated and came out to see." How did the newcomers respond to the meetings? According to Woodworth, it was positive. They saw mighty signs and wonders, she said. "They were confounded and said, 'What meaneth this? Surely we have seen strange things.'"[21]

Two weeks after Judge MacFarland issued his order banning children from participating in the Pentecostal meetings, the services were going strong at the new location outside the city limits—with minor children taking part. One participant was a 13-year-old girl who "lay on the straw covered ground in front of the altar with her shaking hands extended in the air or quiet at her sides from exhaustion."[22]

The closing night of the meetings witnessed a fervent worship exercise by some of the more demonstrable worshipers who broke benches in their exuberance—which no doubt disturbed Woodworth and Foster more than the trouble from the city officials.[23] Foster announced that the meetings would move to a tent at Seward and Elliott streets and continue indefinitely. What about Woodworth's future in Topeka? She had seen enough of the city and made plans to move to Colorado Springs, where she hoped city officials would be more tolerant of Pentecostal worship expressions, and the Rocky Mountain folks less demonstrable.

Woodworth's ministry would continue for another nine years, and she would preach elsewhere in Kansas, but I have found no evidence that she ever returned to Topeka after this 1915 meeting—much to the disappointment of those who stood with her in the bitter struggle in the trenches at

Garfield Park. And they would remember August 1915 as a month of infamy, believing that a religious minority was denied freedom to worship according to the dictates of their heart. This denial is all the more hurtful when they were reminded that it was here in 1901, that Charles F. Parham put the city on the religious map with his Bethel Bible School in the old Stone's mansion—the small beginning that eventually became the Pentecostal Movement of which Woodworth was an integral part.

Practicing Medicine Without a License

The Cox-Harding presidential race captured the attention of the post-war nation in the fall of 1920. Baseball fans were treated to a seven-game World Series as the Cleveland Indians nipped the Brooklyn Dodgers; the 1919 series was also in the news as a probe revealed players were involved in a gambling scandal. After battling for a half century, Women's Suffrage saw the 19th Amendment squeak by ratification during 1920, enabling women to vote in national elections.

Maria B. Woodworth-Etter's attention that fall was not on the presidential race, the 19th Amendment, or the action on and off the baseball diamond. She was in Fremont, Nebraska, under a tent in a battle against the devil, sickness, sin, and the Dodge County prosecuting attorney.

Joseph C. Cook, the prosecuting attorney, probably heaped more public scorn on Woodworth and her co workers than anybody else in the 20th century. And when he could not have Woodworth's pulpit to challenge her claim that people were being healed in answer to prayer, Cook prepared a complaint of four counts of practicing medicine without a license against Woodworth and her helpers. A day before the meetings closed in Fremont, Cook had Woodworth and four others arrested.

The Fremont crusaders in 1920 were neither the first nor the last to have the law step into evangelistic environments and charge leaders with practicing healing without the benefit of a medical degree and license. It was said that John Alexander Dowie, the founder of Zion, Illinois, had been arrested a hundred times. Some 36 years after Woodworth's Fremont incident, a smiling Evangelist Jack Coe is pictured behind bars in the Dade County Jail, Miami. Dowie, Woodworth, Coe, and anyone else who practiced divine healing were broad-brushed as nothing less than religious racketeers.

A Fremont newspaper gave an interesting and surprising slant to the 1920 case. If Cook was antagonistic and hateful, the Fremont *Evening Tribune* was tolerant or even pro-Woodworth and her work. Their favorable news coverage and an editorial no doubt encouraged the 76-year-old evangelist as she labored in the hot, muggy Nebraska weather in a tent crowded with as many as 5,000 people.

In a front page story on September 22, the *Tribune* published a headline giving new hope to the suffering: "Cripples Walking After Prayers of the Divine Healer. Miraculous Cures Accomplished by Woman Who Claims No Reward. Blind See, Deaf Hear."[24] It was easy to see by the blaring headlines and opening paragraph that the writer was impressed with Woodworth and the results: "Two thousand Fremont citizens were stricken dumb with amazement last evening when the evangelist Mrs. Woodworth-Etter, the 'Divine Healer,' straightened the limbs of hopeless cripples, restored the hearing of the deaf and gave power of sight to the blind."

The newspaper continued its uncritical report of the meeting, eliminating the need for paid advertisements. "Skeptics and unbelievers are at a loss for an explanation— but the fact remains hard to deny. Seeing is believing, and the people of this city witnessed miracles performed by this gifted woman, that defy the work of medicine and science."[25]

Numerous cases of people who claimed they were healed and who had given testimonies in the meeting saw their story in the newspaper columns. Some children who had been victims of infantile paralysis were in the testimony lineup. "One little lad, who had to be carried to the platform, was soon able to walk without aid."[26]

The same newspaper published an editorial the next day, praising Woodworth's work in Fremont. Still positive in his views, the writer reasoned that the miracles should not be totally unexpected since the same power that was delivering people from evil habits and giving new life through spiritual conversions at the meetings could also heal the sick. In fact, the writer added, the cure of the soul is more important than the physical healings because that work of the Holy Spirit not only benefits for this life "but for all eternity to follow."[27]

Woodworth was beginning to wonder where this secular newspaper editor learned to preach with such authority and clarity.

Whoever was writing, Woodworth couldn't have agreed more. From the very beginning of her healing ministry in the 1880s, she emphasized the conversion of the soul as being more important than physical healings; but she also believed if both blessings were available, people ought to accept them.

One of the several healing reports Woodworth selected for her 1922 book *Marvels and Miracles* concerned a woman who had been deaf in one ear for 42 years: "The people who stood around, and saw the deaf spirit cast out by the command in Jesus' name, looked on in astonishment—saying in their hearts, 'We never saw it after this fashion.'"[28]

Unfortunately for Woodworth, county attorney J. C. Cook refused to accept the newspaper accounts and the testimonies he himself heard in the tent. And his vote counted more than newspaper writers and Pentecostal evangelists.

Cook wrote a blistering attack against Woodworth that the *Tribune* published on its front page two days after the favorable editorial hit the streets. If the claims Woodworth was making and the paper published were true, Cook reasoned, every good citizen ought to support the meetings. "If they are false," he continued in his long condemnation, "she, and her cohorts, should be exposed and driven from the borders of this county."[29]

There was no question where Cook stood on whether the claims were true or false. He immediately launched into his tirade, which he said was based on a personal investigation of healing reports. "I charge that she has not restored the sight of one single eye; that she has not cured one single case of goiter, cancer, tumor or ulcer; that she has not restored the hearing of the deaf, nor the speech of the dumb; that she has not made one solitary hopeless cripple walk, or brought life to one paralyzed limb."[30]

Now, not only was Woodworth's credibility being challenged, but also that of the *Tribune's* editorial writer. Cook challenged both in a blazing two-gun shootout. If what Cook wrote was true, Woodworth was a fraud and the newspaper had been hoodwinked.

To support his charges, Cook wrote that he had followed up on some of the individuals who supposedly were cured, but could find no one who was actually helped in any way. He summarized his sharp attack on Woodworth and her helpers by denouncing them as imposters, Pharisees, and hypocrites, and accused them of living in luxury "upon the unrequited toil of the unfortunates of this earth."[31]

Shades of Framingham and Topeka!

The shocking Cook shootout would go down on record as probably the most vicious attacks Woodworth experienced in her 35 years of praying for the sick. Yet the healing reports were building like a giant snowball dashing down Mt. Shasta. On the same front page of the *Tribune*, just two columns away from Cook's mudslinging and denunciation, an article told of a woman whose hearing was greatly improved after she received prayer. The article added that each incoming train to Fremont brought "faith hopeful and trusting cripples whose anxious faces are enlightened with a new hope and optimistic thoughts."[32]

The stage was quickly being set for a showdown between Cook and Woodworth. Cook had offered a reward of $100 (and later raised it to $500) for evidence of a single goiter case being healed. Nobody, according to Cook, came forward to answer his challenge and claim the reward. Then, after Cook's critical article appeared in the *Tribune*, Otis Gardner, one of the local leaders sponsoring the meeting, challenged Cook to come to the platform during a service and make his charges in the presence of 5,000 people. Cook was not present the night Gardner threw out the challenge, but he eagerly called Gardner the next day to accept the offer.[33]

Cook was not alone in his demand that people who pray for the sick must not make false claims. Even Mack M. Pinson, one of Woodworth's Pentecostal friends, had written about some who were making false claims in Woodworth's meetings.[34] If they were healed, Pinson wanted to know about it. But he didn't want to hear about the presumption that was being passed off for faith. Too, Pentecostal denominational leaders during the salvation–healing movement of the mid-twentieth century refused to accept all the claims A. A. Allen, Jack Coe, Kathryn Kuhlman, Oral Roberts, and scores of other evangelists were making in their meetings, television, radio, and publications. They, as did the secular press, wanted proof.

As the Fremont meetings continued, the Dodge County attorney continued his crusading efforts against what became the hottest issue in Fremont. If the leaders in the tent would give him a respectable and orderly hearing, he wrote, he would prove his case. "If this woman is controlled by a supernatural power, it is not the power of the Nazarene, but of the devil himself."[35] Cook, from what he wrote in the newspapers, had a high regard for the Christian faith, but obviously believed Woodworth was a fraud. Predictably, Woodworth and the others on her bandwagon labeled this attack as sin against the Holy Spirit.

Who could blame the local tent committee for reconsidering the invitation to Cook to air his tirade from Woodworth's platform? They discussed the invitation and then withdrew it, deciding nothing could be gained from hearing more of Cook's verbal abuse. For the moment, at least, Woodworth and her team had the momentum. But Cook was searching Nebraska law books, and the game had only started.

Cook was not the only problem the Pentecostal believers faced. A windstorm leveled the tent on a Saturday afternoon, so the faithful moved into the city's opera house for a Sunday morning service. While the meeting was in session, a group of men erected another larger tent that was ready that afternoon. As the tent took shape, Cook appeared again and threatened to get an injunction to stop the meetings unless Woodworth could pray for the sick without touching them.[35] But Woodworth had to weigh whether she would obey Joseph Cook or Jesus, who said of His disciples, "They will place their hands on sick people, and they will get well" (Mark 16:18, NIV).

After the committee denied Cook a chance to speak in the tent, he resorted to legal means in an attempt to stop the meetings. He drew up a complaint on September 29, and as a result, Justice of the Peace William M. Stone ordered Sheriff W. C. Conditto to arrest Woodworth, John Saunders, Clyde T. Miller, August Feick, and C. E. Cheatham. The lengthy four-page complaint charged the group with four counts of practicing medicine and surgery without a license, and unlawfully treating and professing to heal.[36]

Woodworth and her co-workers shut down the Fremont revival meeting one day too late. A day before the protracted meetings closed, the sheriff arrested the leaders and placed them under a $500 bond each, which was raised by railroader Otis Gardner and Wallace Smith.[37] Woodworth said the court ordered the sheriff to arrest the leaders during an afternoon meeting, but he refused. "At the close of a very good meeting," she added, "a nice man came and took myself and workers— all of them ordained ministers—before a tribunal where the charge was read to us."[38] More than likely, the sheriff would rather have been fishing or chasing criminals than arresting preachers at the Pentecostal tent, but his choices were limited.

Naturally, the ministers believed they were acting within their rights and responsibilities as men and women of the Gospel to anoint the sick with oil. They pleaded not guilty, and were released when the bonds were satisfied.

That night, September 30, 1920, Woodworth conducted her last service in Fremont. Despite the arrest—or maybe as a result—people came to the platform for prayer, and many others testified of healings they had received in previous meetings. A reporter observed that the entire audience seemed convinced of Woodworth's gift of healing the sick, despite county attorney Joseph C. Cook's opinions to the contrary.[39]

When Woodworth and the others in her party left Fremont for Omaha, some 25 miles away, the news of the arrests preceded them. In Omaha reporters met them at the train depot, hoping they could get comments for their newspapers. Woodworth held her tongue in Fremont, but in Omaha she spoke out: "I'm fighting the battle of the Lord. They may arrest me every day. It doesn't matter. I'm always ready for the next mission."[40]

Joseph C. Cook's celebrated case against Woodworth and the others at Fremont never went to trial. After the five were bound over to the district court and a trial date set, Cook was unable to take part because of sickness. The trial was rescheduled for January 1921, but finally dismissed.

Woodworth was confident of the outcome had it gone to trial: "Of course they had no case against us; but had we desired we could have made a good case against them, so I believe, and have been advised." She added a note that Cook must have scorned, "But I always look to Jesus Christ as my lawyer, and what I feel impressed by him to do, that I make it my business to do."[41]

What happened to the fruit, if any, as a result of the Fremont tent meetings? Did the revival fervor in that fall campaign birth an organized church? According to Woodworth, who maintained correspondence with the group, the work prospered and obtained an initial meeting place— ironically—in the basement of the very courthouse near county attorney Joseph C. Cook's offices![42]

Some of the fruit came to light 70 years after Woodworth left town. A story I wrote on the Fremont meetings appeared in two editions of the *Fremont Tribune* in 1990. Mary Ida Hybl, an elderly woman in Fremont, saw the story and wrote with a thrilling testimony of her father's conversion. Her father, James Hybl, was a drunkard, she wrote, and one night came stumbling along the street where the tent was set up.

He wandered in and became convicted of his drunkenness and life of sin. When Woodworth invited sinners to come to the altar and have their sins washed away, James Hybl responded. The Hybl family's life changed, and they joined the little group meeting at the Courthouse.

Woodworth probably never heard of this trophy of grace while in Fremont—but probably does now.

In 1894—after about 14 years of preaching—Woodworth gave her philosophy concerning people like Joseph C. Cook, who opposed her methods and theology. Acknowledging that the courageous who tell the truth will be persecuted, she gave her response: "We must go on and preach the truth; we've got no time to listen to the howling of the devils. Let us boldly dare, like Hezekiah, to strike for a reformation! Let us purge the priesthood, the temple courts, our own hearts and lives, of every unclean and defiling thing."[43]

Favorite Beatitudes from the Sermon on the Mount encouraged Woodworth when she faced her persecutors: "Blessed are they which are persecuted for righteousness' sake: for theirs is the kingdom of heaven. Blessed are ye, when men shall revile you and persecute you, and shall say all manner of evil against you falsely, for my sake. Rejoice, and be exceedingly glad: for great is your reward in heaven: for so persecuted they the prophets which were before you."[44]

Woodworth was certain of one thing. When Jesus uttered these encouraging words, He looked into the 20th century and saw her struggling against the snarling enemies at Framingham, Topeka, Fremont, and many other battlefields in between.

ENDNOTES

1. Woodworth-Etter, *Marvels and Miracles*, pp. 416, 17.

2. Ibid., *Signs and Wonders*, p. 122. Friends in Oakland gave this 8,000-seat tent to Woodworth in 1889 (see Chapter 5). When the tent was destroyed in 1891, Topeka friends rallied quickly and purchased a new tent so Woodworth could continue the meetings there and around the country.

3. San Antonio *Light,* July 1907.

4. James R. Goff, Jr., *Fields White unto Harvest* (Arkansas, 1988), p. 431. The Stone's Mansion is now the site of a Catholic Church and school.

5. The Topeka *Daily Capital*, Aug. 9, 1915.

6. Ibid., Aug. 30, 1915.

7. My correspondence with Louis Romer, July 20, 1981—66 years after the healing. While searching for Romer in the late 1970s, I made a series of telephone calls to Kansas from my home in Springfield, Missouri, and was shocked to find him living next door to my first cousin in Lowell, Oregon. My story on Romer's healing is told in "Stormy 1915 Topeka Camp Meeting Recalled," in the Assemblies of God *Heritage*, Summer 2001 (a reprint from the Aug. 8, 1981, edition of the Topeka *Capital-Journal*).

8. It is possible that city officials kept children out of the meetings with an all-encompassing statute.

9. A part of the Kansas Session Laws of 1889: Chapter CIV, Children, Protection of. Although this statute does not specify church services, Judge MacFarland could have interpreted the "cruel treatment, willful abuse or neglect" paragraph as fitting the experiences at Garfield Park.

10. *Daily Capital*, Aug. 12, 1915. Alice Romer told the reporter that her son Louis had been healed of St. Vitus's Dance at one of the meetings. This page 1 *Capital* story reporting the police

intervention was titled, "Boy Cured by Miracle Is Taken from Meeting." Woodworth's version of the story in *Signs and Wonders*, p. 429, agrees with the *Capital* story.

11. Ibid.

12. Ibid. The story reported that Louis cried as he was being carried out of the pavilion, and he offered the officers 15 cents if they would release him.

13. Ibid. Mary Romer was placed under arrest and charged with being a "delinquent parent," according to the *Capital*, Aug. 13. Her husband came to Topeka and took his wife and Louis back to their home in Allen. The *Capital* misspelled the boy' s first name; it should be Louis, not Lewis.

14. Ibid., Aug. 13, 1915. Mayor House, Chief of Police Harvey Parsons, Judge McFarland, and several officers attended the pavilion meeting Aug. 12 to ensure the order was obeyed.

15. *Daily Capital*, Aug. 13, 1915.

16. *Signs and Wonders*, p. 428.

17. *Daily Capital,* Aug. 15, 1915.

18. Ibid. The leaders of the meeting had been expecting the police raid and had made arrangements to use the property across the street whenever the ban came on the use of the pavilion. Pastor C. E. Foster was released later that night. Foster, incidentally, was baptized in the Spirit in 1906 at a mission in Topeka. He formed the Grace and Glory Pentecostal movement. Although he is listed as a charter member of the Assemblies of God, he left that group because of his acceptance of "eternal security." His sons, Victor and Clem, followed their father as pastors of the church he started in Topeka, Victory Tabernacle. C. E. Foster died in 1973 (Telephone conversation with Foster's daughter, Stella Lutz, Topeka.)

19. *Signs and Wonders*, p. 429.

20. *Capital*, Aug. 17, 1915. Ibid. The delegates calling on the governor told him they had been holding camp meetings in

Topeka for 9 years and had had no previous trouble.

21. *Signs and Wonders*, p. 430. The next five pages in *Signs and Wonders* contain testimonies of people who said they were healed during the Topeka meetings.

22. "Minors Take Part in Holy Roller Services," *Capital*, Aug. 29, 1915. The reporter said Woodworth "was kept busy throughout the evening meeting treating persons with ailments who sought her assistance. Many of them, after receiving her help, declared they were cured of diseases or infirmities and gave audible thanks."

23. Ibid., Aug. 30, 1915.

24. Fremont *Evening Tribune*, September 22, 1920. According to Woodworth's *Marvels and Miracles*, p. 411, her invitation to hold meetings here came largely from members of the Reorganized Church of Jesus Christ of the Latter Day Saints.

25. Ibid.

26. Ibid.

27. Ibid., Sept. 23, 1920.

28. *Marvels and Miracles*, p. 412.

29. *Tribune*, Sept. 25, 1920.

30. Ibid.

31. Ibid.

32. Ibid.

33. Ibid., Sept. 27, 1920. Cook, in this letter to the paper, again leveled serious charges against Woodworth and her ministering friends, calling them frauds among other things. In *Marvels and Miracles*, p. 415, Woodworth included a testimony by Otis Gardner in which he claims to have been healed of a tumor. After Woodworth moved to Omaha for meetings, two people testified there that they had been healed in the Fremont meetings. Charles W. Savidge, the sponsoring pastor in Omaha,

said the two refused to take Cook's reward money (reported in the Omaha *Evening World Herald*, Oct. 1, 1920).

34. *Word and Witness*, Nov. 20, 1913.

35. *Tribune*, Sept. 27, 1920.

36. Ibid. One of Cook's objections was the vigorous manner in which he said Woodworth handled the sick. He said she would gouge and twist goiters, pushing them out of sight for the moment and then claim the person was healed. Another Pentecostal evangelist, Smith Wigglesworth, was ordered not to touch the sick when he prayed for them in Stockholm.

37. Ibid., Sept. 30, 1920, and copies of warrant, complaint, and transcript of Dodge County, Nebraska court records. C. E. Cheatham, the paper noted, was a black and had been active in the singing and praying. The complaints named three men who had allegedly received unlawful medical treatment from the ministers: Leslie Haurigan, Oscar Monovitz, and Fred Ellmaker.

38. Ibid. The article was titled, "Healer Bound Over to District Court Under Heavy Bonds." Woodworth and the others were staying at the Wallace Smith home while in Fremont. C. E. Cheatham, the newspaper said, had left town before the warrants were issued.

39. *Marvels and Miracles*, p. 416.

40. *Tribune*, Sept. 30, 1920. The same issue of the paper carried a two-column by 11 inch advertisement from Fred's Place, "Ford Expert," with a headline reading, "The Great Healer." Taking advantage of the current healing interest in Fremont, the dealer wrote a poem advertising himself as the healer of sick Model Ts. For those who had no faith to cure their own car by their own hands, Fred's Place would do it: "Now have faith, come to Fred the Ford Expert."

41. Omaha *Evening World Herald*, October 1, 1920. Others helping in the Omaha meeting included August Feick, I. M. Glanville, D. A. Lamere, Mr. and Mrs. John Saunders, Verna Orendorf, Clyde Miller, and C. C. Cheatem (possibly C. E.

Cheatham).

42. *Marvels and Miracles*, p. 416.

43. Ibid., p. 417.

44. *Life, Work and Experience*, pp. 440, 41.

45. Matthew 5:10 12.

CHAPTER 13

The Tabernacle Era

"God showed me one night that I was to build a tabernacle
here at West Indianapolis, Indiana, so that people from all parts
of the country could come in and spend some time in a good
spiritual mission."—*Maria B. Woodworth Etter*[1]

After 35 years of strenuous ministry on the sawdust trail,
it appeared in 1914 that Maria B. Woodworth-Etter's
ministry had come to an end, that someone else would take
up the mantle.

She was sick—deathly sick with pneumonia, which was
brought on after a vigorous ministry during the summer and
fall, trying to keep up with the burgeoning Pentecostal
movement.[2] And during this time, her invalid husband had
given up his valiant fight against the ravages of time, which
had taken their toll on his 71-year-old body. Without Samuel
Etter by her side, Woodworth had reason to retire. After all,
she had preached thousands of sermons from every book in
the Bible. She had prayed for enough sick in her 35-year-
ministry to stretch from shore to shore. She had survived all
kinds of weather in the tents, from rain-soaked and cold to
scorching Midwestern heat. Nobody would have faulted her
for retiring to Indianapolis in 1914.

Now with the pneumonia, which was one of the few
problems Woodworth had permitted to keep her off the road,

she was near death's door. But as she told it many times later, God wasn't through with her yet. She would recover and live another ten years. And during that ten years, she would continue to crisscross the nation in her determination to reach her generation with the Gospel, which she declared would satisfy the needs of soul and body. And not only would she continue to conduct protracted meetings, but she would also build a tabernacle in Indianapolis and write more books and tracts.[2]

Woodworth was certain God had other plans for her and that she would survive the pneumonia. In fact, during her sickness, she said the Lord appeared to her in a vision and assured her that He would raise her up and she would again go out and minister His word.[3] And that's what happened. After her recovery, Woodworth caught a train for Florida and conducted meetings in Tampa during January and February, 1915.

Tampa would be only the first of many cities and camps she would visit during the next ten years with her new lease on life. She would conduct rousing crusades in Philadelphia, Chicago, Atlanta, Los Angeles, and many other cities before she would pass her mantle to a young woman who was beginning to receive national attention—Aimee Semple McPherson. But Sister Aimee would not have the mantle in 1915. God wasn't through with Woodworth yet.

From the very beginning of Woodworth's ministry around Lisbon, Ohio, in the early 1880s, she aimed at strengthening the local church. If there was no local church where she ministered—or none she felt was spiritual enough to nurture her new converts—she would build one. Though she was responsible for planting numerous churches across the country and though she remained in charge of some of the churches for a period of time, she was never a permanent pastor until she established the Woodworth-Etter Tabernacle in the western part of Indianapolis in 1918.[4]

But even then, Woodworth was hardly the pastor type. Just as she could not be closed in to Columbiana County, Ohio, when she began her ministry, neither could she remain in her Tabernacle. Hers was primarily an itinerant ministry; and whenever she felt the tug from a certain part of the country, she would pack her bags, place someone else in charge of the Tabernacle, and hit the road again. Now she could enjoy the best of two worlds.

In addition to her ministry in faraway places, she now had the Tabernacle, which gave her a place of security and a place in which she could minister to close friends. And it would be a place where visitors could come to her for help. Some would even move to Indianapolis just to be with Woodworth and the excitement around the Tabernacle.[5] She had her own dedicated congregation, and the Tabernacle was right next door to her home at 2114 Miller Street. Here Woodworth would minister for the last six years of her life—from May 1918 until her death in September 1924.

Woodworth was no stranger to Indianapolis. As early as 1886, she had held meetings here and had brought the message of divine healing to the state on a wide scale. Just when she moved to Indianapolis isn't known, but she was living here as early as 1912.[6] As in most of the major decisions Woodworth made in her lifetime, she built the Woodworth-Etter Tabernacle after God sent a vision. Because the Tabernacle was built in a near central part of the country, people could come from the east, west, north, and south. They could "come in and spend some time in a good spiritual mission and get established in God," she advertised. She added, "He showed me that the meetings should be of oldtime fashion and power, where people can get spiritual food to supply their needs for soul and body."[7]

Throughout her itinerant ministry Woodworth never put pressure on people to support her ministry, and as a result, many times the offerings were too meager to meet expenses.

A typical experience can be cited from her Oakland meetings during the winter of 1889-90. After being in the bay area four months, Woodworth received an offering of $156—all but $4 went for the new tent.[8] But when she began to build the Tabernacle, she sent out requests for financial help. She reasoned that because the new base was God's idea and it would prepare people to go out in all directions as "flames of fire," believers across the country ought to be willing to support the cause.[9] And the money came in. The Tabernacle went up for the glory of God. Woodworth lived long enough to see her local church impact the city.

Woodworth had dedicated other new buildings—in Springfield, Illinois, and Anderson, Indiana—but this building would "belong" to her. And Sunday, May 19, 1918, was no quiet day in west Indianapolis, for it marked the dedication of the Woodworth-Etter Tabernacle as World War I was winding down.

The well known Canadian evangelist, A. H. Argue, preached one of the dedicatory messages in the afternoon on the subject of setting the church in order to the degree that members of the body would feel free to exercise spiritual gifts.[10]

It appears that the Tabernacle became a model for early Pentecostal churches. It must be remembered that there were few Pentecostal churches of any size when Woodworth built her 500-seat Tabernacle in 1918. True, it never compared in grandeur with Aimee Semple McPherson's Angelus Temple (neither would any other Pentecostal church at the time), but it was a typical Pentecostal church in the formative years of the movement. Would-be church builders with limited finances would consider Woodworth's Tabernacle within reach far quicker than they would McPherson's Temple.

The numerous revival centers which sprang up across the country between 1930-60 in many ways fit the Tabernacle mold. Here an endless stream of visitors and the regular members were treated to any number of evangelists of national and international repute. When Woodworth wasn't preaching, or was out on the road again, a visiting evangelist might be in for two or three weeks of meetings. The visiting speakers, however, would not draw the crowds like the charismatic Woodworth would. When she was out of town, the back section of the church would be roped off to encourage the smaller crowds to sit closer to the pulpit.[11]

The Woodworth-Etter Tabernacle probably had more people coming and going than any church of the day. But many stayed, like the Russell family from southern Illinois. Roscoe Russell remembers how his mother was dying of cancer in their Illinois home. But the sadness in their home would turn to joy, and it all began when an interested friend sent them a copy of Woodworth's *Signs and Wonders*. When they learned that Woodworth had built her Tabernacle in Indianapolis, Roscoe's father took the family to see if all that wonderful healing stuff Woodworth had written in her book was really true. After Woodworth and the Tabernacle believers prayed for Mrs. Russell, she testified that she was completely healed. The happy experience made such a dramatic change in the Russell family that they moved to Indianapolis and became staunch supporters of Woodworth and the Tabernacle.[12]

But Mrs. Russell was not the only member of the family to benefit from Woodworth's faith and teaching. In 1919, only a year after the family had moved to Indianapolis, the teenaged Roscoe developed tuberculosis, which produced a knot on the side of his neck about the size of his fist. Roscoe's mother was quick to take her son to Woodworth. In 1978 Roscoe recalled the event as if it happened the day before. Just as soon as Woodworth was convinced young Roscoe had faith for his healing, the bold evangelist said, "We'll just cut it out with the Sword of the Spirit." Roscoe was hardly prepared for what happened next. "She took her Bible and struck me on the neck with the edge. It hurt! But I was healed."[13]

Roscoe's mother was also involved in yet another unusual manifestation. In a Sunday afternoon service, Mrs. Russell spoke in tongues publicly for 28 minutes. Some wondered why Woodworth didn't overrule and tell Mrs. Russell to be seated. But for almost a half an hour she was free to speak in her "heavenly language."

It wasn't until the next Sunday that the church learned Mrs. Russell's "heavenly language" was actually Romanian, a language she had never learned. A Romanian family had come into the church that Sunday afternoon and heard Mrs. Russell preach a sermon in their own language. They were overwhelmed by the miracle, because only the father in the family understood English.[14]

The husband and father told the congregation the following Sunday that his daughter had been suffering from tuberculosis. Two Pentecostal women came to their house and prayed for the daughter, and she was healed. They wanted to find the Pentecostal church, but didn't know where it was. So they looked around until they found the Woodworth-Etter Tabernacle.

Woodworth and her Tabernacle believers learned to expect such experiences as norm, almost as much as other congregations expected to sing the Doxology at the end of their services.

Roscoe Russell, who grew up to become an Assemblies of God pastor and evangelist, placed the highest seal of approval on Woodworth. He said, "I can remember no one who spoke with greater authority ... she was a great Bible teacher and preacher. She always gave an altar call, with a powerful appeal to sinners." Russell said he saw more people receive the baptism in the Holy Spirit at her meetings than any service he ever attended. "They were not 'aided' in any way. It was just such an outpouring of the Spirit that it was easy to get the baptism." And about money, he said Woodworth taught the people to tithe. "But she never put people under pressure to give. No prosperity kick like we see today ... She was as clean as a hound's tooth, to use a colloquialism."[15] Russell added that Woodworth never lost touch with the common people. They were as welcome in her home as the rich.

When Herman Rose was a teenager, he also attended the Woodworth-Etter Tabernacle and later became Woodworth's youth leader. He described Woodworth as a woman of integrity and with a great love for souls, and he agreed with Russell that her love wasn't just for the people with money. "She loved the poor as well," he wrote for a magazine he edited. "She manifested her love to all kinds of people. She held meetings for an outstanding Negro Christian leader (Thoro Harris) who was an artist, evangelist, and song writer." Rose added that Woodworth's interest was only in the "harvest of souls," and she never organized anything for self-glory.[16]

Another elderly person who remembered being in the Woodworth-Etter Tabernacle as a child was Mrs. Rollie Ellis, daughter of the prominent black leader in the Pentecostal movement, G. T. Haywood. What stood out in her young mind were the many crutches, canes, and wheelchairs left in the Tabernacle as witnesses of healings.[17]

Pentecostals who attended Woodworth's services in the Tabernacle went away with the feeling they had been in an "old-time" worship service. Woodworth would permit the congregation to "take their liberty" but would allow no fanaticism.[18]

Dancing in the Spirit was a rather common manifestation in the Tabernacle. Leland R. Keys, a preacher and teacher, attended services at the Tabernacle and played the piano on different occasions. He said at times everyone on the platform would begin to dance. "It seemed to be a genuine move of the Spirit upon the part of the participants and brought blessing."[19]

Woodworth was slow to accept the dancing as having New Testament precedent, fearing at first that it was something done "in the flesh." But when she did accept it as having spiritual value, she defended the experience as much as she did the heavenly music, which worshipers claimed they heard from time to time. "I soon saw it was the 'Cloud of Glory' over the people that brought forth the dancing and playing invisible instruments. The sounds of sweet, heavenly music could often be heard." Several times she asked the congregation, who said they had heard music from the platform (where they knew there were no instruments to be seen), to be honest and raise their hands if they heard the music. "Many hands went up from saints and sinners ... Often a message in tongues was given in one or more languages and the interpretation. I concluded that this is surely the Lord's strange work, and his strange acts."[20]

Woodworth believed that the demonstrations in her meetings and elsewhere were merely indications that the coming of Jesus was soon, and that the dance and music would be used at the marriage of the Lamb.[21]

Russell described the worship services as what "we think of as old time Pentecost" and recalled Woodworth's manner in leading the church in worship. "She was almost fanatical about people praising the Lord. Many times after the song service was over she would take the service and have people stand and rejoice in the Lord." The services included much singing in the Spirit, altar calls, conversions, and seekers receiving baptism "in the old-fashioned Pentecostal order."[22]

Believers who worshiped regularly at the Tabernacle during the last six years of Woodworth's life would gather early before a scheduled service. Someone would invariably begin an unstructured worship session, all the time watching the backdoor off the platform through which Woodworth would enter.

Then the great moment came. Woodworth would come onto the platform in her patented style, waving her hand and handkerchief and audibly praising God. Frequently Woodworth would step lightly across to the pulpit and begin to sing one of the Tabernacle favorites, one of which was F. M. Lehman's "Elbow Room." And the congregation would join in:[23]

When the gates swing wide on the other side,
Just beyond the sunset sea,
There'll be room to spare as we enter there;
Room for you and room for me.
For the gates are wide on the other side,
On the right hand, on the left hand
Fifty miles of elbow room.[24]

And as the volume picked up, the congregation got "in the Spirit," prompting Woodworth to either march across the platform waving her handkerchief or maybe stand statue-like with her hands raised toward the ceiling and her eyes closed in worship. The congregation and the little general on the platform could almost feel earth receding and heaven coming down.

Herman Rose remembered that Woodworth would whip together a " glory march" in which worshipers could march around the building singing and praising God. Other Pentecostals often call this experience a "Jericho March," which comes from the time the Children of Israel marched around the city of Jericho (Joshua 6). Other Christian believers would label as fanaticism the Tabernacle-shaking worship services at the corner of Miller and Bellmont. But Woodworth justified the dancing and invisible music by quoting Psalm 149:3, "Let them praise his name in the dance: let them sing praises unto him with the timbrel and harp"; Psalm 150:4, "Praise him with the timbrel and dance; praise him with stringed instruments and organs"; and Jeremiah 31:13, "Then shall the virgin rejoice in the dance, both young men and old together; for I will turn their mourning into joy, and will comfort them, and make them rejoice from their sorrow."

And when the three- or four-hour worship service would finally end, the worshipers knew they had been in the presence of the King of Kings and Lord of lords.

During her later years, Woodworth depended on several ministers to preach in her revival meetings and then in the Tabernacle. None was any more faithful and supportive than August Feick, Woodworth's assistant pastor and business manager.

Feick met Woodworth in 1913 and then helped in several meetings before Woodworth asked him to join her team. From that point until Woodworth died in 1924, August Feick was Woodworth's aide de camp. Others would come and go during this period, but Feick felt a call to give Woodworth and the Kingdom his life and service. Photographs taken during the last years of Woodworth's life generally show the short, stocky, sober looking Feick standing like a shadow at Woodworth's side.

Whereas Woodworth would seldom preach with sermon notes, Feick would never preach without them. He was as formal in the pulpit as Woodworth was informal. But they formed an effective and balanced team.

On one occasion, Feick was traveling with others in a car to a town where he was scheduled to speak. A sudden gust of wind snatched Feick's treasured sermon notes and scattered them along the countryside. Feick panicked. He turned to Lyda Paino, a member of the Gospel team, and broke the news she would be the speaker, because he never preached without notes. Lyda Paino was caught by surprise, but Feick insisted he could not speak and that she was the next in line for their Gospel team.[25]

Feick had trouble preaching without notes in a day when it was almost a sin to rely on such devices in Pentecostal churches, but he remained faithfully by Woodworth's side at the Tabernacle and on the road. And when Woodworth died in 1924, Feick took over the Tabernacle and remained in charge until 1933, when he turned it over to Thomas Paino, Sr. and his wife Lyda—an energetic and dedicated couple who had also worked with Woodworth in the early 1920s.

People who knew Woodworth claimed she had a special gift of selecting associates who would contribute to the revival or Tabernacle meetings and who would not embarrass her. Thomas and Lyda Paino were two good examples of Woodworth's ability to select complementary team members.

Thomas Paino's surrender to serve God came when he was in officer's training at Ft. Lee, Virginia, in 1917-18, during the influenza epidemic, which was snatching the lives of men all around him. He had been raised a Catholic and believed in God, but, by his own admission, had little interest in spiritual matters. The epidemic, however, put him in fear of his life, and he vowed to God that he would serve Him if his life were spared.

Little did Paino realize that service to God would mean giving up his Catholic faith, that some family members would disown him, and that he would become a Protestant minister.

It all started after the war when his first wife became ill with tuberculosis, and he took her to Tupper Lake, New

York, for medical help. Mrs. Paino had been converted in a street meeting conducted by a Methodist minister who had in his library Woodworth's book *Signs and Wonders.* The Painos read the book and decided to travel to Indianapolis for Woodworth's legendary prayers.

Although Thomas believed in prayer, he would not attend meetings at the Tabernacle because of his Catholic tradition. But one night a woman invited Paino to attend the services. He told himself that he had committed all kinds of sin anyway, so one more—attending a Protestant service—wouldn't hurt him that much. That night he found his way to the Tabernacle with his ailing wife. It was a night that was to change his life.

Years later Paino described what he saw and heard in a booklet: "At the meeting I heard singing, shouting, messages in tongues and interpretation. The people testified how they were saved, filled with the Spirit, and healed ... God put a hunger in my heart to seek Him. No one had to ask me to go to the altar. I wanted what God had given these people."[26]

That night in Woodworth's Tabernacle was only the beginning in Thomas Paino's spiritual journey. Within a few weeks, on December 26, 1919, he received the Pentecostal experience in the Tabernacle. Years later, the enthusiastic Paino could still say, "It is better felt than told."[27]

While Paino could join right in with Woodworth and her congregation in Pentecostal worship, he found a cold reception from his family. After a short visit, in which he became an outcast, Paino returned to the warm confines of the Tabernacle. Here he offered his services to Woodworth. He learned to lead the song services, pray for people around the altar, and he gave Woodworth assistance in the various other ministries around the Tabernacle. And here is where he met Lyda. When Woodworth went on the road for revival services in Indiana and Ohio, Thomas and Lyda Paino were important members of the team.

Woodworth's prayer and faith encouraged Thomas as a new believer, and her influence would follow him throughout his own ministry long after her death. Two healings stood out in Paino's mind, which helped him in his faith to pray for others. "One was a man by the name of Armstrong who had cancer of the rectum," Paino wrote in 1977. "How that brother would shout and praise God for his healing. The other man was Mr. Kaiser from Petoskey, Michigan, who [had been] paralyzed from his hips down. I heard these testimonies many times."[28]

Woodworth's non-structured school of the prophets—one that featured prayer, Bible study, faith, heart stirring worship, and going out where the sinners lived—produced an outstanding graduating couple in Thomas and Lyda Paino. Though they, too, are gone, their ministry continues in various forms throughout the world.[29]

During the Tabernacle era, Woodworth continued her evangelistic ministry, for it wouldn't seem natural for her—despite the fact that she was in her seventies—to remain in a local church. So after dedicating the Tabernacle in May 1918, Woodworth hit the road again that fall, this time to Ainsworth, Nebraska. And during the next four years, she would preach throughout the Midwest, including Alexandria, Minnesota; Toledo, Ohio; Chicago and Warren, Illinois; Sioux City and Des Moines, Iowa; and Fremont and the Winnebago Indian Reservation, Nebraska.

The Iowa meetings appear to be representative of the crusades Woodworth conducted during this period. She conducted tent campaigns in Sioux City in 1920 and 1921. The Sioux City *Journal* gave ample coverage to the meetings the "hyphenated healer" (Woodworth-Etter) held there in 1920. Their headlines show the editor's interest—which was not without a certain degree of bias and combined with a desire to sell newspapers:

WOMAN SPELLBINDER CONTINUES "CURES"

AFFLICTED BESIEGE TENT OF HYPHENATED "HEALER"

SOME PROCLAIM "MIRACLES"

MRS. WOODWORTH-ETTER "WORKS" ON HOST OF "MOURNERS" AS CHOIR CHANTS AND BODIES UNDULATE—TO BAPTIZE TODAY IN CRYSTAL LAKE.[30]

A week later the *Journal* offered more of their definitive, if not skeptical, headlines:

FAITH "CURES DEFORMITY; PARENTS SAY "HEALER" ENABLED SON TO WALK

SIX OPERATIONS HAD FAILED; BUT WHEN MRS. WOODWORTH-ETTER ANOINTED LAD AND TOLD HIM TO "WALK FOR JESUS," HE APPARENTLY OVERCAME AILMENT.[31]

In another case, it was reported that William Wood of South Sioux City, Nebraska, was healed of spinal meningitis in the 1920 meeting. A sponsoring pastor, I. M. Glanville, said before Wood was healed, "he could not speak, his head lay back between his shoulders; he was as a walking skeleton, twisted and warped out of shape."[32]

But during Woodworth's 1921 campaign in Sioux City, Glanville said Wood was "a great marvel." After the meetings closed, Wood found his own "sawdust trail" in the city park and preached to large crowds. Years later the only remaining sign of Wood's illness was a slight twist in his spine, which Wood regarded as God's reminder to him that he had been healed.[33]

Woodworth set up her tent in Des Moines in June 1921 and stirred the city for several weeks with her preaching, which emphasized the Pentecostal baptism and physical healing. The 4,000-seat tent soon became too small to hold the crowds that wanted to hear the 77-year-old evangelist. A Drake University coed, Berna Glanville, remembered the huge crowds, the excitement, and Woodworth "frozen" in a trance with her hands upraised.[34]

Otto and Viva LaPoint took their two sons, Paul and Phil, to Des Moines and pitched their tent for a week to attend the Woodworth meetings. "The meetings were exciting," Paul told me, "but they were also very noisy—which disturbed the neighbors." He remembers seeing the police come in and warn Woodworth and the organizers that they would have to quiet the crowd by 10:00 p.m.

But that didn't happen, the 91-year-old LaPoint remembers. "The people still prayed, shouted, and sang at the top of their voices after 10 o'clock."

A young man by the name of Charles Leaming, who was reared on a farm near Perry, Iowa, was one of the many who scrambled for a place in the tent every night. But during these meetings, he was unconverted and the services made him miserable.

"I was under such deep conviction I would leave the tent and get a hold of the grass to keep from going back inside and down to the altar."

He later attended Aimee Semple McPherson's L.I.F.E. Bible College and became a leader in the Open Bible Standard Churches, where he was as well known for his trademark singing of the old Gospel favorite, "I'm Going Higher Some Day," as he was for his rousing preaching.[35]

After preaching for several weeks in cities throughout the Midwest, Woodworth could always look forward to the time she would spend at the Tabernacle to regain her strength, just enough strength to get back on the road again. The road was her life. Tents, new people, the sick, sinners coming to an old-fashioned mourner's bench, believers "praying through" to a deeper spiritual experience, testimonies of healing. This was what the road was all about.

Sure, the Tabernacle was a welcome sight after an exhausting campaign in such places as Sioux City and Toleado and Winnebago, but the Tabernacle would always remain a booster station more than it would the powerhouse. The powerhouse was out yonder, out on the road. That is where Woodworth would be as long as she had strength to move, breath to preach, and faith to pray.

ENDNOTES

1. Woodworth-Etter, *Spirit filled Sermons*, p. 202.

2. Maria B. Woodworth-Etter, "Mrs. Woodworth Wonderfully Recovered," The *Christian Evangel*, Jan. 16, 1915, p. 4.

3. Ibid. Woodworth quotes a Dr. E. V. Green who attended her during the sickness: "This result [her recovery] came to you through implicit faith in God's power to heal you. You took nothing but air, milk and eggs, and passed through what is ordinarily fatal in sixty percent of persons seventy two years of age."

4. Woodworth married Samuel Etter in 1903, and for the next decade they lived on a farm near Cisne, Illinois. Although she does not mention this era in later books, her 1904 book (discovered in the 1990s) gives a brief glimpse into this part of their lives. Local newspapers fill in some details. They operated a farm, raised sheep, planned to build a church—maybe a faith home—and drilled an apparent unproductive oil well. Woodworth continued her evangelistic meetings during this period, but it appears the meetings were on a limited schedule.

5.   An advertisement in the back of *Marvels and Miracles* invites believers to move to Indianapolis, "a good place to live," and become a member of the Tabernacle (p. 568).

6.   Alice Reynolds Flower (Mrs. J. Roswell) told me that Mrs. Woodworth took an interest in her and her husband about 1912 and would invite them to her house for food and fellowship. The Flower couple were newlyweds and were getting ready to enter the ministry full time. Mrs. Flower—who was 91 when she talked with me in Jan. 1982—was one of the few people left who knew Maria B. Woodworth-Etter.

7.   *Spirit filled Sermons*, p. 202.

8.   Oakland *Tribune*, Feb. 10, 1890.

9.   *Weekly Evangel*, March 9, 1918, p. 9.

10.   *Marvels and Miracles*, p. 353. It is interesting to note that in this same report (p. 354) the first baptismal service was marked by several messages in tongues which were interpreted and which expressed God's approval, instructions, and prophecies concerning people who were baptized. It was also pointed out in the report that the Tabernacle baptismal formula was in the Name of the Father, Son, and Holy Ghost, which was no incidental matter because G. T. Haywood's Oneness congregation was also in Indianapolis.

11.   Roscoe Russell, taped interview, 1978.

12.   Ibid.

13.   Ibid. The author does not recommend this method.

14.   Ibid.

15.   Ibid. Russell's reference to "prosperity kick" is a criticism of ministries that emphasize receiving material wealth in exchange for faith and contributions. Russell, who died in 1981, said his father was active in the church and was a great admirer of Woodworth, describing her as "all business."

16.   Herman Rose, editorial, *The Railroad Evangelist* Feb. 1979.

In 1922 Rose became youth leader at the Tabernacle, a position
he kept until he left for Bible college in 1925. Rose added that
Woodworth was forgotten now "but not by me, and most of all
she is not forgotten by our Wonderful Heavenly Father." Visitors
to the Flower Pentecostal Heritage Center, Springfield, Missouri,
walk into a store-front church replica designed after one the late
Herman Rose pastored in Indiana.

17. Mrs. Rollie Ellis, telephone conversation in Indianapolis,
August 1979. While in Indianapolis I also talked with Ted Black,
business manager of an Indianapolis church. Black said his aunt,
Ruth Bland of Orangeville, Ontario, Canada, was afflicted with
cancer. She came to the Tabernacle, was healed, and lived
another 25 years.

18. One must keep in mind that fanaticism can be a relative
matter. What is fanaticism to one believer may be a beautiful
worship expression to another.

19. Leland R. Keys, letter to author, May 26, 1981. Keys added,
however, that dancing in the Spirit was not a major emphasis at
the Tabernacle. Old-time Pentecostals will tell you today that a
vast difference exists between their unplanned dancing in the
Spirit and the choreographed church dancing in recent years.
Keys became an Assemblies of God minister, college teacher
and president.

20. *Spirit filled Sermons*, p. 65. Woodworth added that as many
as nine of the most "noted ministers" danced at one time on the
platform. One woman who had been on crutches for five years
was healed in a service and then danced all over the platform,
singing "heavenly music."

21. Ibid., p. 64.

22. Roscoe Russell, taped interview. Russell, in defending the
"falling in the Spirit," said he never saw presuggestions nor
people being pushed over. He said people would move toward
the altar and fall on the floor before they got there. Often those
who fell would receive the Pentecostal experience. In Russell's
opinion, Woodworth would permit nothing superficial: "It was

God. Nothing phony about Sister Woodworth."

23. Herman Rose, taped interview, 1978.

24. F. M. Lehman, "Elbow Room." Copyright 1917.

25. Thomas Paino, Jr., interview, Aug. 1979.

26. Thomas Paino, Sr., "God's Presence Filled the Tabernacle," in Wayne E. Warner, ed., *Touched by the Fire* (Logos Publishing, 1978), pp. 75, 76. Although Paino's first wife did not survive the illness, Paino's conversion was real, and he dedicated his life to the Lord's service.

27. Paul E. Paino, *Living Sacrifices* (Indianapolis: West Side Gospel Tabernacle, 1958), p. 7. This book was published to honor Thomas and Lyda Paino for 25 years of ministry in Indianapolis. A grandson, Troy D. Paino, wrote *Touching Our World With His Hands*, a 75th anniversary book for Lakeview Christian Center in 1993.

28. My correspondence with Thomas Paino, Sr., Sept. 26, 1977. Two others who attended the Woodworth-Etter Tabernacle , Rufus Lentz and Herman Rose, confirmed that a paralyzed man from Petoskey was healed after he had written to Woodworth for a prayer cloth. Rose identified him as Fritz Crisler, a shoe cobbler, who later moved to Indianapolis. It is possible that Crisler is the Kaiser that Paino described. Rose told me, "I heard him tell about this miraculous healing many times. And he would become so happy he would dance and shout for joy."

29. The models for the life-cast preaching couple at the entry of the Flower Pentecostal Heritage Center, Springfield, MO., are Thomas and Lyda Paino—he holding a big Bible and she with a banjo.

30. The Sioux City *Journal*, Aug. 22, 1920.

31. Ibid., Aug. 29 , 1920.

32. Eugene N. Hastie, *History of the West Central District Council of the Assemblies of God* (Fort Dodge, Iowa: Walterick Printing Company, 1948), p. 81. Glanville founded First

Assembly of God, Sioux City, in 1920.

33. Theodore E. Gannon, oral history, 1980; Flower Pentecostal Heritage Center. Tape #A034-036.

34. James and Berna Glanville Crouch, oral history, 1981; Flower Pentecostal Heritage Center. Tape # A112.

35. My interview with Charles Leaming, 1980. "Leaming's Half-Century of Ministry," by William Simbro, *Message of the Open Bible*, October 1979, p. 10 (excerpted from the Des Moines *Tribune*, June 30, 1979).

CHAPTER 14

The Last Hurrah

"When I start to preach and He gives me a new shock of power from His heavenly battery, I feel like I was about 16 years old— Glory! ... They often tell me I had better be in bed. How can I go to bed? I have to tell people about Jesus. Bless God. They say it would do me good to take a little rest. How can I rest when the people are soon going down to death in this great tribulation?"—*Maria B. Woodworth-Etter*[1]

During the spring of 1922, it was easy for Woodworth to think of other springs over the previous 40-plus years. She could reminisce about the meetings she conducted from Petoskey, Michigan, to San Antonio; from Boston to Los Angeles; from Seattle to Tampa. She could recall the struggles and victories, the conversions and healings, the friendships and the sorrows. And no doubt the memories beginning in the 1880s, current revival invitations, and God's continuing call prompted her to sit down and map out an itinerary despite the fact that in July she would celebrate her 78th birthday.

Would anyone want an evangelist who obviously had seen better days? Could she still attract the crowds of the past? Would her health hold up? Would Iowa authorities arrest her when the little boy with lockjaw died? Would she come back to Indianapolis in a casket? She would have the answers to these questions and others during the next few months.

Her 1922 dreams resulted in an itinerary that in part resembled the almost nonstop campaigns of the 1880s. We can only speculate as to what was running through her mind as she set out on this campaign more than 80 years ago that would run from April to September and take her into Texas, Missouri, Iowa, and Kansas—and permitted few days of rest between meetings.

Obviously Woodworth was conscious of the fact that her time on the sawdust trail—her first love when it came to a place to preach—was drawing to an end. And maybe Woodworth was even ready to accept the possibility that the Rapture of the Church would not take place during her lifetime. But if she did accept this possibility, she would keep it a secret.

Whatever raced through her mind when she left Indianapolis, Woodworth knew for sure there were still souls to reach. And despite her age-related illnesses, she knew she belonged out on the trail—in other towns and states.

Somehow the sinners and the sick always looked more needy outside Indianapolis. And as other salvation–healing evangelists, she could deal more easily with those out on the road than she could with the chronically ill at home. On the road, the evangelist–pastor can walk away from the invalid tent and head for another town. But at home, the same chronically ill stare at the preacher through moon-size eyes of hope, people that more than not would go to their graves unchanged.

So when the Indiana countryside began to thaw, Woodworth knew it was time to pack her bags and go to war against the devil in other places. Her itinerant ways were reaching the end of the string, and it was time to hit the road again for at least one last hurrah. She owed it to God and the people who waited for the good news.

Instinctively or supernaturally, Woodworth could have known she would conduct her last major campaign in 1922. And like the anchor runner in the mile relay, she had to give it everything she had. This was no time to sit at home in a rocking chair. Time was short. The destinies of many people were in the balance, and she knew she was God's instrument to reach scores who might otherwise be lost forever. Just as she preached mercy and judgment in the beginning, she preached it in 1922. And she would never let the people forget that the conversion of the soul far outweighed the healing of the body.

As Woodworth's train pulled into the Dallas station, her thoughts must have focused on this Southwestern city 10 years earlier, when she had enjoyed some of her greatest triumphs. Back in 1912, as many as 5,000 people streamed to the big tent and tabernacle, and there the meetings would continue for five very fruitful months. She must have thought of the young Dallas pastor, Fred F. Bosworth, who by 1922 was himself holding healing meetings across the country and in Canada.

Now she was returning to Dallas for possibly the first time since 1912, but under far different circumstances. Ten years earlier, the Pentecostal movement was just getting started in Dallas. Now in 1922, Woodworth was to conduct meetings in one of the many Pentecostal congregations that had sprung up like mushrooms.[2]

The spring storms and flooding had been especially hard on the area, forcing residents to higher ground. Would anyone come to the meetings? More than one evangelist had seen previous popularity dry up with the passing years. Would anyone remember her?

She should not have worried, if she had. Despite a slow start, the small church soon had standing room only to hear the veteran campaigner. And despite the severe cold and pneumonia that hampered Woodworth's speech, she refused to give way to other preachers. Several who had been converted or blessed in some other spiritual or physical way in the 1912 meeting came in to add their testimonies to Woodworth's preaching. One report stated that the "old time" power of God was present at every service, prompting people to fill the altar space as they sought salvation, physical healing, and the Pentecostal experience.[3]

The writer of this report knew he was working with a legend in his time: "It is one of the most remarkable sights of a lifetime, to see this prophetess of great age, still pressing the battle for God, standing heroically for the great fundamentals with His approval in *Signs and Wonders* following."[4]

No doubt the eager Dallas crowd heard Woodworth give her burden for being on the road again and her answer to the critics who said she should be home in bed. "When I start to preach and He gives me a shock of power from His heavenly battery I feel like I was about 16 years old—Glory!" And she followed with an answer to the home-in-bed counsel: "How can I go to bed? I have to tell people about Jesus. Bless God. They say it would do me good to take a little rest. How can I rest when the people are soon going down to death in this great tribulation?"[5]

From Dallas, Woodworth and her party of four moved to nearby Ft. Worth for a two-week campaign with little rest between meetings. F. A. Hale, in writing about the meetings for the *Pentecostal Evangel*, was as amazed at Woodworth's faith and endurance as others who heard her in Dallas: "Although she is almost seventy eight years old," he wrote, "she is just as strong in faith, and God is using her mightily in the ministry of healing and in preaching the deep mysteries of the Kingdom of God."[6]

In addition to her prayers for the sick in Ft. Worth, Woodworth taught on the use of spiritual gifts and then prayed for some 50 Christian workers who sought her help—as opposed to many later evangelists who slip out to a waiting limosine in the alley. She always had time to counsel or pray with someone who was in need. This was her lifetime mission, and nothing would change that passion on this 1922 campaign.

As Woodworth boarded the train at Ft. Worth on her way out of Texas for the last time, it was only natural to assume that she contrasted these two meetings with the giant Dallas campaign in 1912. Despite the much smaller size and impact this time around, she must have felt a deep sense of satisfaction that a newer generation of Pentecostals, as well as the older, flocked to hear her speak and receive her prayers.

But now the Texas meetings were behind her. Another city, this one in southeast Missouri, anticipated that it was their turn to feel the impact of Woodworth's ministry.

Sikeston, Missouri, would be a new area of ministry for the Woodworth journal, but she believed for a long time that the Holy Spirit would go before her to prepare the people for her unique brand of revivalism. No reason to worry about strange areas when one can commit the situation to God, she believed, and let Him work things out for His glory. It was a simple philosophy that worked by faith, but for Woodworth it worked—and more times than she would ever remember.

Sikeston is in a five-state area of Missouri, Illinois, Kentucky, Tennessee, and Arkansas—lying near the Mississippi River in Southeast Missouri. The Missouri "Boot heel," they call this area because of the heel-like shape of the state. Not far away is one of the interesting points of U.S. geography—where the mighty Mississippi and Ohio rivers merge and separate the states. Driving east from Sikeston, the traveler crosses the Mississippi into the southern tip of Illinois, takes a right turn across the Ohio River and enters western Kentucky—all in less than two miles and about five minutes.

Even though the above bridges came after 1922, it is safe to say that each of the neighboring states, and many others, was represented in Woodworth's meeting conducted in the crowded Dorris Theater and outdoors during the months of June and July. They came by ferry boats, trains, autos, horses and buggies, and walking. One of the daily newspapers called the crowd probably the largest religious gathering ever held in the city.[7]

How could Woodworth have been more pleased?

Aaron A. Wilson, an admitted novice young pastor at Puxico, Missouri, was in attendance one night to hear Woodworth preach. Little could he know that Woodworth would not preach, that she and the congregation would listen to him preach.

Before the service began, a woman who worked with Woodworth and who knew Wilson, asked him to lead in the song service. Wilson declined, saying that he had never seen such a large crowd in church, let alone tried to lead that many people in a song service. The woman and then Woodworth assured Wilson that he wouldn't have any trouble and talked him into filling in as the worship leader.

He finally agreed, although he didn't feel comfortable in front of the big crowd. While leading one of the songs, he felt a tap on his shoulder and looked around to see Woodworth standing at his side. She whispered a shocking revelation, "The Lord would have you preach tonight."

Wilson almost lost his place in the songbook. He was certain it was only a dream, that this old veteran of the sawdust trail was asking this small-town pastor to preach. Every young preacher probably fantacizes that he or she would have such an opportunity. Next thing you know, Billy Sunday or Paul Rader will be asking him to preach. And if Wilson had been surprised that they would ask him to lead the congregation in singing, he was now almost in shock. He simply was unable to answer Woodworth.

She was not about to let him off the hook, though, and she had him in a pretty tough place to say no—standing at the pulpit. During the next song Wilson felt the same tap on his shoulder. He didn't need to turn around to know who had heard from heaven again. "Brother," Woodworth whispered with a little more urgency, "don't fail God. He wants you to preach here tonight."

By this time Wilson, who had driven 60 miles to hear the legendary Woodworth preach, knew it was impossible to reject the almost commanding word that he was to bring the message himself. As he sat back waiting for his turn to preach, he decided to preach a sermon on the Second Coming of Christ, a sermon he had preached at Puxico the week before.

But when Woodworth introduced him, he said God changed his sermon and flashed through his mind the question Jesus asked the lame man at the Pool of Bethesda, "Wilt thou be made whole?"[8] Wilson later described this service as one of the high points of his long preaching career: "The Spirit of God preached the whole sermon through me; and I really listened to myself preach."[9]

Woodworth closed the Sikeston meeting on July 2, 1922, and six days later opened her fourth campaign of the season in Ottumwa, Iowa, a campaign that was marred by the death of a young boy whom his parents had brought to the meetings from Illinois. As happened whenever Woodworth preached in Iowa, the Ottumwa meetings during the month of July attracted huge crowds from several states. More than 150 cars were on the campgrounds for a single service, not only illustrating her continued popularity, but also the technological advances from the horse-drawn carriage to gasoline-powered autos. And as in previous meetings, healing testimonies in the Ottumwa campaign were numerous, which—along with Woodworth's presence in the area—boosted the often-maligned local Pentecostal churches.[10]

Woodworth wasn't the only attraction in Ottumwa during July, for the local Chautauqua Association brought the noted William Jennings Bryan to the city for a speech. While Bryan addressed 1,500 people with a speech titled, "We Must Get Back to God and Belief in God's Laws," Woodworth was a few blocks away confidently preaching an apostolic Gospel to more people than Bryan had drawn.[11]

To buttress the faith of scores who gathered in Ottumwa for their miracles, Woodworth introduced people who testified that they had been healed there and in previous campaigns.

• Lawrence Leaming, a young man who was involved in an auto accident and suffered a broken arm and serious internal injuries, came in walking with help and a cane. "His arm was healed and his limbs received strength," according to one report. He discarded his cane and continued to gain strength during the two weeks he was at the camp.

• A young woman who had been deaf since she was four years of age returned a week after she received prayer, "hearing ordinary conversation without difficulty."

• One former epileptic reportedly was healed at Winnebago, Nebraska, two years previously "and has had no attacks during the two years."

- Some said they were still healed as a result of Woodworth's prayers in previous meetings in Des Moines.

In recent years I received a letter from an 80-year-old woman who told about a healing during the Ottumwa meeting—of which Woodworth possibly never learned. Leone Piper wrote that her father was totally paralyzed, suffering with big bed sores on his back, and with the doctor's prediction that he would die within two weeks. But that's when Mrs. Piper's mother heard about the Ottumwa meetings. She placed Fred Attrill on a stretcher and caught a train from near their home, north of Sioux City. "After prayer, he could move a finger," Mrs. Piper wrote in 2000. "And then gradually was totally healed." Mrs. Piper, who was 2 years old when her father was healed, added, "He lived another 30 years. Praise God!"[12]

Meanwhile, back home in Indiana, Woodworth's assistants conducted a revival in the same Pentecostal fashion. Believing a tent set the stage for revival, the church set up for a series of meetings and invited Evangelist Thos. O'Reilly to take charge. Reports of conversions and healings must have reassured Woodworth that the home church was in good hands.

But for the incident involving the injury and death of four-year-old Eldon Stambaugh, the Ottumwa meeting in Woodworth's last hurrah revival tour would have been almost perfect.

H. R. Stambaugh and his family lived on a farm near Vermont, Illinois, some 50 miles southwest of Peoria. Their son Eldon had the misfortune of getting his hand crushed by a rope in a pulley. Then, two days after the accident, the boy developed lockjaw.

Being deeply religious and with strong belief in divine healing, the Stambaughs chose to pray and trust God rather than seek medical help for their son. Others in the area prayed, too, but in the words of Mrs. Stambaugh, "There wasn't enough power at home," so they brought the boy to Ottumwa for Woodworth's prayers.[13]

Woodworth did pray for the boy. But when she learned that the parents had not taken the boy to doctors, she advised them to seek medical help immediately. By this time, a week had passed since the accident. The Stambaughs apparently rejected Woodworth's counsel and remained in their tent set up in the park.

Somehow a Wappelo County judge heard about Eldon Stambaugh's condition and immediately ordered Sheriff George H. Giltner to take the now feverish boy from Stambaugh's tent and admit him to Ottumwa's St. Joseph Hospital. Stambaugh disagreed with the order, but did permit the sheriff to take the boy out of his custody. If his 4-year-old son died, he threatened the law officer that he would pay for it: "You can persecute us in this world, but you can not in the next."[14]

Tragically, the next day Eldon Stambaugh died of lockjaw, and his parents were charged with manslaughter.[15]

The Stambaugh case brought up a sticky question concerning total dependence on prayer and faith for healing. Fortunately for Woodworth and the other leaders in Ottumwa, they had advised the parents to seek medical help for the boy. Although Woodworth prayed for the sick during the biggest part of her over-45-year ministry, she did not rule out medical help, as evidenced by an interview she had with an Atlanta *Journal* reporter in 1914 regarding her ailing husband. "Yes, I've had doctors see him. He takes medicine," she replied. "I don't tell people not to see doctors, you know; but I do tell them, when doctors have failed to cure them: 'Come to the Lord.'"[16]

She did not rule out medical help, but she often expressed the view that believers who are not healed remain sick because their faith is weak—the position she took in her husband's case.

As the Ottumwa meetings came to a close, Woodworth was anxious to put the unfortunate Stambaugh case behind her and set her sights on neighboring Kansas—the cradle for the modern Pentecostal movement. She counted many friends in the state and had conducted numerous revivals here, including the Topeka campaign in 1915, when police stormed in and broke up the meeting (see chapter 11).

Now in 1922, she bypassed Topeka to fill an engagement at the annual Woodston Camp Meeting, some 40 miles north of Hays, where 1,500 people gathered in a tent, hoping and praying that God would meet with them under the trees.

They were not disappointed. Neither was Woodworth.

One report from Woodston stated that some 40 people were converted and another 50 received the Pentecostal baptism. "The Spirit fell in torrents, the Spirit-filled praises and shouts of glory sounded like the voice of many waters."[17] Others reported that they were healed of physical ailments ranging from dropsy to goiters. And the crowd could hardly believe that Woodworth had just celebrated her 78th birthday as they listened to her preach twice daily during the hot month of August.

James Musgrove, an area young man who was an Army veteran and well known for his drunkenness, saw something at the Woodston meeting from which he would never get away. His mother was a godly woman, supported the local Pentecostal church, and looked forward to the annual camp meetings. One of her prayers for the 1922 meeting was that James would surrender his life to God. But James liked his liquor and had little interest in spiritual matters.

That is, until he saw Woodworth pray for a man who was swollen way out of proportion with dropsy, a disease that causes a retention of an abnormal amount of body fluids.

The ailing man was wearing size 54 overalls, much too big for his normal size. As James Musgrove watched Woodworth lay her hands on him and pray, he could hardly believe his eyes. The overalls suddenly loosened around the man's legs.

Somehow Mrs. Musgrove's prayers were beginning to take an effect on her son. And even though James walked out of the 1922 camp unconverted, that one healing had a profound effect on his life, which helped bring about his conversion later.[18]

Several ministers from non-Pentecostal denominations attended the Woodston meetings because of their interest in what Woodworth believed was nothing less than the Acts 2 baptism in the Holy Spirit. Woodworth and other Pentecostals were happy to explain the Scriptures and pray with them. Among the ministers in attendance were a Methodist, a Presbyterian, a United Brethren, and a Free Methodist.

One of these ministers was drawn to the meetings after reading Woodworth's *Signs and Wonders*, which by 1922 had been on the market for six years. "He would watch the sick as they were prayed for," August Feick wrote, "and looked on in amazement as they touched Jesus by faith." The minister returned to his Nebraska church and wrote that he had decided not to mention the Woodston experiences, because "my people do not believe that way." To avoid confusion, he chose a text, which would steer him away from what would be a radical experience. He wrote, "But when I came before my congregation, before I knew what I was doing, I found myself preaching from a different text." He told the congregation what had happened to him the previous week and then worried that he had gotten himself in trouble. He could relax. "My people came to me from all sides," he added, "and wanted to hear more about Pentecost."[19]

A missionary couple who had served in China attended the meetings with a desire to hear someone—who did not know Chinese—speak the dialect, which they understood. They said they heard it at Woodston: "A man who had been seeking his baptism for over seven years and had just received it, was in the meeting happy as a new born babe. While the whole audience was praising God with uplifted hands, this man kept repeating in perfect Chinese, 'Open thy mouth, open thy mouth, open thy mouth!'"[20]

The missionaries, and others who heard the story later, went away more than ever convinced that the Pentecostal experience of the 1st century was being repeated in the 20th in an obscure place under the trees near Woodston, Kansas.

But like all good things, the Woodston meeting came to a close. Woodworth and her workers packed their bags, said their last good-byes to the believers, and made their way to the train station.[21]

It had been a great spring and summer, but as Woodworth boarded the train, she turned her back on the West for the final time. She was almost at the end of the sawdust trail, and she believed that this trail connected with the golden streets of heaven of which she often talked and for which she urged others to prepare.

If Woodworth suspected the spring and summer campaign would be her last hurrah—the last of the old time itinerations that had established her place in American church history beginning in the 1880s—she would never admit it, at least not now. She had been predicting the Lord would come in her lifetime, and she wasn't ready just yet to go any other way.[22]

ENDNOTES

1.   Woodworth-Etter, *Spirit filled Sermons*, p. 158.

2.   Feick, *Life and Testimony of Mrs. M. B. Woodworth-Etter*, p. 74. The sponsoring church was new and had about 50 members.

3.   Ibid.

4.   Ibid, by C. W. Harned.

5.   Woodworth-Etter, *Spirit filled Sermons* p. 158.

6.   F. A. Hale, "Woodworth-Etter Meeting, Fort Worth, Texas," *Pentecostal Evangel*, July 22, 1922, p.

7.   From Sikeston *Daily Herald* as quoted in *Life and Testimony* of M. B. Woodworth-Etter, p. 76. The Sikeston *Standard* also published reports of the meetings, June 20 and 22; July 4 and 6, 1922. However, the very positive and subjective June 20 story, "Pentecostal Revival,"—which in tone resembles Luke's writing in the Book of Acts—appears to have been written by one of Woodworth's staff members rather than a newspaper reporter. August Feick quotes a long positive letter to the *Standard* editor from the July 4 edition, in his *Life and Testimony*, pages 76-77, written by Evangelist G. R. Aubrey, Evansville, Ind.

8.   John 5:6.

9.   My taped interview with Aaron A. Wilson, Aug. 4, 1978, Flower Pentecostal Heritage Center, tape no. 716. Wilson never had another opportunity to hear Woodworth preach, but she did give him a copy of one of her books that encouraged him in his efforts at Puxico. Wilson later pastored in Kansas City for more than 30 years and served as an Assemblies of God executive presbyter. He was one of the speakers at the funeral service for

another well known Pentecostal evangelist, Dr. Charles S. Price. Wilson told me he never heard anyone criticize Woodworth and her ministry and described her as having no showmanship: "She was just the most humble little thing I ever saw in my life." In Sept. 1979, I corresponded with retired pastor and missionary Henry B. Garlock who compared the three best-known women evangelists of the 20th century: "Aimee McPherson, Kathryn Kuhlman were, to my way of thinking, more like theatrical performers; Mrs. Woodworth was not showy at all, no fancy clothes, no spectacular gimmicks. In those early days no one would have tolerated anything that smacked of entertainment."

10. *The Iowa Latter Rain Evangel*, Sept. 1922, p. 6. The local chairman of the Ottumwa meeting was Joe Darner, who corresponded with me in 1978, providing a poster which was used to advertise the meetings. In 1984, I interviewed him at his home in Ottumwa (tape at Flower Pentecostal Heritage Center, tape nos. 541-42). Two local pastors, A. D. McClure and Lottie Peters, assisted in the meetings. Evangelist Nellie Cox conducted the morning services. The meetings were conducted in a grove on West Park Street in a new tent seating 2,000. Thirty-five tents for campers were also set up.

11. Ottumwa *Courier*, July 26, 1922. The August 2, 1922, *Courier* estimated Woodworth's closing crowd on July 30 as 1,800; local chairman Joe Darner estimated "at least 2,500" attended the closing service, according to the report in *Life and Testimony*, p. 78.

12. "Father Healed in 1922 Meeting," Leone Piper. *Assemblies of God Heritage*, summer 2000, p. 28.

13. Ottumwa *Courier*, July 17 , 1922. Mrs. Stambaugh made this comment at the inquest conducted in Ottumwa. Witnesses called to testify at the inquest included the parents, Joe Darner, and Woodworth.

14. Ibid., July 14 , 1922.

15. Ibid., July 15, 19, 1922. In answer to my query, Mrs. Osie V. Leonard, clerk of Wapello District Court, stated that the court

had no record of a trial held in Ottumwa (letter, Nov. 17, 1981). The charges were dropped against the Stambaughs, according to a relative in 1982.

16. Atlanta *Journal*, April 13, 1914. This position seems to contradict Woodworth's views in her book *Questions and Answers on Divine Healing*. However, as noted in Chapter 10, evidence shows the bulk of *Questions and Answers* was borrowed from another author. The Stambaugh case was not reported in religious publications nor in August Feick's *Life and Testimony*. Evidently the writers believed such reporting would be counterproductive to faith in God's ability and willingness to heal the sick—still a common practice among healing evangelists in the 21st century.

17. S. H. Patterson and Fred Vogler, "The District Council Camp Meeting," *Pentecostal Evangel*, Sept. 30, 1922, p. 11.

18. James Musgrove's daughter, Leota Morar, related this story to me, Jan. 28, 1982. Musgrove's son Derald served as the superintendent of the Kansas District of the Assemblies of God. S. H. Patterson and Fred Vogler, in their report to the *Pentecostal Evangel*, Sept. 30, 1922, stated that a man was brought in on a cot who was suffering with dropsy and that the day after he received prayer, the swelling disappeared. It is possible that this is the dropsy patient Musgrove saw.

19. August Feick, "Camp Meeting," by August Feick, *Pentecostal Evangel*, Oct. 14, 1922, p. 29. Unfortunately, no name is given for this Evangelical minister from Nebraska to permit follow-up.

20. *Life and Testimony*, p. 85. Although this report does not give the names of the missionaries, the Sept. 30, 1922 report above in the *Pentecostal Evangel* stated that a missionary couple to China, the Rev. and Mrs. L. M. Anglin, attended the meetings and "gave such stirring, Spirit-filled messages that they created a sweet and keen interest for the foreign work."

21. Woodworth made one stop between Woodston and Indianapolis. She conducted a five-day campaign in Kansas City, Kansas, for Pastor Henry Hoar who had been healed in an

earlier Woodworth meeting in Sioux City, Iowa. A photograph of the Kansas City meetings shows a weary looking Woodworth on the tent platform, posing with other ministers and what appears to be a choir.

22. Woodworth would go to Evansville, Indiana, for a two-week meeting in Nov. and Dec. 1922. Then in 1923, the only prolonged meetings outside of Indianapolis were in Cincinnati, May; Wynnburg, Tenn., Sept.; and Louisville, Oct., for a total of seven weeks. In Jan.1924 she conducted her last out-of-town revival in Toledo, Ohio.

CHAPTER 15

Falling Shadows and a Woman's Legacy

"For years I have been longing to meet Sister Woodworth, and have been talking about it more in recent months. I have longed to hear her preach and be at her meetings … Tomorrow Mrs. Woodworth's tabernacle will be open and I will have the desire of my heart. Glory!"
—Aimee Semple McPherson, 1918[1]

As the shadows lengthened for Maria B. Woodworth-Etter, and she passed her 80th birthday in July 1924, we can almost hear her intercessory prayer—asking God for more strength and just a few more good years. Just as she had rationalized in the past, she must have honestly believed a great revival would come if she could have only a few more good years. The people at the Tabernacle needed her. The people out on the road needed her.

In 1914, God answered that prayer with healing and strength. But now in 1924, there would be no new lease on life. There would be no ten years more for Woodworth. Not even one. Others were about to claim her legacy.

The Woodworth-Etter legacy would include very little material substance. She began her life in poverty, and when she died on September 16, 1924, she had accumulated very little material wealth. But despite the lack of the good things in this life, friends and acquaintances across the country would argue that the Woodworth-Etter legacy was rich in something more enduring than gold, silver, precious stones, or real estate. The lives she touched and influenced on the sawdust trail from the early 1880s to 1924 could never be counted or weighed by our high tech computers. And these lives in turn touched and are touching countless others, a process that continues to multiply.

Touching lives, that seemed to be Woodworth's greatest ministry. And when one touches people with love and concern, it's pretty hard to measure that kind of contribution. You know it's there, but visible results are something like only the tip of an iceberg.

And what she did for women is the biggest hidden iceberg of all.

Men held a strangle-hold on the 19th century pulpit, and few women could break that grip. Society dictated that women belonged in the home. Churches agreed and added their own interpretation of Scripture that forbade a woman to usurp authority over men. Preaching, in their thinking, did just that.

A strong voice for fundamentalism, and against women in the pulpit, John R. Rice, wrote, "Feminism in the churches is a blight that has grieved God." Rice, who laid out his tirade against women in *Bobbed Hair, Bossy Wives, and Women Preachers*, added, "I have no doubt that millions will go to hell because of the unscriptural practice of women preachers."[2]

The restrictions against women preachers was built into the infrastructure of the church. And Rice in the 20th century, and others in the 19th, were constant reminders that the Kingdom would be better served if women were listening to sermons rather than trying to preach them.

Frances Willard's 19th century dream still seemed like a long shot for would-be women preachers, even when Maria Woodworth-Etter reached the end of her life in 1924. Willard predicted for women, "The time will come when these gates of Gospel Grace shall stand open night and day, while woman's heavenly ministries shall find their central home within God's house." Several 19th century publications supported women's rights in the ministry, including Phoebe Palmer's *Promise of the Father; Holiness Tracts Defending the Ministry of Women*; and Catherine Booth's *Female Ministry: or Woman's Rights to Preach the Gospel*. These writers acted as burrs under the saddle and helped prepare women and the church to accept the inevitable.

So, along came Maria Beulah Woodworth, a 35-year-old Ohio farmer's wife. In 1880 she accepted the challenge to break through the heavy restrictions men had used to protect the pulpit as their own domain. More than a century later she is still a role model of the female salvation–healing enthusiasts who dream of hitting the big time as itinerant and television evangelists—or for liberty to simply speak to a group when men are present.

In addition to Woodworth, the two best known women evangelists of the twentieth century were Aimee Semple McPherson and Kathryn Kuhlman. And it is safe to say that, in many respects, Aimee and Kathryn owed at least some of their success to one woman who gained national respect for women in the pulpit—Maria B. Woodworth-Etter.

Despite the fact that she was a role model for McPherson and Kuhlman, Woodworth met only one of her successors. And that was only once when she and McPherson met briefly in 1918.[3] The setting for that historic meeting was in the Tabernacle shortly after it was built and during the influenza epidemic. Aimee was on a trip of destiny, passing through Indianapolis from her home on the East Coast. It was a trip that would lead her to California, where her name would shortly after be identified as the glamorous young woman evangelist and founder of Angelus Temple and the International Church of the Foursquare Gospel.

Aimee's new seven-passenger Oldsmobile, the "Gospel Car," carried the 28-year-old evangelist, her mother, her stenographer, and her two children.[4] As they neared Indianapolis, Aimee was concerned that the influenza epidemic would prevent them from attending one of Woodworth's church services. She wrote an entry in her diary, which was later published in her book *This Is That*: "For years I have been longing to meet Sister Woodworth, and have been talking about it more in recent months. I have longed to hear her preach and be at her meetings." She added, "Tomorrow Mrs. Woodworth's tabernacle will be open, and I will have the desire of my heart. Glory!"[5]

Aimee prayed and believed God for everything, not the least of which was being able to see Woodworth and being in her service. Praising God in her diary, she called the city officials' decision to lift the ban a "marvelous thing."[6] The next day she visited with the 74-year-old Woodworth, and then she attended a meeting in the Tabernacle that night, adding an entry to her diary regarding their meeting: "We rejoiced and praised the Lord together. The power of God fell; even though there were only a very few at the meeting, the Lord was there showering His blessings upon us."[7]

It is obvious that Aimee respected Woodworth and appreciated the trail of tears and victories she had blazed for women to enter the ministry—not only as missionaries and Sunday school teachers, but also as evangelists and pastors—the path Aime Semple McPherson now walked.

If Woodworth had a mantle to pass, no doubt this young woman who visited with her on October 31, 1918, took a good look at it and dreamed of the not-too-distant future when she too would be as well-known. Aimee Semple McPherson must have thought about that the next day as they headed the big Gospel Car toward the west and her place of destiny.

Did Woodworth accept Aimee as having an authentic Pentecostal ministry and one who could pick up her mantle? Would Aimee's separation from Harold McPherson affect her ministry? I have uncovered nothing in print concerning their relationship except for the one meeting in Indianapolis in 1918. However, I talked with Bertha Schneider, Detroit, Michigan, in 1981. Mrs. Schneider traveled with Woodworth, and, on one occasion, Woodworth and Aimee were in the same city.

Members of Woodworth's party attended one of Aimee's services on their night off, but Woodworth chose not to attend. Mrs. Schneider said Woodworth expressed concern about the direction Aimee's ministry was going with theatrical performances and other popular attractions.

The legendary English evangelist, Smith Wigglesworth, also came under Woodworth's influence according to a man who heard them both on different occasions. Carl M. O'Guin believes Wigglesworth was in some respects one of Woodworth's disciples. "His motto," O'Guin recalled, "was, 'I'm not dealing with you, but the devil in you.'" O'Guin added that he is certain Wigglesworth picked up that motto from Woodworth.[8]

Those who study the Pentecostal movement or heard Woodworth would probably agree with O'Guin when he defined Woodworth's role: "Sister Woodworth was surely a chosen vessel of the Lord. She served her day and generation and was something of a John the Baptist to the great Pentecostal outpouring of our time."[9]

Maria B. Woodworth-Etter's most visible legacy can be traced through the Thomas Paino, Sr., family. It was his conversion in the old Tabernacle in 1919 that started a chain of events, which today is an outstanding legacy in itself.

Overlooking Interstate 465, at 47 Beachway Drive in Indianapolis, is the beautiful and spacious Lakeview Christian Center, the home for 2,000 worshipers. Woodworth never saw this complex, because it wasn't constructed until 1969, but it is an outgrowth of the Tabernacle she founded in 1918. She planted the seed, and one of her converts, Thomas Paino, Sr., and his descendants watered and nurtured that seed until today. It has grown into a mighty redwood.[10]

Whenever members of the Woodworth-Etter Tabernacle era, few in number today, look at the multifaceted Lakeview complex, they are reminded that it is there for the glory of God and as a memorial to Thomas and Lyda Paino, and Maria B. Woodworth-Etter.

And the association continues. Thomas Paino, Jr. became co-pastor with his father in 1956 and later senior pastor, serving until 1994. (Ronald J. Bontrager succeeded Paino.) During the latter half of the 20th century, Thomas Paino Jr.'s leadership resulted in several new ministries: Lakeview Manor, a 184-bed convalescent center; Lakeview Christian Academy with an enrollment of 400; Lakeview Village, a 90-unit senior citizens' apartment complex; Lakeview Place, a 50-unit senior citizens' apartment complex, Summit Place West, a 60-unit assisted living facility, plus single dwelling units for senior citizens.

Annually, during the last 15 years of Thomas Paino, Jr.'s ministry, the church sponsored missions projects and missionaries around the world with an annual missions budget of a million dollars.

But Thomas Paino, Jr., is not the only family member who perpetuates the Woodworth-Etter and Paino legacies. Resulting from the conversion of Thomas Paino, Sr., three other Paino children pastored or co-pastored large churches.

In Fort Wayne, Indiana, everyone has heard of Paul E. Paino, founder of the huge Calvary Temple, which his son Paul Craig now pastors. Betty Jean Paino Johnson co-pastored with her husband, M. C. Johnson, another Calvary Temple, this one in Springfield, Illinois, of which their son Mark now is senior pastor. Edwina Paino Duncan and her husband Harold Duncan formerly pastored Century Assembly, Lodi, California.

Then there are third-generation Painos involved in various ministries. Lakeview Christian Center alone has produced more than 100 preachers. This most visible legacy through the Paino family continues to grow and reap rich dividends for the Kingdom of God every day.

A legacy should include family descendants. But one branch of Woodworth's family until 1975 hardly knew she existed. And then the discovery came almost by accident, simply because Tom Slevin had an interest in his family tree. Much to his surprise, Slevin learned that his great-great-great-grandmother, Maria B. Woodworth-Etter, had been a famous evangelist and founder of a church not too far from his home in Indiana. Slevin asked his mother about their famous ancestor, but Mary Slevin could give her son little help, because her mother and grandmother had told her nothing about Woodworth.

Tom Slevin would not give up that easily.

He read Woodworth's books religiously; and the more he read, the more he became interested in spiritual matters. In a short time, he was converted and became active in a local church. It wasn't long before the Slevins met a preacher who had known Woodworth personally. The preacher, Roscoe Russell, told the Slevin family more about Woodworth, but more important, they agreed, was that Russell pointed Mary Slevin to Woodworth's Lord and Savior.

Now Mary Slevin wanted to be baptized, and what better place could she find than the church her great-great-grandmother founded at Indianapolis in 1918! Thomas Paino, Jr., the pastor of Lakeview Christian Center at the time, honored Mary's request and baptized her in 1979.

Maria Woodworth-Etter died in 1924—long before Mary and Tom Slevin were born—but the rediscovered legacy has changed their lives. They are doing their part so that present and coming generations will know and learn to appreciate Woodworth's important family and spiritual legacy, and they won't have to wait until they are adults, as Mary and Tom did.[11]

For more than 45 years, Woodworth believed and preached the imminent return of Jesus Christ, that He would "rapture" the believers into heaven. Woodworth just knew it would happen in her lifetime. In her earlier years she was critically lumped with Seventh-Day Adventists and others who were setting dates on Christ's return, based on their own personal prophecies or their peculiar interpretations of the books of Daniel and Revelation. That kind of exercise embarrassed them and caused a lack of trust in other so-called "words" from the Lord.[12]

Although Woodworth eliminated the date setting in her eschatology in later years, she still made the Second Coming an important part of her preaching—so much so that people in her audiences could almost hear the trumpet sound and the graves bursting open as she preached.

But something took place on April 1, 1921, that gives the idea Woodworth was beginning to question whether or not she would live to see the Second Coming. On that day, three months short of her 76th birthday, she walked into an attorney's office and made out her last will and testament.[13]

She still hoped and believed the Second Coming would take place before her death. But, if it didn't, she wanted to make certain what little property she owned would be divided according to her wishes—not the wishes of a probate court.

Throughout life Woodworth gave away far more than she kept for herself. And in death few material possessions remained to divide. To her only living child, Lizzie C. Ormsby, Woodworth bequeathed $1,000. But Lizzie died the month before Woodworth's death and never collected anything except "money advancements," which the will stated had been made "at divers times."[14] Because of Lizzie's death, the $1,000 bequest was voided according to terms of the will, and this amount remained with the estate, to be used for "religious purposes."

Woodworth rewarded the faithful August Feick by appointing him executor of her estate and willing to him the remaining possessions, which included the Woodworth-Etter Tabernacle, personal property, her books, publications, and copyrights.[15] Woodworth's desire was that Feick and his successors would hold her estate "in trust for the use and purposes therein stated, namely: the support, maintenance and perpetuation of the work of the 'Woodworth-Etter Tabernacle' and generally for the advancement of the Christian religion."[16]

It seems extremely unfair and tragic that just before Woodworth's life ended, she would see the death of the last of her six children. But she had committed the lives of her other children to the Lord, and the 60-year-old Lizzie's death was according to the will of the Lord as far as she was concerned.

Woodworth had lost her other five children at early ages before she went into the ministry. And throughout her long ministry she could always count on her remaining daughter, Lizzie Ormsby, to stand with her in faith. When she had no other person to whom to turn, Lizzie was always there. That was in the past. Now even Lizzie was gone, the victim of a streetcar accident in Indianapolis, August 7, 1924.

At her daughter's funeral, Woodworth bravely stood at the Tabernacle pulpit and spoke about the "earthly house" that will be dissolved and replaced by a permanent body in heaven. Many times in this life, Woodworth told the mourners, "we have more thorns than roses."[17]

Then Woodworth, always the evangelist at heart, made a strong plea toward family members, telling them that she believed God had a purpose in Lizzie's sudden death. It was a call to the family, she reasoned, "Some children have thus far not taken heed; we should heed the call. God is calling each one of us. May God help us all to be ready when we receive the summons to come up higher."[18]

Woodworth had not been well during that summer of 1924, and it wasn't certain she could even participate in her daughter's funeral. But she reached back, like she did when gangs tried to tear down her tent, and found her hidden strength. Not only did she preach the memorial service at the Tabernacle, but also when her daughter's casket was being lowered into the grave, she continued to encourage the family and friends to have faith in God, to look into the heavens and not into the grave.[19]

At the close of her graveside exhortation, the aged veteran of the sawdust trail summoned a little more strength and began to sing one of her favorite songs, a song that she had used from the Atlantic to the Pacific and one that had touched thousands of emotions during her passionate altar calls:

Oh, brother, seek a home
In that new bright world;
For I didn't come here
For to stay always,
Oh, brother seek a home in Heaven.

Little could Woodworth have known as she stood at her daughter's grave in the Memorial Park Cemetery that these same friends, and many others, would return the next month for her own funeral. But she had just sung, "For I didn't come here for to stay always." And those who supported her in this trial could see that the feeble soldier of the sawdust trail would not have long in this life unless she experienced another 1914-type miracle.

Just before Christmas 1923, Woodworth developed a bad case of gastritis and then dropsy. At times she was too weak to walk to the services at the Tabernacle next door. But that didn't stop her from getting there, because devoted friends would carry her. She even conducted a January revival in Toledo, Ohio.

When she celebrated her 80th birthday during the 1924 summer tent meeting, she determined that she would get there somehow. And she did. August Feick remembered the emotional scene as the friends affectionately carried her in: "As she entered the tent, the saints arose and praised God. The power fell wonderfully, her body was readily quickened so that she walked back and forth on the platform praising the Lord and exhorting the people to be ready to meet God."[20]

"Ready to meet God. Ready to meet God." Woodworth never let the people forget that text.

Her own meeting with her Maker happened on Tuesday, September 16, 1924, at the age of 80. The Ohio farm woman, who was called to preach 50 years earlier, had finally passed her torch to others. The little woman, who fought against unbelievable odds, had finished her course.

Woodworth's fame and exploits in earlier years had been emblazoned on the front pages of national newspapers. But, ironically, a new generation of editors knew nothing—or didn't care—of her evangelistic ministry on the sawdust trail. The *Indianapolis News* published only a simple and brief note of Woodworth's death and funeral on one of the back pages.[21]

Woodworth was pastor of the Tabernacle at her death, but the death certificate listed her occupation as evangelist, and rightfully so. She was an evangelist from the day God called her in Ohio until the day she died in Indianapolis. That was her calling. That was her passion for nearly 50 years.

And the marker in the Memorial Park Cemetery, which she shares with John and Lizzie Ormsby, reads:

EVANGELIST

M. B. WOODWORTH-ETTER

1844-1924

Thou Shewest Unto Thousands Lovingkindness[22]

A hyphen between her dates of birth and death is the smallest of the characters and says nothing of her amazing story. The tents on the sawdust trail are gone and forgotten. The difficult struggles of a woman doing what many claim only men are called to do have ceased. The sick and dying would no longer come to her for help. She had made her last emotional altar call. She had helped break the male domination of the pulpit and paved the way for other women—aspiring women preachers and teachers and missionaries, who would be called from other farms, other crossroads, other backwoods, other countries, and other cities.

When followers across the nation and around the world would hear of her coronation day, they would pause to thank God that Maria B. Woodworth-Etter came their way. The inscription on the cold marble monument probably sums it up best:

"Thou Shewest Unto Thousands Lovingkindness."

ENDNOTES

1. Aimee Semple McPherson, *This Is That* (Los Angeles: Echo Park Evangelistic Association, 1923), p. 149. Because of the tragic influenza epidemic, public buildings were closed. Authorities lifted the ban the day before McPherson arrived in Indianapolis.

2. John R. Rice, *Bobbed Hair, Bossy Wives, and Women Preachers* (Murfreesboro Tenn: Sword of the Lord, 1941), p. 59. Quoted in Ruth A Tucker and Walter Liefeld, *Daughters of the Church* (Grand Rapids: Zondervan Publishing House, 1987), p. 14.

3. One can find some interesting comparisons between McPherson and Woodworth. Both were born on farms; they were married as teenagers; their first husbands died; they continued using first husbands' names after they remarried: Woodworth-Etter and Semple McPherson; they became well known as evangelists before establishing their own churches; they were healed and practiced faith healing; they were Pentecostal; they established churches which they called tabernacles (Aimee's Angelus Temple was originally called Echo

Park Revival Tabernacle); they both died in September:
Woodworth, September 1924, and Aimee 20 years later in 1944;
and Aimee's death came in the year that some would remember
as the 100th anniversary of Woodworth's birth. In longevity,
Woodworth lived to be 80; Aimee, 54. The youngest member of
this evangelistic trio, Kathryn Kuhlman, reached the age of 68
(1908-76). Woodworth was closing her big St. Louis meeting in
October 1890, the month Aimee Kennedy was born on a small
farm near Ingersoll, Ontario, Canada. Woodworth was 46 at the
time and had been preaching for ten years. Kathryn Kuhlman
was also born on a farm, near Concordia, Missouri, in 1907.

4.   Aimee Semple McPherson, *The Story of My Life* (Waco,
Texas: Word Books, Inc., 1973), p. 102. When Mrs. McPherson
arrived in Los Angeles, she was invited to conduct meetings at
Victoria Hall, where a Pentecostal congregation was meeting.
The building would seat about 1,000, but it soon became too
small. The meetings were moved to the 3,500 seat Philharmonic
Auditorium. The campaign helped establish Aimee as an
effective evangelist among not only Pentecostals but also among
other evangelicals. Here in Los Angeles she would found
Angelus Temple, the International Church of the Foursquare
Gospel, and a Bible school.

5.   McPherson, *This Is That*, p. 149.

6.   Ibid. Edith Blumhofer wrote a definitive biography, on
Aimee Semple McPherson: Everybody's Sister; Daniel Mark
Epstein's popularly written biography, *Sister Aimee*, was
published in 1994.

7.   Ibid., p. 150.

8.   Carl M. O'Guin, letter to Thomas Slevin, June 2, 1980.
O'Guin heard Woodworth preach in 1915, just as he was
beginning his own ministry, and described her as "blunt spoken,
direct in what she said. Did not try to be smooth or diplomatic
in public relations." I found no evidence that Woodworth and
Wigglesworth ever met, but it is possible because Wigglesworth
visited this country several times. Wigglesworth conducted
services at the Tabernacle after Woodworth's death during the

winter of 1925.

9. Ibid.

10. Thomas and Lyda Paino began their pastorate at the Tabernacle in 1933. An arsonist destroyed the building in 1946, but Paino—doing much of the work himself—rebuilt from the ashes. Later the church purchased ground on Beachway Drive, and the 1946 building became the home of Westside Assembly of God.

11. Tom and Mary Slevin, interviews and correspondence with author. Tom Slevin has uncovered numerous newspaper stories reporting Woodworth's meetings dating back to the 1880s. They were compiled, along with many others at the Flower Pentecostal Heritage Center, in Roberts Liardon's *Maria Woodworth-Etter, The Complete Collection of Her Life Teachings* (Tulsa: Albury Publishing, 2000).

12. Perhaps Edgar Whisenant gave the best-known date setting prophecy in recent years with his *88 Reasons Why the Rapture Will Occur in 1988*. And Harold Camping, a Christian radio network owner in Oakland, predicted the Rapture would happen in Sept. 1994. Obviously, both had to explain why their prophecies failed.

13. Last Will and Testament of Maria Beulah Woodworth-Etter, Marion County Probate Court, Indianapolis, Indiana, No. 119862, probated Sept. 17, 1924.

14. Ibid., item four.

15. Ibid. item two. Roscoe Russell, who grew up in the Tabernacle, remembered that Woodworth's relatives contested the will, but the matter was settled out of court.

16. Ibid., item three. The net value of the estate was set at $11,648.38. Of this amount, August Feick received personal property valued at $710, and the Tabernacle and furnishings were valued at $10,929.38 (Inheritance Tax Report, Marion County Court, Estate No. 69 22745, Case No. 2852, March 21, 1925). Today's tax laws would prevent an individual receiving

non-profit property.

17. Feick, *Life and Testimony*, p. 118.

18. Ibid., p. 119.

19. Ibid.

20. Ibid., p. 122. Although Woodworth seldom preached during the latter months of her life, she wanted to be there to encourage the speakers and the crowd. And often she would deliver a short exhortation or offer prayer for the sick.

21. The *Indianapolis News*, Sept. 19. 1924. Earl W. Clark, who was married to Woodworth's granddaughter Beulah, conducted the funeral. The death certificate stated the cause of death as acute dilation of the heart (Indiana State Board of Health, Certificate of Death #28557).

22. Several Scripture references are engraved on an open Bible: Jeremiah 1:17 19; Revelation 1:7; 1 John 3:1, 2; Psalm 91; Mark 16:15 18; and 2 Timothy 4:7,8.

APPENDICES

"Women's Rights in the Gospel"

A Sermon by Maria Woodworth

A nd when the day of Pentecost was fully come, they were all with one accord in one place" (Acts 2:1). "And it shall come to pass in the last days, saith God, I will pour out of my Spirit upon all flesh; and your sons and your daughters shall prophesy, and your young men shall see visions, and your old men shall dream dreams" (Acts 2:17; Joel 2:28-29). "And suddenly there came a sound from heaven as of a rushing mighty wind, and it filled all the house where they were sitting. And there appeared unto them cloven tongues like as of fire, and it sat upon each of them. And they were all filled with the Holy Ghost, and began to speak with other tongues, as the Spirit gave them utterance" (Acts 2:2-4).

There was wonderful excitement; the people came rushing in great multitudes from the city to see what was the matter. They saw these men and women, with their faces shining with the glory of God, all preaching at once; all anxious to tell what God had done for them and a dying world. Conviction went like daggers to their hearts. And, just as it is today, when the power of God is manifest, instead of yielding, they cried out, "Too much excitement," and began to fight against God; they said, "These people are mad, are drunken with new wine," and mocked them.

Peter gets up to defend the cause of Christ. He refers to Joel 2:28-29. "And it shall come to pass in the last days, saith God, I would pour out of my Spirit upon all flesh; and your sons and your daughters shall prophesy, and your young men shall see visions, and your old men shall dream dreams, and on my servants and on my handmaidens I will pour out in those days of my Spirit; and they shall prophesy" (Acts 2:17-18) ... Paul speaks as if it were very common for women to preach and prophesy.

"Every woman that prayeth or prophesieth with her head uncovered dishonoreth her head" (1 Cor. 11:5). "The same man had four daughters, virgins, which did prophesy" (Acts 21:9; Eph. 4:11).

Paul worked with the women in the Gospel more than any of the Apostles; Priscilla and Phebe traveled with Paul preaching and building up the churches (Acts 18:2-18, 26; Romans 16).

He and Phebe had been holding revivals together; now she is called to the city of Rome; Paul cannot go with her, but he is very careful of her reputation, and that she is treated with respect; he writes a letter of recommendation: "I commend unto you Phebe, our sister, which is a servant of the church (which signifies a minister of the church) at Cenchrea, that ye receive her in the Lord as becometh saints and that ye assist her in whatsoever business she has need of you, for she has been a succourer of many and of myself also" (Rom. 16:1).

This shows that she had authority to do business in the churches and that she had been successful in winning souls to Christ. He is not ashamed to say she had encouraged him; he speaks in the highest praise of a number of sisters who had been faithful workers in the work of the Lord, who had risked their lives in the effort to save souls, and not he alone, but all the churches of the Gentiles sent their thanks.

Paul said, "Let your women keep silent in the churches." So saith the law. We are not under law but under grace. "And learn of their husbands at home." What will those do who have no husbands? Do you suppose they will remain in ignorance and be lost? And if some women had to depend on their husbands for knowledge, they would die in ignorance.

Paul referred to contentions in the churches. Paul says you had better not marry. How many agree with Paul? How many obey? He is referring to contentions in the churches, that it is a shame to bring up questions and have jangling in the house of God. He writes to the brethren, "I hear that there be divisions among you, and I partly believe it" (1 Cor. 11:18).

"Help those women which labored with me in the Gospel, with Clement also, and with other my fellow laborers whose names are in the book of life" (Phil. 4:3). There were also several women who were prophetesses (Luke 2:36; 2 Kings 22:13-15). Huldah, the prophetess, the wife of Shallum, dwelt in Jerusalem, in the college, and they communed with her, and she said unto them, "Thus saith the Lord God of Israel."

[Names other women in the Bible, such as Miriam, Deborah, Esther.]

Paul says there is no difference, but that male and female are one in Christ Jesus (Gal. 3:28). Let us take Jesus for our pattern and example and see no man, save Jesus only.

Women were called and commissioned by the Angel sent from Heaven, and by the Lord Jesus Christ, to preach the Gospel (Matt. 28:5-10).

The cowardly disciples had forsaken the Savior and fled. Peter denied the Savior and swore he never knew him, but many women followed him and stood by the cross, and went to the sepulchre and saw the body laid away; the great stone was rolled against the door (Matt. 27:55-61). These women went home and brokenhearted, but they returned to pay a last tribute to their dear friend. They spent the night in preparing spices to embalm the body of their Lord. They came to the sepulchre as it was coming day. The grave was empty. The Lord was not there. As they stood weeping two Angels stood by them, and said: "Fear not ye ... And go quickly, and tell his disciples that he is risen from the dead."

Observe the wonderful mission that Jesus had intrusted to these weak women to preach the first resurrection sermon; to risk their lives in gathering together the followers of Christ, where the wonderful meeting was to be held. But just like many today, they would not believe. Peter said, "I will not believe your report." Thomas said, "I will not believe except I see the prints in his hands and feet."

In the midst of all these discouragements they went on with the work and had grand success. Jesus met with and preached to them; they were all made to rejoice. They were called by Angels, and the Lord from glory, and sent to preach the Gospel. The names of four women were given and there were many others.

God is calling the Marys and the Marthas today all over our land to work in various places in the vineyard of the Lord; God grant that they may respond and say, "Lord, here am I; send me."

"I will pour out in the last days of my Spirit"; that refers in a special manner to these last days in which we are now living. God is promising great blessings and power to qualify His handmaidens for the last great harvest just before the notable day of the Lord comes. We must first be baptized into Christ by the one Spirit, that is to be born of the Spirit; then we ought to be anointed with power and wisdom. The Spirit ought to be poured out like oil on our heads, to give us knowledge of the deep things of God. The Lord says we shall prophesy.

Paul says desire spiritual gifts, but rather that ye may prophesy (1 Cor. 14:1). It makes no difference how many gifts we have, if we have not the gift of talking, and teaching, it will not avail us much. The Lord has promised this greatest gift to his handmaidens, and daughters. In the third verse, Paul explains what it is to prophesy.

[Tells of the Samaritan woman Jesus spoke to at Jacob's well.]

She left her pitcher and took the well of salvation with her, and running to the city, went up one street and down another, with her face shining with the glory of God. Perhaps the people would have scorned her an hour before; now they saw and felt the change. "Look what he has done for me. He will do the same for you."

The people left their stores, their places of business, left their parlors and kitchens, and came out in great multitudes to see the Savior of the world. There was a great revival there at the well. Jesus went into the city and stayed two days. The wave of salvation went on and on. This was the result of one sermon by a weak woman.

My dear sister in Christ, as you hear these words may the Spirit of God come upon you, and make you willing to do the work the Lord has assigned to you. It is hightime for women to let their lights shine; to bring out their talents that have been hidden away rusting, and use them for the glory of God, and do with their might what their hands find to do, trusting God for strength, who has said, "I will never leave you."

Oh, the fields are white, for the harvest is great and ripe, and it is ready for the Gospel sickle; oh, where are the laborers to gather the golden grain into the Master's garner?

The world is dying, the grave is filling, hell is boasting; it will all be over soon.

God left the glorious work of saving souls in the hands of the church. What is the church composed of? Men, women and children. We are putting up a building of God; everyone has a part in this building ... Whatever we do for Jesus, with the right motive, is precious in his sight.

We are sons and daughters of the most high God. Should we not honor our high calling and do all we can to save those who sit in the valley and shadow of death?

*Published in Woodworth-Etter, *Signs and Wonders*, pp. 210-16. Excerpted here.

"Woodworth's Wand"

MOST MYSTERIOUSLY MOVING MASSES MAKING

WICKED WILDLY WEEP, WRETCHED WIERDLY WAIL

SKEPTICS STAND SILENT; SCORNING, SCOFFING, SNEERING

AMAZEMENT! AWE! ASTONISHMENT! AMUSEMENT! APATHY!

TWENTY THOUSAND PEOPLE AT THE WOODWORTH REVIVAL MEETING

Some Notes Concerning a Wonderful Gathering—How They Do and What They Do

Muncie Daily News. Sept. 21, 1885. (Paragraph breaks are added for ease in reading. The spelling and grammar errors remain as published.)

> *"The devil is mad And I am glad.*
> *Oh my soul! Praise the Lord! Glory to God!"*

The above quoted lines, chanted hundreds of times by thousands of people, were heard by twenty thousand people gathered in a small grove in the edge of Madison County yesterday. Laying aside the immensity of the assemblage there was perhaps never before such a gathering of people as was gathered together yesterday to hear and see Mrs. Woodworth, the great revivalist, who has achieved considerable local notoriety. On divers occasions in this portion of the State there has been as large and larger assemblies of people, but never before was one so singular and peculiar in its noisy demonstrations, and manifestations.

It was similar to a circus crowd with its bustling curious throng of motely curious pleasure seekers; it might be likened to a grand rally gathering with its enthusiastic leaders and boisterous demonstrations; it was like a vast audience listening to a great speaker on momentous questions, with its quiet respectful attention; it looked some like a big temperance picnic and might possibly remind one of church. The wonderful demonstrations of the meeting as we will note later, affected the audience in so many different ways as to make everything seem exceedingly singular, the crowd was simply immense and impossible to estimate.

The tent where the meetings were held is in a ten acre grove thirteen miles northwest of Muncie. Of this grove, fully half of it was so compactly filled with wagons that walking about among them was impossible, save by climbing over them. A large wood to the north had fully as many wagons, and contiguous fields were liberally occupied. About the speaking stand in the afternoon there was a dense mass of people, reaching many rods in several directions, and more than that many were assembled in the adjoining places. Not caring to submit our own estimate, we supply several "old inhabitants" figures which were 20, 000. Now we will attempt to give a faint idea of Mrs. Woodworth's MODUS OPERANDI as observed and noted by the writer. There was in the woods a tent about forty feet by sixty feet, in the center of which was a platform raised about two feet, and upon this two chairs, upon which the woman stood. These chairs were held by two men, so there would be no danger of her toppling off—chairs and all. Around this was rude benches extending from the pulpit or altar about fifteen feet on two sides. Upon these benches were the converts, contrite and submissive, as they said, before the power of the Holy Ghost. Upon these chairs in the centre, stood Mrs. Woodworth, a handsome, somewhat stately lady, who looks to be on the sunny side of forty. She was dressed in black, sparingly trimmed with black lace, rather short sleeves, and a white neckdress. Her hair was braided, dressed high on her head and confined with a conspicuous, old-fashioned tortoise shell black comb. She was commencing her discourse as the writer elbowed himself up to the edge of the stand. She evidently understands human nature thoroughly, and seems to move her people more by the fear of hell than by the love of God. She jerks each sentence out with little reference to the previous or following one. Talks, rapid, fluent, nervously and disconnectedly on many subjects. She tells her hearers that the Holy Ghost is about knocking at the heart of each one and may never come again, and if they do not heed its call he may be angered and they will be damned irrevocably and unredeemably.

After one of these passionate, wild, wierd appeals, their weeping and wailing among the converts, piteous supplications from the affected unconverted, and joyful, jubilant exclamations from the enthusiastic followers of the revivalist. When this spiritual manifestation had subsided, she continued her talk in a slightly different strain, always suiting her words to the thoughts, doubts, and fears of her hearers. By observing her listeners she seemed to read with an exquisite nicety what was passing in their minds, and know how to control the mind of the larger portion of the audience as one. After she had finished her talk, which at times was singularly eloquent, she commenced singing; the audience joined in with a noise that was deafening and appalling. The very tent seemed to swell and collapse as the thundering manifestation would grandly increase in volume, transfixing one with mute awe, astounded and dumbfounded. Decreasing in volume in regular cadences, the noise would slowly die away, leaving oppressively near yet seemingly distant a low moaning, muttering, weird, supernatural and unearthly, sending a convulsive shudder over the most passive and indifferent, and almost unconsciously your lips would move as if to utter the same praises. At the same time Mrs. Woodworth had risen to a dread and awful majestic grandeur. Her lips moved, but she said nothing. Throwing her head back she gazed upward with a reverential and earnest, though frightful and terrible, yet fascinating, and with an alluring charm her hands supplicantly and helplessly extended in the direction of her gaze and her whole frame was quivering as though laboring under intense excitement. She controlled the audience in marvellous, miraculous and not easily accountable way.

She would majestically raise up to her fullest height and the manifestations of the audience would increase to terrible proportions, and then she would crouch low and couchant and serpentinely cringe away, as if from abject fear, the deafening voice would decrease to the low, moaning wail. The demonstrations decreased as the distance increased from her as though her violent agitations produced vibrations, which lost intensity with distance. The most violent crowded on the stage, jumped up and down, wrestled, shook hands, hallooed and pushed off the exhausted, and when worn out their places were filled with fresh converts.

One can not imagine the sight that confronted the writer, who stood on that platform and looked around at the indescribable confusion. Dozens lying around pale and unconscious, rigid and lifeless as though in death. Strong men shouting till they were hoarse, then falling down in a swoon. Women falling over benches and trampled under foot. Children crying and weeping as though their parents were dead. Aged women gesticulating and hysterically sobbing, as though their sons and support had been cruelly murdered. Men shouting with a devilish, unearthly laugh, jubilant as if the arch angel had been conquered.

Everyone was affected. The skeptic stood with folded arms and a smile of scorn. The grim stoic stood by with grim indifference illy expressed. The light hearted apathetic trembled with a smile of amusement and passed jocose remarks, which fear counterfeited with unreality, and the affected undecided were read [red] with terror. It affected people for rods and rods away. A big wagon load of people forty rods away were noticed, who heard the voice, stopped their team and commenced a wild demonstration of joy among themselves. People ran up and gathered around the wagon, and soon they were surrounded with a concourse of people having a little meeting of their own, with all its wildest characteristics. A man heard the "hallelujah," jumped up and hollowed "Glory to God!" and fell down in a trance, from which he did not wake for hours. And while the subject is broached we will say a word concerning these.

A person when they "get em" gets stiff. One fellow "got stiff" during services and straightened upright and stood like a post with a man holding him up. As he attracted so much attention, and there was not enough room to lay him down, it took three men to break him at the back and double him up so he could be put on a seat. When in a trance their condition becomes highly abnormal, their pulse becomes slow, they get cold and look dead. Sometimes they lay that way for hours and even days. They "take lem" without the slightest of "provocation." It is a funny sight to see them stretched out in the tent and laying over the woods.

A BIG COLLECTION

In the afternoon yesterday the meeting was held on a raised platform in the open air, where Mrs. Woodworth stationed herself on one side with a woman beside her, who held the hat in which to put their "mite." For forty minutes the people passed in front of her two and three abreast, at the rate of fifty a minute, everyone shaking hands with her and throwing in money literally by the hatful. We truthfully say that the hat was emptied several times before the collection was finished. Several five-dollar bills were noted and but little less than quarters. We will not imperil our reputation for truth and veracity by giving an estimate of the amount taken in.

GRAND FINALE

We are done, dear reader. We have done our best to describe the meeting, and Mrs. Woodworth could have done no better than her best. We are afraid that our soul is lost. We have long pined for religion, but somehow could never work our mind to the proper condition. Yesterday we tried to get in at wholesale rates but failed, and we are convinced that the only thing we can do with religion is write about it and publish religious notices in the hope of getting a free pass *a la* R. H.

APPENDIX C

The Glory of the Lord

A Sermon by Maria Woodworth

A nd the glory of the Lord abode upon Mount Sinai; and the cloud covered it six days; and the seventh day he called unto Moses out of the midst of the cloud. And the sight of the glory of the Lord was like the devouring fire on the top of the mount in the eyes of the children of Israel" (Exod. 24:15,16).

We read with wonder the supernatural displays of God's power and glory, but how many comprehend that we, too, may behold them? The people seem to think that these manifestations were for the early followers. We do not find any such teachings in the word of God. Lord, help us to know that our God is the same forever. God would ever dwell with his people. He does not want to live apart from them. His delight and pleasure is to ever be with them. He would walk with them; and wherever the footsteps of God have been among his people he has left a beautiful pathway of light and glory.

This significant sermon is a reprint from *The Life, Work and Experience of Woodworth Beulah Woodworth* (pp. 432-441), published in 1894. It is significant because it documents Woodworth's Pentecostal preaching prior to the 20th century Pentecostal movement.

God delights to reveal his arm of power; he rejoices to show forth his glory. He maketh a way in the sea, and a path in the mighty deep. His glory is for his people. He wants to bestow it upon them. O, that his people should reject it! O, that he should come unto his own, and his own receive him not! God has ever desired to manifest himself unto his children. In the ancient days he made himself known in various manifestations of his power.

He descended upon Mount Sinai in fire and smoke, and a cloud of glory covered the mount; his voice was heard in the thunder; he revealed himself in the lightning; he went before Israel in a cloudy pillar by day, and hovered over them in a pillar of fire by night, and the glory of his presence was with them. In the apostolic days God revealed himself, through the blessed Holy Ghost, in many miraculous ways.

He came to Saul of Tarsus in the brightness of the noonday sun, and changed him from a bold persecutor to a bold preacher. He came to the amazed disciples upon the transfiguration mount, and the Old Dispensation and New held heavenly converse. He came upon the church with such magnifying power that she presented, not simply one of the phenomena, but the grand phenomena of history. In all these exhibitions of his power the people recognized the presence of God and gave him the glory.

That there came a time when there was an interruption of the communication of God with his people, was not due to God's plan. God has told the people that if they would hearken unto his voice he would give them counsel. But they apostatized, and God withdrew himself. God will never dwell with an apostate people, nor will his voice be heard in their midst. God never speaks in the heart where the whispers of Satan are heard. It is only the pure in heart who shall see the manifestations of God.

We are living in the last days, and the glorious times of the early Pentecost are for us. If, as in the days of Samuel, there could be a return of the "open vision" and the interrupted communication of God with his people restored, the great decline of the power of the church would be arrested. The Holy Ghost is no longer with us in primitive Pentecostal power. Instances of marked faith-power, of unction in preaching, of wondrous displays of the Holy Ghost, are painfully inconspicuous and exceptional. The church is merely a negative barrier in restraining the floods of wickedness, when she should be a positive, aggressive force in driving back evil. Sorrowfully we must acknowledge that the glory of the former days has departed.

Now, there is a reason why we do not see the wonderful displays of God's power among the people. There is a hindrance. The trouble with the people today is, that they believe that this power was for the early church only, and we have taken the views of our ancestors and abided by them. We have not tested God and met his conditions, and seen whether he would pour down his Spirit. We have not met the conditions, such as would ask God to display his power. We have believed that God has taken this power from the church; and when one does put forth the faith and believe these days may be for us now, such a one is called a crank, a hypnotic, etc.

The glory of God was withdrawn from the temple because they had abandoned him. He told them that so long as they would obey his laws he would be with them; but it was because they forsook God that he withdrew his presence from them.

The Lord is always ready to do his part. Though his true believers may be few, he will be to them a mighty host. "Fear not, thou worm Jacob, and ye men of Israel, and I will help thee," saith the Lord. God's people are in the minority.

Wherever God's people were engaged in warfare the numbers of the Lord were the smallest. But whenever the battle was fought in the strength of the Lord, then God fought the battles for them and delivered them. God will make the minority victorious when the fight is in the strength of the Lord.

The masses of people are not looking for signs and wonders to-day. They do not want to see them. The preaching of God is foolishness to them that believe not. We preach the Gospel as the Lord gives it to us. Bless God, his people obey the spirit, and where the spirit is they recognize it. Where you see these manifestations—the lame leap as an hart, the sick healed, people stricken down with the power, etc.—it is a visible sign of God's wonderful presence. Jesus said: "I will send you the Holy Ghost and he shall abide with you forever!

"But oh, how many of God's professed people despise the Holy Ghost! In many places where the people profess to follow God the Holy Ghost has been driven out; and there are thousands to whom the Holy Ghost has come for the last time. We are not going to stay here very long. We are bound for judgment, and the time has come for us to get out from the traditions of men. The Holy Ghost is our leader and teacher. We must depend upon him for our teachings.

The glory of the Lord covered the mountain for those six days; and the people saw it and believed it. They saw the visible power of God. Do we look for the visible power in our midst today? Moses lived with God forty days and forty nights, shut up with God without nourishment. Now, you don't believe that. I believe it. I believe the whole Bible. God help us to believe the whole Bible or throw it away.

Now, they had to do something. They made a consecration; repented of their sins and shortcomings; they made a new consecration to God, and then they were ready for duty, and then expected the glory and the visible signs and wonders.

It was just the same at the time of Pentecost. The one hundred and twenty came together, forsaking everything, and tarried in earnest prayer and consecration for ten days, waiting for the enduement of power to fit them for life's service. And they didn't wait in vain, for while they were yet praying the Holy Ghost came upon them in wondrous power, the city was shaken, and three thousand souls were converted in a single day.

If we were ready to meet God's conditions we would have the same results, and a mighty revival would break out that would shake the world, and thousands of souls would be saved. The displays of God's power on the day of Pentecost were only a sample of what God designed should follow all through the ages. Instead of looking back to Pentecost, let us always be expecting it to come, especially in these last days. God help us to get into line and come together as one man.

In the 19th chapter, God came again in the bright cloud. In the 14th verse, Moses came down from the mountain and the people washed their clothing. This was the emblem of purity. This was the sign of the inward cleansing. We must be sure we have a pure heart. We can never expect to have these visible manifestations of God unless we are children of God. The people were in a condition to meet God— clean bodies, clean garments. God help us to get the cleansing power.

The people trembled when they heard the sound of the trumpet; and the mountain quaked because the Lord descended into the mount. The people prayed for the power to be stayed. That's the way today. They were not right, some of them. And so it is now. People pray for these demonstrations of God to be stopped. They do not want a visible sign of God's presence. The cloud of glory hung over them. God help us to pray for the cloud of glory to hang over us. The cloud over them by night, that had the appearance of fire, and the pillar of cloud by day, were visible signs of God's presence with them.

I will turn to the 3rd chapter of 2nd Corinthians. I want the dear people to know why we preach the power and believe in these signs. [Reads portions of the chapter, with special reference to verses 3, 7, 8, 9 and 11.] "Forasmuch as ye are manifestly declared to be the epistle of Christ ministered by us, written not with ink, but with the Spirit of the living God; not in the tables of stone, but in the fleshly tables of the heart."

Oh, God, help us to know whom this means. The fleshly tables of our hearts. Praise God for the new covenant. We may now come within the veil, into the most holy place. The apostle wants us to understand that we can come so much nearer to God. He writes his law on the fleshly tables of our hearts. God wants us to be walking Bibles! He wants us to be a living ark, bearing about the glory of God! Our body is the temple. He lights our lamp and it becomes brighter.

Then we have the epistle written in our hearts. Bro. Paul says we have treasure in an earthen vessel: "But if the ministration of death, written and engraven in stones, was glorious, so that the children of Israel could not steadfastly behold the face of Moses for the glory of his countenance; which glory was to be done away: how shall not the ministration of the Spirit be rather glorious? For if the ministration of condenmation be glory, much more doth the ministration of righteousness exceed in glory. For if that which is done away is glorious, much more that which remaineth is glorious."

Well, if the glory of God was displayed in wonderful manner in the old dispensation, how much brighter should it burn in the temple of our bodies today. Bro. Paul says the letter killeth: it is the Spirit that giveth light. God gives us light today! God gives us light! Paul says the old was done away when the middle wall of the partition was broken down; but that which is more glorious has come to stay. Christ said: "I will send you the Comforter."

Those who have the courage to stand up and tell the truth will be persecuted. But we must go on and preach the truth; we've got no time to listen to the howling of devils. Let us boldly dare, like Hezekiah, to strike for a reformation! Let us purge the priesthood, the temple courts, our own hearts and lives, of every unclean and defiling thing, and bring all to the storehouse, putting God to the proof, whether he will not open the windows of heaven and pour us out a blessing, that there shall not be room enough to receive it. Whenever the beauty of holiness is found in God's temples, the shekinah will flood them with the glory of the Lord!

APPENDIX D

"Neglect Not the Gift That Is in Thee"

Instructions to Ministers and Christian Workers

A nd this Gospel of the kingdom shall be preached in all the world for a witness ... and then shall the end come" (Matt. 24:14). "The Holy Ghost said, Separate me Barnabas and Saul, for the work whereunto I have called them" (Acts 13:2). They had been called and were working, but now they were to be set apart in a special way. The Holy Ghost has to call you, qualify you. Jesus Christ has to send you forth.

"And when they had fasted and prayed, and laid their hands on them, they sent them away. So they, being sent forth by the Holy Ghost, departed" (Acts 13:3, 4).

Has God sent you? The Holy Ghost has to qualify you. Our laying on of hands would do no good unless the Holy

This exhortation is excerpted from a sermon Maria B. Woodworth-Etter preached at Chicago's Stone Church, July 17, 1913, and published in *The Latter Rain Evangel*, August, 1913, pp. 13-17. Following the sermon, Woodworth and others laid their hands on 70 "elders, evangelists, and helpers" and prayed for them. A. H. Argue, who took part in the Chicago meetings, said the meetings resulted in the "mightiest visitation from God of these latter days" (*The Latter Rain Evangel*, p. 3). For more on this meeting, see Chapter 9.

Ghost comes in to work mightily. The Holy Ghost said, "separate." These men had been called and chosen; chosen for the special work to which they had already been called.

Don't be puffed up by the miracles, don't get your eyes on them, but keep your eyes on Jesus. You are not saved by miracles. You are saved and kept by the power of God. The miracles are the works of the Holy Ghost. You will get a reward for the works of the Holy Ghost that are wrought through you; they are going to make your crown, but they will never save you. If a hundred thousand were healed through my prayer today, I could not pin my salvation to that. We are not saved by works, but through faith in Jesus, through living, constant faith and prayer. We are kept by the power of God. The works are thrown in and there will be a great reward for them; our crowns will be the brighter.

You must have the Spirit resting upon you if you are to do anything for God, either at home or abroad. You are not fit for work unless you have it, and those who serve at home must have it the same as those who go to China or Africa. God is not calling everyone to the foreign field, but God is calling everyone in some way. Many make the mistake of going out when God has not called, and many spend all their time running around to camp-meetings. Let us make every place a tent of meeting with the Lord and the Spirit may fall on us.... And if you are not called to the foreign field get to work in the place in which God does call you to labor.... The seventy that Christ sent out had power, and how much more should we have power now that Christ is glorified? So we are expected to do all these great things set forth in the last chapter of Mark.

Now in the twenty-fourth chapter of Matthew it says this "Gospel of the Kingdom shall be preached to all nations as a witness and then shall the end come." Friends, you and I cannot go out and preach as we used to do. Many sermons that God wonderfully blest in the past I cannot preach now. I used to preach hell fire, so you could nearly see the fire, and it took effect then, but the call today is for a different ministry. It is not so much in the might of preaching but in the demonstration of the Spirit. Sinners are more hardhearted than they used to be. You can preach hell until they see the blaze and yet they will stand and look you calmly in the face; but let them see the mighty power of God manifested and they are convicted.

The Lord has given me a special mission to bring about a spirit of unity and love and God is raising up people in every land who are reaching out after more of God and saying, "Come and help us. We want the spirit of love. We want the signs and wonders." The Lord showed me last night as I lay awake the most of the night, to gather together the ministers as far as I could that we might see eye to eye, preach the same Gospel and have the same signs following. The word is going forth and the multitude is going to take it up and publish it everywhere—this Gospel of the Kingdom, our last commission.

His ambassadors must stop all contention, all hair-splitting theories must be dropped; this hobby and that hobby with continual harping on finished work or sanctification that antagonizes the saints must be put away. We are to go out and lift up Jesus.... The ministry of healing brings people more than anything else and if you can lay hands on the sick and they recover you won't have to preach to empty seats. You produce the goods of heaven and people want to see the goods. Let the word go forth in demonstration and power so people can see what God has for them. There will be no failure in your ministry when they see the power of the Lord present to heal.

There is loving unity here. So far as I can see there is not a dissentient voice. There is not much wildfire. God will not permit it and no one dares to chime in saying, "I am a dove" when he is a raven. No one dares to join us but to magnify God. Those just starting in the life of the Spirit will run off in the flesh more or less, but if they are honest they will recover themselves and fall into their places. There is room for everything in a meeting but the devil. We don't want to give him a place.

Let Jesus have the pre-eminence. The more He is held up, the deeper people get in love with Him, the quicker they will drop everything else. So let us hold up Jesus and herald the coming of the King. Show them the great danger of the Tribulation. Preach Jesus and hold on to God until signs follow. There is something wrong unless they do follow. Don't wait until you have any special gift. Believe you can do it and it will be done. Not only send forth the prayer but look to God for courage, command the devil to go and you will see victory perched on your banner.

Don't denounce churches. Don't denounce the Catholics. Catholics won't come in for fear you will denounce them. I never mention Catholics. I never denounce any particular church. We can show the signs of the formalist in a general way, and they see they have been fed on chaff, and they know they are frozen to death and will want to get alive. Paul said to Timothy, "Stir up the gift of God which is in thee." If there is any gift God is showing you you ought to have, you can receive it by the laying on of hands. It is not so much what you say about the baptism in the Holy Spirit but what they see you have. We can talk until we are hoarse and they won't be convinced, but the power of God convinces them. Don't wait for manifestations before you go forth and do something. When you are weakest, then you are strong. Let us go out and work miracles. Then the people will glorify God.

Selected Biographical Index